Para
Pe

com os amigos sempre
amigos de
Josiah Blackmore

MOORINGS

MOORINGS

*Portuguese Expansion and the
Writing of Africa*

JOSIAH BLACKMORE

University of Minnesota Press
MINNEAPOLIS
LONDON

The University of Minnesota Press gratefully acknowledges the generous assistance provided for the publication of this book by the Victoria University Senate, University of Toronto.

The map of Portuguese explorations and settlements in West Africa was originally published by the Hakluyt Society. The Hakluyt Society was established in 1846 for the purpose of printing rare or unpublished voyages and travels. For further information, see www.hakluyt.com.

Material in chapter 1 was published in an earlier form as "Imagining the Moor in Medieval Portugal," *Diacritics* 36.3–4 (2006): 27–43, published by The Johns Hopkins University Press. Material in chapter 3 was published in earlier versions as "Africa and the Epic Imagination of Camões," *Portuguese Literary and Cultural Studies* 9 (2002): 107–16, and as "The Monstrous Lineage of Adamastor and His Critics," *Portuguese Literary and Cultural Studies* 7, published by the Center for Portuguese Studies and Culture, University of Massachusetts, Dartmouth.

Published by the University of Minnesota Press
111 Third Avenue South, Suite 290
Minneapolis, MN 55401-2520
http://www.upress.umn.edu

Library of Congress Cataloging-in-Publication Data

Blackmore, Josiah, 1959–
    Moorings : Portuguese expansion and the writing of Africa / Josiah Blackmore.
        p. cm.
    Includes bibliographical references and index.
    ISBN 978-0-8166-4832-0 (hardcover : alk. paper)—ISBN 978-0-8166-4833-7 (pbk. : alk. paper)
    1. Africa—Historiography. 2. Africans in literature. 3. Muslims in literature.
4. Imperialism in literature. 5. Historiography—Portugal—History—To 1500.
6. Historiography—Portugal—History—16th century. 7. Portuguese literature—History and criticism. 8. Portugal—Colonies—Africa. 9. Africa—Description and travel. 10. Africa—Foreign public opinion, Portuguese. I. Title.
    DT36.3.B58 2009
    960′.22072—dc22
                                                                    2008032085

Printed in the United States of America on acid-free paper

The University of Minnesota is an equal-opportunity educator and employer.

15 14 13 12 11 10 09   10 9 8 7 6 5 4 3 2 1

This book is dedicated to the memory of my father

JOSIAH H. BLACKMORE II
(1934–2007)

lo mio maestro e 'l mio autore

Contents

Note to the Reader

Throughout this book quotations of primary sources are first given in the original language followed by translation into English. Quotations of non-English secondary sources are given only in English. All translations are mine unless otherwise attributed.

The chronicles of Gomes Eanes de Zurara studied here are quoted from editions that retain Zurara's orthography and grammar. These editions, with their respective abbreviations, are:

Ceuta *Crónica da Tomada de Ceuta por El Rei D. João I*, ed. Francisco
        Maria Esteves Pereira
Guiné *Crónica dos feitos notáveis que se passaram na conquista da Guiné por
        mandado do Infante D. Henrique*, ed. Torquato de Sousa Soares

For full bibliographic information, see the Works Cited at the end of this volume.

Acknowledgments

I gladly acknowledge the support and encouragement of many individuals and institutions throughout the long process of writing this book. As always, my students and colleagues at the University of Toronto have provided engaging discussion (and tolerance) of this project and have asked hard questions at just the right times. Ricardo Sternberg, David Higgs, Suzanne Akbari, David Rojinsky, Stephen Rupp, Kenneth Mills, Robert Davidson, Néstor Rodríguez, Sanda Munjic, and Walid Saleh offered scholarly conversation and help. I am very grateful to Victoria University in the University of Toronto for the award of a Victoria Senate Grant in support of this book. Miguel Torrens of the Robarts Library helpfully acquired books and journals. Outside Toronto, I presented parts of the book's arguments to receptive and demanding audiences at Bridgewater State College, the University of Massachusetts–Dartmouth, the University of Colorado–Boulder, the University of Chicago, Cornell University, Columbia University, Stanford University, the University of the Witwatersrand, and a Faculty Weekend Seminar on José de Acosta at the Folger Institute. To the facilitators and conveners of those institutional occasions I express my gratitude. In particular, it's a pleasure to thank Leora Lev, Anna Klobucka, Victor Mendes, Vincent Barletta, Lisa Voigt, Pedro Schachtt Pereira, Simone Pinet, Bruno Bosteels, Patricia Grieve, and Michael Titlestad. I also gratefully acknowledge the University of Toronto and the Connaught Foundation for the award of a Chancellor Jackman Research Fellowship in the Humanities in 2003–4, which afforded crucial research and writing time and funds.

This book benefited from the comments and criticisms of several other colleagues and friends. The anonymous readers for the University of Minnesota Press offered helpful criticisms. K. David Jackson continues to be an ideal scholarly interlocutor. João R. Figueiredo, James Burke, Gregory Hutcheson, and Barbara Weissberger all came to the book's aid on several occasions. For other favors and support, thanks to my sisters Anne Wessels-Paris and Judith Dann, and to Nancy Ratey, the late Kathleen Randles, and Manuela Marujo. Anything good that I do I owe to my parents, Josiah H. Blackmore II and Joyce Blackmore, and to my father's unsurpassed example as a scholar and a gentleman.

The University of Minnesota Press has followed *Moorings* from the beginning with unwavering good faith. I thank Doug Armato for his support. To Richard Morrison I give thanks first as one of the early and steadfast friends of this project and then for cheerfully tolerating more delays and shifts in schedule with this book than with any of our previous collaborations.

INTRODUCTION:
INTO AFRICA

ON AUGUST 21, 1415, a company of soldiers under the orders of King João I of Portugal disembarked from a fleet of ships anchored off the coast of Morocco and went ashore to seize the city of Ceuta. According to chronicler of the Portuguese court Gomes Eanes de Zurara (or Azurara, 1410?–74?) in his *Crónica da Tomada de Ceuta* (Chronicle of the Capture of Ceuta), Ceuta was in Portuguese hands by the end of the day. At a certain point, the chronicler writes, one of the king's men approached the Moorish castle and paused and glanced upward at its walls

> sobre o quall uio estar huũa gramde bamda de pardaaes. Nom ueedes disse elle comtra os outros como aquelles pardaaes alli estam assessegados, que me matem sse Çalla bem Çalla com todollos outros nom he partido dalli, e leixou ho castello uazio. ca sse assy nom fosse, nom estariam alli aquelles pardaaes assy dassessego. (231)

> on top of which he saw a large flock of sparrows. "Don't you see," he said to his companions, "how those sparrows are calmly perched there, a sign that, on my oath, says that the prophet Çalla bem Çalla along with all the other Moors must have fled and left the castle empty, for otherwise those sparrows would not be so calm?

Zurara tells us that indeed no Moor remained within the walls to resist or fight. Relieved, the conquerors thanked God who "por semelhamte maneira os posera em posse de todo" (in such a way had placed them in possession of everything, 232).

Zurara's semiotic overlapping of Moors and birds symbolically renders the capture of Ceuta as portentous, an expression of the providential mandate that was often considered both motive and justification for Portuguese maritime expansion and which is a leitmotif throughout the record of Portuguese empire in the fifteenth and sixteenth centuries. Though it is possible, as Malyn Newitt observes (*Portuguese Overseas Expansion* 11), to identify the first steps of Portuguese overseas expansion with an expedition to the Canary Islands in 1341, the capture of Ceuta traditionally stands as the first action of Portuguese—and European—maritime empire that will soon lead to the Iberian voyages to the Americas, Asia, and the Pacific.[1] The historical role of Ceuta is as important as its symbolic dimension in European thought of the time. Peter Russell argues that Ceuta is significant "[n]ot only in an ideological and political sense but also in an institutional and administrative one . . . the experience of ruling Ceuta would give birth to models which spread overseas in the wake of Portugal's maritime expansion" (*Prince Henry* 51), while Francis M. Rogers advocates for the place of Ceuta in the European mind-set by noting that "Ceuta and the maritime discoveries captured the imagination of Portugal and the world to a far greater extent than other events of Portuguese history" (*The Travels* 71). If Ceuta is the initial event of European imperial and colonial campaigns that will gain momentum through the fifteenth century and last to the twentieth, and will include the interests not only of Portugal but of other nations such as Belgium, England, France, and Spain, then Zurara's anecdote of the birds serves as an appropriate marker of this fact etymologically: "to inaugurate" derives from the Latin *inaugurare*, which means "to take omens from the flight of birds, to consecrate and install after taking such omens or auguries" (*Oxford English Dictionary*). Alongside the interpretation of Ceuta as the beginning of European imperialist voyaging and colonization in the early modern era, some scholars read the Portuguese capture of the city as an end to or culmination of the ideology of *reconquista*, or Reconquest. For Rogers, who opts for a heroic reading of the Portuguese action on the city, "it sealed the Reconquest and was a crowning chivalric achievement" (*The Travels* 8).[2] Andrew C. Hess thinks along similar lines when he eschews Ceuta as the first step of Portuguese seaborne imperialism and finds a continuation of a crusading zeal, so that "at the time the arrival of the

Christians on the African side of the strait appeared to be no more than an extension of old practices" (*Forgotten Frontier* 12–13). If the mentality of a crusade constitutes the "old practices" identified by Hess, it is also true that newly developing commercial interests in North Africa also lay behind the armature of a Holy War.[3]

However the Portuguese campaign against Ceuta might ultimately be viewed—as the first identifiable action in the historical trajectory of early modern European imperialism or as a culminating manifestation of a medieval crusading mentality that promoted Christian–Moorish inter-action in conflictive terms—the fact remains that the invasion initiated a new series of encounters and contacts with Africa and its inhabitants and served as a catalyst for a Portuguese culture of writing on Africa that exists to contemporary times. The primogenitor text of this tradition is Zurara's *Crónica da Tomada de Ceuta*, followed by three other chronicles on Morocco and the exploration of the West African littoral. In Zurara, Africa is in essence an ideologically new place since, after 1415, Africa was no longer merely a site of commercial interaction but became both the harbinger and first arena of empire. Zurara ignores the Portuguese his-torical familiarity with the North African city in favor of his immediate chronistic objective which is to narrate the arrival of the Portuguese in another guise, that is, as conquerors in an incipient national practice of maritime expansion. Zurara's narrative of the capture of Ceuta is already part of an expansionist mentality that has identified the city as the real and symbolic initiation of imperial campaigns, so that Africa and its peoples are mapped, appropriated, and incorporated into a rapidly expanding imperial-mercantilist *oikoumene*. We may regard Zurara's historical narratives, then, as texts in the tradition of Portuguese/European writing that foundation-ally lay out some of the characteristics of the imperial discourse of en-counter in non-European spaces and the exploitation of those spaces and the peoples in them.

Moorings is a book about the Portuguese culture of writing on Africa in the first century and a half of maritime expansion, from Zurara's chronicles in the mid-fifteenth century to the epic poem *Os Lusíadas* (The Lusiads, 1572) of Luís de Camões (1524?–80). The book explores, through readings of representative texts, the Portuguese textual fashioning of Africa and its peoples and how they were depicted and brought into the expansionist imagination. It is, from one perspective, a book of imperial discourse analysis, one that—I hope—will catalyze other studies of Portuguese writings on and about Africa in both the colonial and postcolonial periods. It seeks to delineate the inchoate practices of writing that accompanied, and, at the same time, were the product of, maritime expansion and voyaging.

The traditional, even stereotypical, figure of the African in medieval and early modern cultures was usually the Moor, most often an Arabic-speaking, (North) African Muslim. Thus the Moor, as the emblematic representative of Africa, presides over the arguments in the pages that follow. With the gerundive *mooring* I mean to designate a practice of excogitating or fashioning Africa textually within an expansionist mentality or zeitgeist, of creating a Portuguese "gnosis" (to borrow V. Y. Mudimbe's term) of Africa and its inhabitants. *Moorings* also gestures toward narrative practices—such as those in Camões or Álvaro Velho's account of the voyage of Vasco da Gama—that recall the oceanic origins of texts on Africa and the stops and pauses of maritime journeying, the hiatus in forward movement of an itinerary or planned course over land or sea. Such stops typically allow for the encounters between Africans and Europeans, the dynamic of human interaction that serves as the backbone of military, commercial, and religious imperial pursuits. In Camões, this kind of mooring or pause permits the realization of an expansionist design: moments of suspended nautical movement allow the personages of *Os Lusíadas* to construct historical narratives (such as Vasco da Gama's long historical peroration to the King of Melinde) that are part of Camões's creation of a collective, historical memory of Portugal as the head of Europe. Portugal emerges as "the source of power and organization" (Nicolopulos 240) in the geography of the *Lusíadas* and in the historiographic dimension of the poem. The nautical moorings allow that historiographic dimension to unfold.

In using the term "Moor" to name the African I do not mean to repeat the imperialist practice of reducing the demographic diversity of Africa to an undifferentiated mass of otherness with one label. Rather, I employ this etymon since it was part of the lexical and conceptual currencies of the late-medieval and early-modern periods and so was a component of historical and imaginative thought. This premise shares an affinity with

Nabil Matar's formulation of the Moor in early-modern English culture
as a "representation of the non-European non-Christian in the Renaissance [that] was not so much dependent on facts and experience as on
cultural molds and imaginary portraits" (14).[4] This formulation has the
advantage of understanding the figure of the Moor as constructed by ideologies, literary traditions, or historical circumstances, though England
and Portugal differ in their relationships to the African continent and in
the presence of Moorish elements within each national culture. Matar's
"non-European non-Christian" distinction often dissolves in the case of
Moors born in Portugal or Moors who converted to Christianity during
expansion but who still retained traits of Moorishness.

The chronological scope of *Moorings* is defined by the works of Gomes
Eanes de Zurara in the fifteenth century and the publication of Camões's
Os Lusíadas in 1572. These two writers bracket, in my view, the formative
years of Portuguese imperial discourse and for this reason the book's
arguments fall between these two poles. Both Zurara and Camões redact
ideologically informed works, but from different ends of the temporal
spectrum and as responses to different historical circumstances. Zurara
records the campaign against Ceuta, the governorships of Pedro de Meneses and Duarte de Meneses in Morocco, and the sub-Saharan explorations
and conquests of the Infante D. Henrique, or Prince Henry ("the Navigator"), in Guinea. Zurara held the post of Keeper of the Royal Archives of
the Torre do Tombo and *cronista-mor* (chronicler-major or royal chronicler), appointed by Afonso V (Prince Henry's nephew, reigned 1438–81) in
1454 as successor to Fernão Lopes (ca. 1383–ca. 1460). Lopes had been
charged by João I to redact the "Crónica Geral do Reino" (General Chronicle of the Realm), and this included the first two parts of the *Crónica
de D. João I* (Chronicle of King John I), the history of the monarch who
was the founder of the House of Avis and whose six sons (including Prince
Henry) came to be known, in Camões's famous expression, as the "ínclita
geração" (illustrious generation) owing to their preeminence in Portuguese politics and culture. Zurara's first task was to complete the chronicle Lopes had begun, and this he did by writing the third and final part
of the *Crónica de D. João I*, more commonly referred to as the *Crónica da
Tomada de Ceuta*. Zurara's historiographic output would eventually include
three other chronicles, all of them narrating the Portuguese exploration

and conquest of northern and western Africa in the first five decades of expansion. These chronicles, with their dates of completion, are *Crónica dos feitos notáveis que se passaram na conquista da Guiné por mandado do infante D. Henrique* (Chronicle of the Notable Deeds That Occurred during the Conquest of Guinea by Order of Prince Henry, or, more commonly, the Chronicle of Guinea, 1453), the *Crónica de D. Pedro de Meneses* (Chronicle of Pedro de Meneses, 1458–64), and the *Crónica de D. Duarte de Meneses* (Chronicle of Duarte de Meneses, 1464–68).[5]

Camões, on the other hand, writes after the conquest of Africa, India, and Brazil, and after the establishment of complex colonial administrations. He is an "innately" expansionist figure in that he was born once maritime empire was well under way, but when he redacted his epic, imperial fervor was somewhat on the decline. Zurara's chronicles are ideological in that they are written as part of the official machinery of the expansionist state, and Camões's poem is ideological in its attempts to resuscitate an imperialist zeal among his countrymen and reinstate a determination to vanquish Portugal's competitor imperial power, Islam, especially in the form of the Ottoman Turks.[6] *Os Lusíadas* recapitulates, synthesizes, and poetically reconstrues the mainly prose historiographic tradition that is the poem's immediate textual antecessor, the tradition inaugurated by Zurara. The poem takes as its historical basis the 1497–99 voyage of Vasco da Gama to India, which opened the Indo-Portuguese maritime trade route known as the *carreira da Índia* (India voyage) and which was the cause of most of the dramatic shipwreck narratives contained in the *História trágico-marítima* or *Tragic History of the Sea.*[7] Although the poet identifies the attainment of India as the pinnacle of epic achievement, and since the skeins of historical and mythological narrative culminate in Gama's arrival in Malabar (Calicut), it is understandable that much criticism reads the *Lusíadas* as a poem "about" India. Yet the first five of the poem's ten cantos take place in Africa, so that Africa acts as a principal space for the formation of the mythological and historiographic structures of thought that serve Camões's ideologically driven poetic imagination. Camões allows historical narrative to occur in Africa; he allows his protagonists and antagonists to linger on Africa's sands and along its coastlines in order to build stories, predict the future, construct the entire history of Europe and Portugal, and mingle with the classical gods and the governing energies of the cosmos that direct the efforts of explorers and mariners. Africa is Portugal's first conquest in the poem in that Portuguese presence in it allows for the creation of the narrative of *Os Lusíadas,* Portugal's most developed expression of the ideologies of empire that resides at the heart of the country's literary and cultural canons and of its identity as a voyaging, seafaring nation. In a general sense, this book documents the textual culture on Africa that made Camões's poem possible.

A few definitions of working concepts are in order. I use "expansion" or "expansionist" as synonymous with "empire" and "imperial" throughout this book. Thomaz ("Le Portugal et l'Afrique") defines expansion as the "military occupation, peaceful colonization or simple commercial presence [of Portugal]" (161) abroad. This definition provides an idea of the range of activity and endeavor encompassed by "expansion," though I would add nonpeaceful colonization to Thomaz's definition, and, more importantly, the production of texts and documents as a characteristic practice of expansion. "Empire" and "imperial," moreover, designate a spectrum of activities—for example, geographic exploration, descriptions of the natural world, slaving raids, inland travel, or simple trading encounters—that vary considerably with regard to stated or putative objectives and do not always imply Portuguese power or domination over indigenous or colonial subjects. Thornton writes of the considerable African resistance to Portuguese expansionist interests while also noting the generally peaceful relations between African states and Portugal in the sixteenth century ("Early Portuguese Expansion" 122–23). Pagden remarks that for the Portuguese in Africa, at least until the mid-fifteenth century, trade was more profitable than conquest (64). Indeed, given the often shifting purposes and unexpected contingencies of "imperial" actions, it is difficult, if not impossible, to identify one consistent form, definition, or practice of Portuguese empire. Costa ("La presencia de los portugueses") argues, in the context of the Portuguese presence in Asia, for "the substitution of the notion of empire with that of network. The many spaces occupied by the Portuguese did not form a territorial unity but, on the contrary, a discontinuity" (438). Hespanha makes a similar claim in a comparison of Portuguese and Spanish empire when he notes that "Portuguese empire in the Orient did not constitute . . . a single, territorial entity, but a discontinuous political space. . . . it was, first and foremost, a non-monotonous network of political relations" (18). These observations might equally well be applied to the Portuguese presence in Africa. What both these critics make clear is the necessity of undoing any notion of "empire" as a unified or cohesive exercise of power in which Europeans, Christians, or Portuguese always wield the upper hand in encounters with non-Europeans.[8] In the Portuguese context, imperial or expansionist writers document several reasons for expansion, such as the fight against the infidel, the search for slaves or gold, chivalric honor, a providential plan, and obedience to the Christian faith—and oftentimes all in the same text.[9] Sometimes, but not always, imperial activity attempts to establish a power differential in favor of the Portuguese, such as in combat or in the capture of slaves. Other circumstances find Portuguese explorers in situations of humiliation or defeat. Joan-Pau Rubiés's comments on imperialism and textuality in the New World recognize what was a common practice in early Portuguese empire, namely, that

> any interpretation of the literature of travel and discovery must be an exercise in cultural history which acknowledges the apparent contradictions between the rhetoric of triumphant imperialism, too often portrayed as a one-sided force both by critics and apologists, and the ambivalence of the actual encounter with an indigenous world, human and natural, which was neither passive nor homogeneous. ("Futility in the New World" 75)

There were structures of empire and colony, for example, in the Portuguese presence in the Kongo, where commercial and political relations and exchanges (satisfactory to both sides of the colonial divide) were established and maintained for centuries and which stand as a caution against reading this interaction in modern, colonial terms (MacGaffey 260). Or, P. E. H. Hair notes that

> [i]n Guinea, as in maritime Asia, the Portuguese presence can be defined, not so much as one of eager imperial conquest and predatory rule as one of opportunist co-existence with "native" political and economic units, within an existing and vigorous commercial network to which the Portuguese contributed useful middleman services. ("Discovery and Discoveries" 21)

Newitt speaks of an "informal empire" in Morocco in which private cas-
tles were built, private deals were struck with local Moroccan chiefs, or
freelance raids (that is, unauthorized by the Crown) were pursued (*Portuguese Overseas Expansion* 71–72; "Formal and Informal Empire" 8–12).
Jonathan Hart's comment is also apposite: "[t]he textual messiness—the
descriptions, opinions, proclamations, asides and other forms of verbal
record and report—makes difficult any single notion of imperial expansion" (1). Hart's observation has the advantage of concentrating the messiness of empire at a textual level, and could be expanded to include the
proliferation of genres that accompany expansion in Africa.

The terms "to discover" (Portuguese *descobrir*) and "discovery" (*descobrimento* or *descoberta*), so often used in conjunction with the expansionist
fifteenth and sixteenth centuries, carried particular meanings in documents of the time not always consonant with modern understandings.
Samuel Eliot Morison uncovers possible meanings of these Portuguese
terms based on passages from Fernão Lopes de Castanheda and João de
Barros, two of the preeminent Portuguese historians of Portuguese Africa
and Asia and whose works greatly influenced Camões. Morison observes
that "[*descoberta* means] the discovery of a land the existence of which
was already known to the Portuguese by fact or rumor; *descobrimento* . . .
implies both 'discovery' and 'exploration.' . . . Often it is only from the
context that one can tell which meaning is intended" (8–10). Wilcomb E.
Washburn cites historian Edmundo O'Gorman as providing the most
extensive treatment of "discovery" (here in the context of Columbus and
the New World): "'Discovery' implies that the nature of the thing found
was previously known to the finder, i.e., that he knows that objects such as
the one he has found can and do exist, although the existence of that particular one was wholly unknown" (quoted in Washburn 13).[10] "Discover,"
then, does not necessarily mean "to come upon for the first time." The Portuguese explorers did not always "discover" Africa in the modern sense,
though they did "discover" parts of it along the lines indicated by Morison and O'Gorman. Mudimbe argues that this fifteenth-century "discovery" of Africa "meant and still means the primary violence signified by the
word" (*The Idea of Africa* 17) as the origin of the slave trade. In Portuguese
explorations of both coasts of Africa there was sometimes a folkloric idea
of what lay beyond the bounds of lived experience, and oftentimes it

conflicted with what was actually encountered. Africa, then, both was and was not a "new world."[11]

The most frequent term used by expansionist writers to denote the arrival and presence of Portuguese in foreign lands is not "empire" but *conquista* or "conquest." It is Zurara who invests this term with the meaning it will carry as Iberian empire expands as the strategic use of force over the "barbarians" and/or the (divinely approved) campaigns of trade, slaving, or colonization on a large scale. In writing of imperial Spain, J. H. Elliott notes that "[t]he word *conquista* to the Castilian implied essentially the establishing of the Spanish 'presence'—the securing of strongpoints, the staking out of claims, the acquisition of dominion over a defeated population" (44). In a series of fifteenth-century papal bulls authorizing a Portuguese trade monopoly over Africa, there is a sense of legal right inherent in *conquista* that extends beyond Africa to the "Indies." Zurara's understanding of *conquista* in the expansionist idiom will be repeated by subsequent official or state-appointed writers.

Moorings, then, engages the Portuguese textual matter of Africa to the time of Camões as an important moment in the history of western expansion and reveals some of the mechanisms that create imperialism as a discursive practice. The rapidly evolving field of postcolonial studies makes such an analysis urgent, as does the fact that the Portuguese documents—in scholarly discussions of early modern Iberian empire within North America, at least—recede from critical view because of the (over)emphasis on the texts produced under the Spanish, English, or French crowns. The focus in *Moorings* on the early documents of expansion reflects the fact that there is still much left to be done in considering how empire functioned discursively in its initial years. Roland Greene, for instance, subscribes to the idea that postcolonialism begins with colonialism (424), an assumption I share. Barbara Fuchs has suggested a slight retooling of terminology in her postulation of "imperium studies" as both a critical approach and a disciplinary label to designate the contemporary analysis of early-modern empire and its textual productions. She notes, for instance, that

[w]hen discussing early modern imperialism, the temptation is to turn to postcolonial criticism, yet it clearly behooves critics working on earlier

periods both to develop theoretical concepts better suited to our field, and
to historicize postcolonial concepts in order to expose the early modern
foundations of later imperialist representations. ("Imperium Studies" 71)

Without engaging postcolonial criticism directly, *Moorings* might be
thought of as one possible response to the critical and methodological
necessity Fuchs identifies.[12] The distinction between colonialism and imperialism, especially in the realm of discourse, is often elided in favor of
"colonial" as the more common term. Yet that distinction is worth noting
here, especially because it bears on Zurara and Camões. Ania Loomba
defines imperialism as "the phenomenon that originates in the metropo-
lis, the process which leads to domination and control" (12) and colonialism as "[i]ts result, or what happens in the colonies as a consequence of
imperial domination" (ibid.). Zurara and Camões do not on the whole
occupy themselves with Portuguese colonial presence; their texts are more
imperial in that they focus on a practice of establishing power through
knowledge of other lands that radiates outward from the metropole and
returns in the form of a text. Camões is silent about Portuguese colonies—
in fact, he ignores the colonial history of the entire west African coast in
favor of the ideological factors that, for the poet, always and necessarily
motivated expansion into Africa. Camões structures his poem on an ideal
of maritime, expansionist itinerancy originating in Portugal and Lisbon,
as does Zurara. According to Loomba's definition, Zurara and Camões are
practitioners of imperial, not colonial, discourse.[13]

Chapter 1, "Encountering the African," briefly explores the textual background of the Portuguese expansionist writing of Africa. It considers
medieval formulations of Moors and Moorishness in historiographic and
poetic sources, and outlines the ways in which the Moor occupies different conceptual and geographic zones, thus making Moorishness a marker
of boundaries that are not fixed but shifting. In this fluidity of limits,
Moorishness is an interior, as well as exterior, quality. The chapter also
considers the "in-between" nature of Portuguese writings on Africa from
certain theoretical postures, especially the influential conceptual vocabulary of discursive imperialism elaborated in Edward Said's *Orientalism*.

The "African In-Between" proposes that, in the map of European imperial discourse, Portuguese writings on Africa challenge critics to rethink
the conceptual role Africa played in the idea of the East or the Orient as
the putative counterpart to European Christendom.

Chapter 2, "Expansion and the Contours of Africa," studies the historiographic and nautical writings that were the predecessors of Camões's
influential poetic fashioning of Africa and maritime itinerancy in *Os Lusíadas*. Nautical movement and passage through space forms part of the
exercise of imperial power, and demonstrates how Africa was gradually
subsumed into the Oriental enterprise of India through nautically oriented writing. In this discussion, I explore the strange in the conceptual
world of expansion. The strange functions as part of a mental framework
in which displacement and alienation are metaphors for a shifting and
evolving gnosis of Africa. I finally consider how Africa was infixed into
the imagination or *imaginatio*, a standard component of medieval and
early-modern theories of vision and cognition. This physiological imagination has important claims to make about Africa and the process of perceiving and writing about Africa in Zurara and Camões that prepares for
a portion of the material in chapter 3.

Chapter 3, "The Monster of Melancholy," examines the episode of the
phantasmal monster Adamastor in *Os Lusíadas* as the most significant
moment about Africa in the poem and connects this episode to prevailing ideas on the imagination and melancholy in Camões's time. The chapter argues that the episode, central to many interpretations of the poem,
indelibly infixes Africa into the voyages traced through space and mind,
and posits that Adamastor's melancholic monstrosity invests him with a
cultural and hermeneutic currency. Melancholy and monstrosity inform
the Camonian idea of Africa as both historiographic and imaginative realities. The conquest of Adamastor by the Portuguese is part of the metaphoric erotics of imperial voyaging as represented by the iconic figure
of the expansionist ship, and the chapter concludes with an analysis of
Manuel de Faria e Sousa's influential commentary on *Os Lusíadas* in the
mid-seventeenth century. Faria e Sousa's critique stands as a milestone of
Camonian criticism and is perhaps the most important secondary source
on Camões's rendering of Africa in the history of the poem in its inscription of Adamastor into an expansionist, cartographic imperative.

1

ENCOUNTERING THE
AFRICAN

FOR PORTUGAL ON THE EVE OF EXPANSION, Africa was familiar and strange, a known place across the modest parcel of sea between the Algarve and Ceuta, and, farther south, an unknown expanse of land that glimmered black under the equatorial sun. It was at once a historical reality and a vast, limitless land of myth, monsters, and biblical time. Like Adamastor in *Os Lusíadas*, it was simultaneously spectral and concrete, imminent and distant. In the early fifteenth century it became, for the Portuguese, a laboratory of expansion, the primordial space of imperial and colonial campaigns. Africa's borders were crossed and plotted by explorers, colonizers, slavers, traders, and missionaries; almost from the moment of the arrival of João I's army in Ceuta, the continent and its inhabitants became a motor of textual productivity in the form of chronicles, letters, reports, navigational rutters, and geographic treatises. As Africa's west coast was gradually explored under the orders of Prince Henry, old ways of thinking gave way to new empirical realities. And for Portugal, as for Spain, Africa was part of the demographics and history of home in the figure of the Moor, simultaneously an other and a closer, more intimate presence. The voyages of exploration along the west African littoral, round the Cape of Good Hope, and onward to the eastern shore and the Indian Ocean, generate the multitude of writings that shape Africa for Portuguese imperialism in the late-medieval and early-modern periods and conscript it into the imaginative and ideological frameworks of expansion.[1] As a first step in understanding how Africa and its inhabitants were variously and diversely shaped in the Portuguese imaginary, it is best to begin with a brief look at how Moors, Africa, and other inhabitants of the continent were defined and conceptualized prior to expansion in the medieval period. The medieval precedents to expansion collectively shape the Moor as a historical, living presence in Portugal as well as a marker of boundaries in the arenas of sex, race, and spirituality. The quality of being a Moor— or Moorishness—can be determined by factors that are anything but stable or predetermined. The medieval understandings of the Moor and Africa will migrate to some extent into the writings of expansion and the ideological campaigns forged in African spaces.

SOME MEDIEVAL FORMULATIONS

Let us begin by considering the word *Moor,* a shifting and slippery label in medieval Iberia. Prior to the campaigns of maritime expansion initiated by Portuguese travelers in the fifteenth century, the Moor (Portuguese *mouro,* Castilian *moro*) was the emblematic African in the Iberian literary and historical imagination. *Moor* is alternatively denotative and connotative, precise and imprecise, historically accurate and imaginatively construed. Etymologically, geographic writings gave birth to *mouro* as a generic label. The word derives from Latin *maurus,* an adjective meaning "Moorish" or "of the Moors" that referred to the inhabitants of Mauritania, a region of North Africa comprised of two provinces and frequently described by classical geographers. In his *Geography,* for example, Strabo, in speaking of Libya (i.e., Africa), mentions the Moors or Maurusians (from *Maurusia,* the Greek word for Mauritania) as "a Libyan tribe living on the side of the straight opposite Iberia" (157). Pliny the Elder includes Tangier in his *Historia naturalis* (*Natural History*) as part of Mauritania, and in it live "the Moors (from whom it takes its name of Mauretania), by many writers called the Maurusii" (231). Pomponius Mela, like Strabo, juxtaposes Mauritania and Spain as facing one another across the sea and identifies the mountains Jabal Musa and Gibraltar as the Pillars of Hercules (41–42). *Maurus* was one of the many terms used to describe the peoples of Africa in classical texts, and often coincided with the Greek and Latin terms for "Ethiopians," which were, as Frank M. Snowden Jr. observes, words synonymous with blackness of skin (5).[2] In the Middle Ages, Isidoro de Sevilla (Isidore of Seville) reiterates an etymological connection between darkness of skin and the name Mauritania in his *Etymologiae* (Etymologies) by noting that "Mauritania takes its name from the color of its peoples, since the Greeks called blackness *maûron*" (2:189).[3]

In a study of medieval texts written in Latin in Spain, Nevill Barbour provides some specifics on the various understandings of *maurus*, in addition to the related terms *sarraceni* (Saracens) and *arabes* (Arabs). Barbour acknowledges the common understanding of *mauri* and *sarraceni* as designations for the Muslim inhabitants of Spain or al-Andalus and notes the etymological link to Mauritania (253–54). However, the location of Mauritania as a geographic space is unstable:

> [W]hile the name Mauritania meant properly the former Roman provinces, Mauritania Caesariensis and Mauritania Tingitanis, corresponding to the present western Algeria and north-eastern Morocco, Latin writers sometimes used it not only to cover all North Africa but also the whole of the African continent as far as the Equator, beyond which geographical knowledge did not then [754 CE] extend. From this it followed that there were black as well as white *Mauri*. (255)

Maurus could, then, from an early date, be a catchall term for Africans in the pens of Iberian writers. So varied were the understandings of *maurus* in the early Middle Ages, in fact, that by the eighth century "'Mauritania' [became] a word, like Christendom, whose geographical significance depends on the context" (Barbour 258). This is a crucial point because it establishes that Mauritania—and, by extension, Moor—was vulnerable to the exigencies and positionalities of writers and discourse, even though putatively what was being referenced was the "objective" fact of geographic boundaries. Mauritania ceases to be a fixed region in Africa and becomes an itinerant and constructed zone of religious, linguistic, and racial alterity whose existence and location reflect culturally or politically determined perspectives and objectives. The location of Mauritania, then, far from being a predetermined "fact," can, in large part, depend on who's doing the looking.

Vernacular uses are equally broad along the lines sketched by Barbour, both in Portugal and in Spain. In Portugal, *mouro* is often the same as *mourisco* or *muçulmano* as designations for an Arabic-speaking Muslim. L. P. Harvey notes the terminological vagueness of *moro* in medieval Spain by observing:

Moor (*moro*) . . . is a historical term which is authentic in the sense that it occurs in source materials of the period, but it is a term we can rarely use nowadays. It is not merely geographically imprecise, leaving us uncertain whether the person it describes is of North African origin or simply a Muslim, it is ambiguous with regard to the value judgment it implies. Often *Moor* conveys hostility, but there are contexts where Muslims refer to themselves as Moors with evident pride. (*Islamic Spain* 1)

The related term *morisco* (a Muslim converted to Christianity) presents similar difficulties: "*Morisco* illustrates particularly clearly the dangers inherent in vocabulary. . . . [B]y employing [it] . . . we are tacitly accepting and approving of the forcible reclassification of this group of Muslims as something other" (ibid. 3).[4] Harvey is correct in observing the historical authenticity of the word *moro,* yet the very factors he cites as militating against *Moor* as a useful label advocate, in my view, for the critical interest of this word/concept. The slippages and imprecisions of *mouro* are precisely those that construe the term as a marker and principle of difference.

In literary and historical texts the Moor appears in a number of guises before expansion in Africa in the fifteenth century. José da Silva Horta ("A imagem do Africano") surveys several medieval texts, focusing on the conflation of blackness and Africa in the form of the Moor or Ethiopian in historiographic, hagiographic, and Christian doctrinal texts and noting the usually negative connotations of this conflation. Blackness most often appears as a visible sign of sin or spiritual waywardness, often with diabolical associations; thus the blackness of the African is a spiritual darkness. In historiographic texts, such as Alfonso X of Castile's *General estoria* (General History), the Moor is in fundamental "politico-religious" ("A imagem do Africano" 50) opposition to a presumed Ibero-Christian, historical status quo. In poetic texts such as Alfonso's *Cantigas de Santa Maria* (Songs of Holy Mary, hereafter CSM), Moors appear as the foe or foil to Christianity. These devotional lyrics, which often mix the religious poem of devotion and praise with historiographic narrative since many of the *cantigas* take specific historical events as their basis, sing the triumph of Christianity over Moors as the representatives of paganism or Islam. This unilateral view of Moors responds to the didactic purposes of these songs, for they were meant to instruct as well as laud the Virgin, and does not exemplify a more personal prejudice on Alfonso's part against Moors or Muslims, as Bagby (166) claims. The Moors of the CSM are predominantly archetypes within the salvific logic of devotional verse, as either the enemy of Christianity or the possibility of conversion, and as such are the products of a kind of discourse rather than an indication of what in modern terms we might call the racial or ethnic bias of the poet. A similar view of Moors appears in the pages of Alfonso's legal treatise known as the *Siete partidas* (Seven Parts). Here, Moorishness is solely a matter of faith with no visual exteriorization (such as dark skin) or linguistic tags (such as speaking Arabic). In the seventh *Partida*, Alfonso defines *moro:* "[m]oros son una manera de gente que creen que Mahomat fue profeta et mandadero de Dios" (the Moors are a people who believe that Muhammad was the Prophet and Messenger of God, 5:1438).[5] Moorishness is hence an internal quality, all the more dangerous because it is not readily apparent to the eye.[6] Alfonso adds that "[e]nsandecen á las vegadas homes . . . et desesperados de todo bien reniegan la fe de nuestro señor Jesucristo et tórnanse moros" ([m]en sometimes become insane and lose their prudence and understanding . . . and those who despair of everything, renounce the faith of Our Lord Jesus Christ, and become Moors, 3:1439). Alfonso distinguishes between being a Moor at the outset in the first citation and becoming a Moor—or "turning Moor"—in the second, which, for the Learned Monarch, appears to be worse. To "turn Moor" is a form of insanity that leads to an act of apostasy, so that the question remains open of the possibility of curing Moorish converts of their Moorishness. Moorishness can be an act of will as much as it can be a spiritual belief, and as such enters the much dicier (from a legal perspective) arena of unlawful transgression.

Immediately preceding Alfonso's definitions of Moors is a section on Jews (*Partida* 7, title 24), who, like Moors, are defined by their faith, but a faith that marks the body visibly in men with circumcision. Furthermore, Alfonso orders that all Jews, both men and women, must bear marks on their heads so as to be immediately recognizable; to be caught without the mark incurs a fine or a lashing (*Partida* 7, title 24, law 11). We might think of Alfonso's legislated mark of the Jew as a revival of the mark of Cain in Genesis, bestowed on Abel's fraternal murderer as a sign of both damnation and divine protection.[7] But in Alfonso's *Partida,* the mark serves simply to identify and indict, not to protect. Jewishness and Moorishness comprise a legal demographic, a line that cannot be crossed without punishment, as Alfonso's injunctions against sexual intermingling between Christians and Moors or Jews demonstrate.[8] In the CSM, by contrast and unlike the invisible nature of Moorishness in the *Siete partidas,* Moors bear visible marks of their "incorrect" faith. The inscription of Moorishness on the body occurs through beards, blackness, and ugliness. CSM 46 tells the story of a Moor who plunders a Christian village in the Holy Land and brings back a statue of Mary as part of his booty.[9] The statue begins to lactate, and the astonished Moor converts to Christianity along with his comrades, "estes mouros barvudos" (these bearded Moors, l. 59). Beards identify Moors, a kind of infidel counterpart to the beard as a symbol of Christian honor in medieval epic. The Moor possessed by the devil in CSM 192 and who is freed from diabolical power by Mary is likewise bearded, as are the Moors who lay siege to Marrakech in CSM 181 and are terrified by the emblems of Christianity wielded by their enemies. These visible, hirsute markings, in addition to blackness, which is linked to Satan (CSM 185, 329) it is important to repeat, function as part of a moral-didactic narrative whose purpose is the immediate distinction between Christians and Moors. The white and black world of the CSM visualizes spiritual demarcations that do not allow for porosity. This capacity for visualization in the imagery of the CSM facilitates comprehension of the various lessons or exempla in these songs of Marian devotion.

Opposed to the sober readings and definitions of Moors and Moorishness in the *Siete partidas* and the *Cantigas de Santa Maria* are the ludic treatments in the corpus of Galician-Portuguese insulting joke poetry known as the *cantigas de escarnho e mal dizer* (songs of mockery and insult, hereafter CEM). These *cantigas,* composed between the late twelfth and early fourteenth centuries, jokingly lampoon aspects of daily life in Iberia, from sick mules to selling fish to fashion to sex, religion, and even poetry itself. A number of these poems bring Moors to this vibrant and often hilarious poetic corpus. Transgression of various kinds frequently provides the tensions that are jokingly exploited in this poetry. In the case of Moors, this transgression is characteristically sexual, so that boundaries between sex and religion or race are dismantled and frequently fused.

Moors often display a high level of sexual prowess and energy and invite incursions into the forbidden zones of sodomy and fornication; Moors demarcate the realms of "deviant" sexual practices and occasion transgression into these realms.[10] By way of example, consider two *cantigas*, CEM 229 and 297, the first by Joan Soárez Coelho and the second by Martin Soárez.[11] Both poems take as their target one Joan Fernándiz. In these *cantigas*, the poets relate Joan Fernándiz to sex through an unnamed *mouro*. In CEM 229, Joan Soárez Coelho ridicules Fernándiz because a Moor is sleeping with his wife under his own roof. Liu reads this *cantiga* to mean that the Moor and Fernándiz are one and the same person, and that Fernándiz in essence cuckolds himself because he is most likely a Muslim convert to Christianity; Fernándiz is "simultaneously intended as both the adulterous Moor and the newly Christian husband, who has been cuckolded, paradoxically, by none other than his past self" (105). Liu bases this interpretation on the rubric to CEM 297, which reads "esta outra cantiga fez d'escarnho a un que dizian Joan Fernándiz, e semelhava mouro, e jogavan-lh' ende" (this other *cantiga d'escarnho* was written against one Joan Fernándiz, who resembled a Moor, and that's the joke against him). Other CEM mention Fernándiz and contain allusions to his circumcised member, so there is an intertextuality or interreferentiality that might be assumed to underlie the jokes against Fernándiz and that the poets would have assumed their audiences knew. Liu argues that these allusions "fuse religious and sexual practice in a constant reminder of [Fernándiz's] convert status" (106). In CEM 229, then, Moorishness as a quality that can be changed or discarded is the butt of the joke because it allows for the boundaries separating legally distinct groups to be redrawn comically so that a man may commit adultery with his own wife. Fernándiz's unorthodoxy in carnal matters becomes even more pronounced in CEM 297, a poem which hints that Joan Fernándiz keeps a Moorish boy with him, hidden from public view, for sexual gratification. For readers of the *Cancioneiro da Biblioteca Nacional* (Songbook of the National Library [of Lisbon], the codex in which CEM 297 appears), one more layer of equivocal complexity is added by the rubric to the poem, which contains the key phrase "semelhava mouro" (resembled a Moor). There is an ambiguity in the meaning of *semelhar*, "to resemble," "to appear like," or "to be similar to," that seems to advertise the joke in the poem. Most uses of *semelhar* in the CEM denote a visible similarity or likeness between things, so that one reading of the rubric is that Joan Fernándiz displays readily identifiable traits of Moorishness, such as dark skin, dress, mannerisms, or perhaps even speech. If Fernándiz is a Muslim convert to Christianity, then his similarity to a Moor is a physical trace or vestige of a quality that no longer exists internally, that is, his Islamic faith. Yet, given the same-sex innuendoes in CEM 297, *semelhar mouro* (to resemble a Moor) may imply that Fernándiz is "like a Moor" in his deviant sexual practices—in fact, the joke here might be that Joan Fernándiz not only looks like a Moor but acts like one too, sexually speaking.

Roughly contemporaneous with many of the CEM in Portugal is the writing of genealogical histories known as *livros de linhagens* (books of lineages). The most well known of these is by D. Pedro, count of Barcelos and bastard son of D. Denis, king of Portugal (and grandson of Alfonso X) from 1279 to 1325. D. Pedro's *Livro de Linhagens* was probably composed between 1340 and 1344. In the political turmoil of mid-fourteenth-century Portugal, D. Pedro was exiled to Castile, where he came into contact with the fecund intellectual culture promoted by Alfonso X. He returned to Portugal and composed his *Livro*, a text that combines the tracing of genealogical lines of descent of the Portuguese nobility to biblical times interspersed with short historical narratives. These narratives sometimes mix the historical and the fantastic, and include some of the earliest Arthurian literature in Iberia. One of the narratives recounts the battle of Salado waged in October 1340 in which Portuguese and Castilian armies joined forces to defeat the last Muslim attempt to invade the Peninsula (Livermore, *A New History of Portugal* 89). Another narrative recounts the story of King Ramiro II of León, who "cobrou a terra a Mouros" (took lands from the Moors, 204) and fell in love with the sister (Ártiga) of a Moorish king in Portugal, Alboazar Alboçadam, who reigned over the territories between Gaia and Santarém. This narrative is known as the *Lenda de Gaia* (Legend of Gaia).[12] It tells of Ramiro's adultery in abducting the beautiful Ártiga, her conversion to Christianity, and her eventual marriage to Ramiro—all of this against Alboazar Alboçadam's wishes. The story is one of adultery, abduction, vengeance, and Moorish–Christian romantic entanglement. Ramiro and Ártiga's offspring are listed at the close of the narrative, and the story, in its depiction of Moorish–Christian interaction

as both erotic and hostile, may, as Miranda suggests, combine legendary
and factual accounts of the origin of the Maia aristocracy. Pedro's frequent
references in his narratives to the fabled loss of Spain to the Moors by
King Rodrigo—a staple of Reconquest ideology—and the fashioning of
the flow of Luso-Hispanic history into an often anti-Islamic and Christian chivalric telos are countered by stories of erotic adventure that undo
the clean social and historical separation between Christian and Moor.[13]
The erotic currency between Moor and Christian in this narrative exposes
hostilities, both veiled and overt, that contravene the supposed genteel
idealizations characterizing Moorish–Christian coexistence in the literature of maurophilia (literally, "Moor loving"), traditionally epitomized in
Iberia with the sixteenth-century novel *El Abencerraje*.

We bring to a close this brief consideration of medieval Moors with
two examples from the early fifteenth century, after the invasion of Ceuta
but before Zurara's redaction of the *Crónica da Tomada de Ceuta*. The first
is the *Leal Conselheiro* (Loyal Counselor, completed ca. 1438), a philosophical treatise composed by D. Duarte, one of João I's sons. The *Leal
Conselheiro* considers, in essayistic and frequently autobiographical form,
the moral and spiritual values for living well (*viver bem*), especially for
those charged with the onus of governance. The book frames the moral-
ity of responsible living and leadership in a strict Christian mold. In a
commentary on the sin of *ira* (ire), Duarte considers the "passions" that
can result from this sin, including hatred (*ódio*). The discussion of hatred
centers on the *guerra dos mouros* or war against the Moors and the ethical quandary that such an action presents. The topic is timely, because
Duarte wrote in the aftermath of the capture of Ceuta and the continued
pursuit of Portuguese interests in Morocco and North Africa. Duarte
proposes his topic of reflection: "por que razom fariamos contra elles
pelleja, ou moveriamos guerra, pois soportavamos antre nos vyverem
judeus e outros mouros taaes como elles?" (for what reason could we fight
against them or wage war, since we allowed Jews and other Moors like
them to live among us?, 62). He concludes that the *guerra dos mouros* is
just if the Moors themselves—and we are to assume here African, not Portuguese, Moors—persist in denying the Catholic faith through the "delib-
eraçom de suas voontades" (deliberate acts of will, 62). Furthermore,
"[n]os e todos senhores catholicos lhe devemos fazer guerra pera tornar

suas terras a obediencia da santa madre igreja" (we and all Catholic lords should wage war to convert their lands to the submission of Holy Mother Church, 63). Although Duarte doesn't use the word *conquista*, this statement is tantamount to a defense of forceful military conquest. The extent and magnitude of oppresive force ("prema") used in such campaigns is to be determined by the Pontiff (63), and the king has the right as well to determine how his subjects will "matar, ferir e roubar" (kill, wound, and rob, 63), and Duarte advises that these actions should be tempered with "piedade" (pity).

Duarte's defense of the *guerra dos mouros* was most likely first drafted as a defense of a planned attack on Tangier in 1437; thus, we probably should understand Duarte's apologia of the war against the Moors as a reference to a specific military attack. Duarte's eventual offensive against the North African city ended in disaster; it had been conceived as an attempt to continue the pursuit of Portuguese interests in Morocco that had been initiated with the capture of Ceuta. Maintaining these African interests had been fraught with difficulties, and the Tangier plan was meant to support the presence in Ceuta and facilitate progress inland against the Muslims (Diffie and Winius 71). The attack on Tangier was a cause of considerable disagreement at court. Duarte's brothers João, Henrique (Prince Henry), and Pedro all weighed in on the proposed action against "Benamarim" (or "Belamarim," that is, western Morocco). Three documents exist that contain the princes' opinions. João argues at length against the attack, noting, inter alia, that "reason" (*syso*) often contravenes the code of chivalry and honor, and that such aggression is not necessarily in the service of God and might occasion severe financial loss; Henry, as one might expect, fully supports the proposal as consonant with service to God; and Pedro, while acknowledging that battling enemy Moors might well be honorable, opines that the cost in terms of men and money strongly militates against such a plan.[14] The controversy is a particularly good example of the monetary and military interests at stake behind the religious rhetoric that will increasingly surround references to the *guerra dos mouros* in expansionist documents, beginning with the chronicles of Zurara. The supposed spiritual antagonism of Moors boils down to their obstruction or resistance to Portuguese designs of a much more practical nature, and the *guerra dos mouros*—once a conceit in the medieval era that accompanied the "reclaiming" of Christian lands within the borders of Iberia—has become a catchall expression for aggressive campaigns against Moors in Africa and their natural resources.

THE AFRICAN IN-BETWEEN

In the fifteenth century, the voyages of exploration along the west African or "Guinean" coast pursue the coast as far south as it will reach. The writings that record these voyages, such as Zurara's chronicles or the Italian Alvise Cadamosto's eyewitness narrative, reflect an African-bound project of conquest, a view of exploration that sees only the western littoral and the encounters, including slave raids, on its sands and in its inlets. Even when "India" is referenced in Henrican documents the term refers to northeast Africa (Russell, *Prince Henry* 121). With Vasco da Gama's voyage to India at the end of the century there is a shift in expansionist texts and explanations about the reach of Portuguese *conquista* in that now Africa has become a middle ground in a larger and more "epic" progression of empire in the attainment of India and the East.[15] Sixteenth-century writers will, with hindsight and to varying degrees, make the voyages along Africa part of an ineluctable and gradual revelation of the ultimate Indian objective and therefore as constituent of a kind of teleology of expansion and maritime imperial travel. The "Moor," "Guinean," or "Ethiopian," terms that often are inconsistently applied, reflect shifting encounters with Africa as the limits of the known expand. Africa and the *mouro, negro, guineu,* or *etíope* become part of an expansionist culture that combines taxonomic observation with chronistic narrative as a foundational mode of imperial discourse. The Portuguese encounters with Africa, distinct from those of other European countries because of the geographic and historical proximity of the continent to Iberia, produce a body of texts that recognize the enterprise of Africa as a discrete undertaking while also situating that enterprise within a larger purview that ultimately encompasses India and America. Africa occupies its own place in the expansionist writings of Portugal, between the extreme East and the West—an African in-between, as it were. This interstitial space poses certain questions about the conceptual tools and vocabularies common in imperial/colonial studies as they intersect with the Portuguese fashioning of Africa.

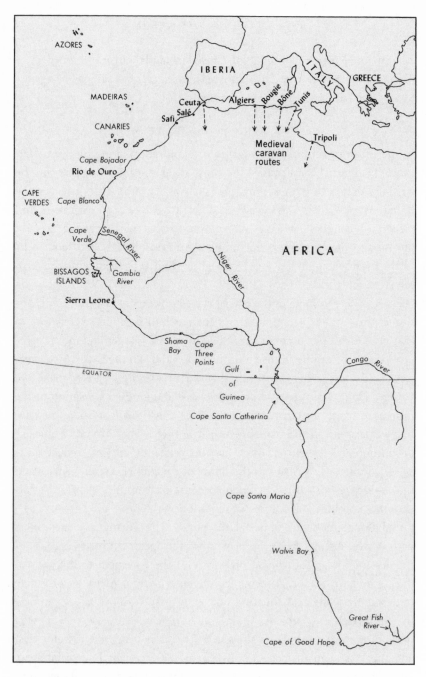

Map detailing major landmarks in the Portuguese exploration of West Africa from 1415 (Ceuta) to 1488 (Good Hope). From Diffie and Winius, *Foundations of the Portuguese Empire, 1415–1580.*

Arguably one of the most influential books in contemporary colonial studies is Edward Said's *Orientalism*. The tenets of Said's theories concerning the West's construction of the Orient have become commonplaces in much critical work: among them, that Orientalism is an ideologically driven, hegemonic practice of discourse with supporting institutions and vocabulary; that the ideological construction of the Orient participates in formulations of western European identity or the European "self"; that Orientalism is a Western strategy for dominating, structuring, and having authority over the "Orient" as a construct rather than as an "inert fact of nature" (*Orientalism* 4); or that Orientalist discourse is more about European power over the Orient than it is a veridic discourse. In the years since its publication, Said's formulation of Orientalism has been criticized for a number of its assumptions and arguments, including that of an unchanging or static concept of cultural interaction with a "hegemonic, active West imposing an idea upon a subordinate, passive East" (Hadfield 1) or the Eurocentric nature of Said's models, which leads to a "monolithic" character of Orientalism and essentialist contrasts between East and West (Cass 27, 39).[16] It has also been argued that Said proposes a more or less homogeneous concept of "empire," and the result of this assumption is that there is an assumed, internal consistency to Orientalist discourse. "Said asserts the unified character of Western discourse on the Orient over some two millennia," Dennis Porter observes (181). Even if we allow that debates on Orientalism have taken place only within the parameters set out by Said, as Robert Irwin claims in his rebuke titled *Dangerous Knowledge*, the fact remains that Said's book has provided a conceptual vocabulary for much of imperial studies (or "imperium studies," as Fuchs proposes), however much we might disagree with or modify the presuppositions or applications of that vocabulary. In that fact the influence of *Orientalism* cannot be overlooked; Cass notes how some scholarship has admittedly stretched and contorted Said's original concept but "into new and fascinating shapes" (38). Bringing Orientalism into contact with imperial practices and cultures outside of Said's original intentions and parameters can generate provocative ideas about Orientalism as a shaping characteristic of imperial discourse and can bring the textual, imperialist practices of nations not included in *Orientalism* to the scholarly table. The Portuguese textual matter of Africa is a case in point. The question is, then, in the late-medieval and early-modern Portuguese discourse on Africa, how might it be possible to define a Portuguese Orientalism, or, to follow Christopher L. Miller's lead in his study of French texts, a Portuguese Africanist discourse that postures with and/or against Saidian Orientalism? In posing this question I am not suggesting that Said be modified or rewritten to fit the Portuguese textual matter of Africa. Rather, I wish to bring some of Said's precepts into contact with Portuguese ideas about Africa. For the sake of convenience, I will use the term "Orientalism," though it is probably better, as K. David Jackson suggested in an MLA paper, to formulate the Portuguese imperial/colonial relationship to the East in terms of "Orientalness." Such a term has the advantage of acknowledging a distinct Portuguese practice of fashioning and experiencing the East prior to the Anglo–French engagements with the Orient studied by Said, while still notionally retaining some of the postulations about the importance of discourse as an ideological practice of empire, a discourse that is anything but unified and that is a result of different historical moments and purposes. And here we find the first note of dissonance between Saidian Orientalism and Portuguese empire in Africa (and later, in India): this was not an imperialist practice that fashioned non-Western spaces solely on a discursive level but also as the result of lived and concrete experience. Jackson's idea of Orientalness might thus be understood to gesture toward the Portuguese experiential nature of the East as opposed to the Saidian Orient that is abstracted through scholarly disciplines and literature. The Portuguese texts do not exoticize the spaces of empire to the extent present in Said's arguments but bring them nonetheless into often very ideologically driven agendas. The discussion here seeks to fill a gap in Orientalist debate by bringing Portuguese materials to the fore.[17]

In *Blank Darkness*, Christopher L. Miller makes a critical rapprochement between some tenets of Saidian Orientalism and French writings on Africa from the eighteenth and nineteenth centuries. In Miller's reading, *Orientalism* is part of a reappraisal of European knowledge that studies arbitrary judgments made by discourse (15). Miller delineates an Africanist discursive practice that, in accordance with the Saidian construction of the East, is born in Europe of European ideas (5) and is a European attempt to fill an empty space called "Africa" (6). A central aspect of Orientalist discourse is the creation of a monolithic Other and its opposition to the European. But unlike Orientalist writings, with their assumed prerogative of knowledge and authority, knowledge of Africa "has tended to be proffered with caveats; Africanist authors frequently call their own authority and mastery of the subject into question" (19). These Orientalist and Africanist discourses, nonetheless, manifest a "will-to-truth" (16). For Miller, Africa and Africans are the locus of gaps, breaches, and failures in understanding and knowledge (20), and (black) Africa constitutes a nullity, a nonspace that exists negatively until there is a European colonizer to fill it.

In Portuguese writings, Africa occupies a place in the expansionist imagination that is at once a named geographic space (or the parts of the continent that will gradually come to be referred to collectively as "Africa") as well as a less-defined geographic directionality referred to as the Orient. Once Vasco da Gama reaches India, for instance, eastern Africa was subsumed into an expansive geomercantile territory that defined the central arena of Portuguese imperialism. This territory was known as the *Estado da Índia* (State of India), "the name given by the Portuguese to all their possessions and trading-posts between Sofala and Macao, or, in a looser sense, to the whole of maritime East Africa and Asia from the Cape of Good Hope to Japan" (Boxer, *Race Relations* 41).[18] Even before the *Estado da Índia* was delimited, "Africa" was a geographic idea that frequently was combined with the East or India. In speculating on what the term "India" meant for fifteenth-century Portuguese, Randles notes that "India" was applied to all territories that lay east of the Mediterranean, beyond Islam, and south of the Sahara ("Notes" 21). Randles further observes (22) that the state of geographic knowledge in Portugal at the time is hard to assess, with almost all of our information coming from Zurara's *Chronicle of Guinea*. In that chronicle, Zurara describes the large region of western Africa designated as "Guiné" as well as its inhabitants. The Senegal River is the dividing line between the "terra dos mouros" (land of the Moors) and the "terra dos negros" (land of the blacks); at one point, Zurara equates the Senegal River with the Nile:

> E esta gente desta terra verde he toda negra e porem he chamada terra dos negros ou terra de guinee por cujo aazo os homeẽs e molheres della som chamados guineus. que quer tanto dizer como negros. E quando os das

carauellas viram as primeiras palmeiras e aruores altas . . . bem conhecerom
que eram preto do Ryo do nillo da parte donde vem sayr ao mar do ponente
ao qual Ryo chamam de Çanaga . . . (225)

And the people of this verdant land are all black and for that reason it is
called the land of the blacks or the land of Guinea, for which reason the men
and women are called Guineans, which is the same thing as saying black.
And when those on the caravels saw the first palms and tall trees . . . they
well knew they were close to the Nile at the point where it flowed into the
western sea, which is there called the Senegal . . .[19]

In the following chapter, Zurara summarizes biblical and ancient geographic knowledge about the Nile, culled, as Léon Bourdon and others
note in the French translation of the chronicle, from the *General estoria*
of Alfonso X (182n1).[20] Here, Zurara claims that the Nile flows through
Mauritania, thereby linking the "land of the Moors" to the venerable
waterway. The point is that the Nile was considered to divide "India" from
"Africa," so that, in this logic, lands south of the Senegal technically could
have been considered India (Randles, "Notes" 24). This was one of the
reasons the Portuguese may have sought the kingdom of Prester John in
Africa as opposed to the subcontinent (sometimes referred to as "Upper
India"), because the mention of India in a fourteenth-century copy of
the apocryphal letter of the Prester now in the National Library in Lisbon
may have been understood as meaning African lands.[21] Another instance
in which Zurara's separation of the eastern and western spheres occurs
in chapter 2 of *Guiné*, where the chronicler, in an apostrophe to Prince
Henry, refers to the farthest points reached by Henry's expeditions:

Espantãme aquelles vezinhos do nyllo cuja grande multidom tē ocupados
os termos daquella velha e antiga cidade de Thebas porque os veio vestidos
da tua deuysa E as suas carnes que nũca conhecerõ vestidura trazē agora
roupas de desuayradas collores. . . . E que fez esto senom largueza de tuas
despesas e o trabalho de teus seruidores mouidos per teu vertuoso engenho
pello qual tresmudaste nas fijns do ouriente as cousas criadas e feitas no
ocidente. . . . Oo tu . . . que te metes no laberinto de tãta glorya. por que te
estas ocupando con as naçōoes ouryentaaes. (21)

I am astonished by the dwellers of the Nile, whose great numbers possess
the ancient and venerable city of Thebes, since I see them clothed in your
livery, and their flesh that never knew any covering, is now adorned in cloths
of many colors. . . . And what has caused this but the largesse of your purse
and the labor of your servants inspired by your virtuous will, by which
you carried to the ends of the East that which was made in the West? . . .
Oh Prince . . . you who enter the labyrinth of such glory, why do you busy
yourself with the nations of the East?

What, precisely, Zurara means here by the "East" and by "nations of the
East" has been the subject of some discussion. In his edition of the chronicle, José de Bragança notes that Zurara's reference to the "dwellers of
the Nile" refers to the blacks living by the Niger, which was thought to be
a branch of the Nile (16n5). The East Zurara mentions has led some scholars to argue that Henry's expeditions had already reached, by land, not
only Egypt but also India and perhaps Malacca, and that these expeditions
were kept secret by the so-called *política de sigilo* (policy of secrecy) by
which Portugal was supposed to have imposed a strict code of silence
on travelers and kept any documents resulting from such travels under
lock and key in order to protect its commercial interests from competi-
tors such as Spain.[22] Zurara's often unclear notions of world geography
will probably make this an unresolvable question, but it is important to
acknowledge that these references to the East may mean Africa, according to the geographic inconsistency of "India" in the fifteenth century.
Even if Zurara theoretically considers eastern Africa and Asia as an "Orient" opposed to the West, the regularly blurred boundaries between East
and West in the chronicle inevitably draw sub-Saharan Africa into these
notions of Orientalness. The inconsistent use of toponyms and the general confusion of (Eastern) geography in Zurara, then, including the shifting and inconsistent uses of "Ethiopia" (which was considered part of Asia),
conflate Africa with the East and thus make it apposite to theorizations of
Orientalist–Africanist discourse. Furthermore, if we think of the "East"
not as a strictly denotative geographic term but rather as a relational term,
as Daniel Martin Varisco points out in his readings of Said (61, 66), and
which ultimately requires us to treat "[t]he very notion of Europe . . . as
an invention" (61), the Zuraran concept of African space places the East

as laterally adjacent to Europe but also relocates it southward.[23] Africa is an intermediate and shifting space that is both Eastern and non-Eastern and is the first term of the conceptualization of the East to be developed later in the sixteenth century (such as in João de Barros) when "India" comes increasingly to refer solely to the subcontinent.

In medieval patristic and geographic writings, as Suzanne Conklin Akbari points out (20), the world was conceived of in three parts (Asia, Europe, and Africa) and the Orient was continually in the process of being re-formed (31). The shifting space of the Orient and the tripartite division of the world in the medieval period are echoed in Zurara's conflation of sub-Saharan Africa and Ethiopia/Egypt through the path of the Nile; they maintain Mauritania as a discrete geographic entity (one of the parts of Africa) distinct from the land of the blacks below the Senegal. As a third term interposed between West and East, then, it is possible to understand Africa in the years of expansion as a non-Western Other. The aprioristic superiority of Christian culture over the barbaric gentile or Moorish heretic, the supposed readiness of African indigenes to accept Christian conversion, or the sometimes—but by no means consistent—presence of a passive native population confronted by the (military) might of Portuguese expeditions might seem to conform to Said's notions of positional superiority or the inherent passivity of "Oriental" or non-European cultures. In such a situation, we might also be inclined to find the Saidian binary opposition between Self and Other. But such similarities are provisional. The third term of Portuguese (or Iberian) Africa as a space of otherness is not geographically distant like the Orient described by Said, nor is it exotic in a way that recalls the novelistic narratives that underlie Said's analyses. The geographic and historical proximity of Africa to Iberia is different from the distances separating the Orient from Said's Anglo-French writers of the nineteenth and twentieth centuries. The question of the Other—the Moor, or the sub-Saharan African—in expansion reflects the intertwined histories of Africa and Iberia that defy simple categorization. On the other hand, as Diogo Ramada Curto reminds us, from a methodological perspective Saidian Orientalism is a mode of imperialism that reveals the perspectives of those who wield power ("Introdução" xiii), and, in the case of Portuguese texts like the histories of João de Barros, allows for the reconstitution of the several means and manners of the mediation between power and knowledge (xiv).[24]

Africa's stereotypical role as Europe's Other glosses over the relational intricacies of the African or the Moor to Portuguese or Iberian cultures. The idea of Africa-as-other, outside of the Iberian context, has received influential expression, such as Hegel's *Lectures on the Philosophy of World History*, in which the German philosopher provides an excursus on the geographic basis of world history. There, Hegel proposes that Africa consists of three distinct parts: North Africa, Egypt, and sub-Saharan Africa or "Africa proper." For Hegel, North Africa forms a "single unit with Spain" (173) and is oriented toward Europe; Hegel perpetuates the non-Iberianist trope that Africa begins at the Pyrenees. Egypt has a destiny as a great and independent culture and has nothing to do with North Africa because it is not near the Mediterranean. The longest section describes Africa proper (i.e., black Africa). It "has no historical interest of its own" because its inhabitants live in "barbarism and savagery [without] an integral ingredient of culture" (174). Here history is "out of the question" because there is no subjectivity (176); man has not progressed "beyond his immediate existence" (177). Without explicitly saying so, Hegel resuscitates a medieval view of Africa as a space made up of discrete regions; Hegel's three divisions correspond roughly to the regions of Mauritania, Ethiopia, and the Torrid Zone, though a Torrid Zone that is now inhabited. Like the medieval conceptualization of Africa (when that label was in fact used) as in parts, Hegel proposes the quasi paradox of immediately proximate lands that are discontinuous. Hegel's comments are an example of the idea that the "African has an absolute alterity to the European" (Snead 63) and stands as a "discrete otherness" (64).

In Iberia, the African as a "discrete otherness" is a problematic idea. The coexistence of Muslim, Jewish, and Christian cultures in the form of *convivencia* (living together or coexistence) means that any notion of a binarized, Moorish Other dissolves.[25] In fact, as most theorists of Orientalism tacitly presuppose, it is the Christian European that is assumed to be the neutral ground zero of the self in constructions of otherness. Such arguments would have us believe that this Christian ur-Self is somehow natural, a posture exemplified in the Iberian case, for example, by the ideology of the Reconquest as a "rightful" reappropriation of Christian territories or in the expansionist understanding of *conquista*. In medieval Spanish culture, Mark D. Meyerson notes that the "other" was often "a neighbor or a known quantity who had to be rendered 'other' if society

were to function as rulers and religious elites of all groups" (xiv). Jean
Dangler points out that one of the tenets of medieval alterity was that it
"girded epistemological and ontological modes that integrated rather than
expulsed the divergent" (2), and that shifts in alterity coincided with the
modern creation of the other as someone to restrict and disempower (6).
One incarnation of the Moor as a figure of alterity is the Saracen, and
Dangler notes the methodological necessity, exemplified in John V. Tolan's
Saracens, of historical analysis according to specific time periods and social
contexts (3) that recognizes that there is no diachronic, uniform concept
of Moorish or African otherness. Jeffrey J. Cohen's study of English and
French representations of the Saracen works toward freeing the Saracen
from the overly facile strictures of the Self/Other binary opposition by considering how literary depictions dovetail with the universalizing claims of
psychoanalysis.[26] In the case of "Oriental" cultures in Spain, as Tofiño-
Quesada argues apropos of nineteenth-century perceptions of the country
by foreign travelers (143), there is a paradox inherent in the idea of Spanish Orientalism: as a country that orientalizes and colonizes the African
Other, Spain is often described as Oriental itself. Similarly, Mahmoud
Manzalaoui speaks of the overpolarization of Self and Other in Saidian
Orientalism and notes that, in Spain, "the study of the East is precisely
not a study of the Other, but a recovery of part of the Self" (838, emphasis in original). The same claim could be made about Portugal, although
"Eastern" cultures (Arabic, Hebrew, or Moorish) were not as present to
the degree they were in al-Andalus. Nonetheless, the Arabic, Hebrew, or
Moorish sectors of Portuguese society means that there existed an a priori
Orientalness to the "self" within the borders of the home country that was
the seat and origin of imperialism.

    If medieval and early-modern *convivencia* in Spain constitutes one socio-
historical forum for questioning otherness and Orientalist tenets, expansionist Portugal constitutes another. The nature of Portuguese empire in
Africa varied greatly from time to time and region to region, so that it is
a mistake, as Wyatt MacGaffey notes in the case of Portuguese colonial interaction in the sixteenth-century Kongo, to read those relations in modern, colonial terms (260). It is necessary not to construe the imperial or
colonial relationship solely in terms of dominance versus subjugation, a
construction that tends to polarize the subjugated other from the European

colonizer and thus distorts the variegated encounters in Africa. The Portuguese spaces of imperialism and colonialism align more with Mary Louise Pratt's postulation of the contact zone as "social spaces where disparate cultures meet, clash, and grapple with each other, often in highly asymmetrical relations of domination and subordination" (4). Consider the Arabic-speaking Moorish slave trader in Africa who facilitated the trade in sub-Saharan captives, or the *mussambazes,* African traders who worked for the Portuguese and acted as their commercial agents in the Indian Ocean trade (Newitt, *East Africa* xix).[27] Moors were often complicit in the exercise of power over other Africans, and, because of the historical presence of Moors in Portugal, are already and necessarily part of the culture that produced expansion. Throughout the late-medieval and early-modern periods up to Camões, the operative distinction made between Portuguese imperialist voyagers and African Others is not "Portuguese" versus "African" but "Christian" versus "Moor," "infidel," or "pagan." Yet, as Chandra Richard de Silva points out, even "Christian" is not an altogether accurate term; though all Portuguese shared at least an ostensible bond through Christianity, there was a minority of New Christians grouped under the "Chrisitan" label who were reluctant converts from Judaism, and not all of them were Portuguese (296). In a study of early-modern Portuguese presence on the Swahili coast, Jeremy Prestholdt argues that the "other" is too limiting a concept for understanding the many situations of intercultural exchange and that scholars should be wary of employing this concept as an easily transportable conceptual tool (384). Prestholdt presents evidence that overturns the idea that "totalizing conceptualizations of the Other were necessarily present in every historical encounter between Europeans and non-Europeans" (399).

In an oft-cited analysis of colonial discourse, Homi Bhabha argues that "[t]he construction of the colonial subject in discourse, and the exercise of colonial power through discourse, demands an articulation of forms of difference—racial and sexual" (67), and, furthermore, that "[t]he objective of colonial discourse is to construe the colonized as a population of degenerate types on the basis of racial origin, in order to justify conquest and to establish systems of administration and instruction" (70). In the Portuguese writings on Africa prior to Camões, the construction of Africans as degenerate types is frequent, if not consistent, and the basis of the differentiation is usually religious and often also linguistic. Sub-Saharan Africans in particular receive the most degrading characterizations as bestial or barbaric, though as military foes they are often depicted as formidable. What we do not find in the Portuguese material is emphasis on sexual difference or on the sexuality of the African as a characteristic of his alterity to European paradigms of civility. The pre-Camonian writings on Africa do not characteristically shape expansionist travel and appropriation in erotic terms; they do not participate in a tradition of "male travel as an erotics of ravishment" or depict Africa as "libidinously eroticized" (22) that McClintock claims predated the writings of Columbus. The "racial" aspect of the African, however, requires comment.

"Race" as an applicable term to medieval and early-modern culture has generated a fair amount of critical discussion, especially in regard to texts composed during imperial expansion and the establishment of a supposedly natural power differential in favor of European colonizers when confronted with indigenous populations of differing physiognomies and spiritualities. A major point of this debate is the degree to which modern understandings of "race" may be said to obtain in the culture of expansionist encounter, such as Zurara's descriptions of black Africans. In the light of such problems, some scholars prefer the term "racialist" to point to an inchoate, premodern practice of negatively differentiating non-European civilizations from European ones on the basis of physical traits, religious practices, or language. The modern use of the word race, according to Ivan Hannaford, is "to claim that there [are] immutable major divisions of humankind, each with biologically transmitted characteristics" (17). The biological determinism of modern racist thought does not always or easily map onto earlier time periods. Hannaford goes on to note that the words for "race" in European languages in medieval and premodern times carried meanings distinct from modern usage: "'race' entered Western language late, coming into general use in Northern Europe about the middle of the sixteenth century" (5).[28] In fifteenth-century Portuguese, according to James Sweet, *raça* referred to groups of plants, animals, or humans that shared traits through a common genealogy (144); it is important to note that the characteristics of a shared genealogy, in the case of humans, were usually not physical but religious.[29] Zurara does not use *raça* to refer to Moors or Africans but instead uses *geeraçom* (generation)

the "new human" that attends the emergence of anthropological discourse (212), then this new brand of human and discourse is part of the ideological reinvention of Africa that expansion and Zurara's chronicle instantiate. Zurara's terminology for natives is inconsistent; for example, *mouro* is alternately distinct from, and synonymous with, *negro* (black), *mouro negro* (black Moor or blackamoor), or *guinéu* (Guinean), and refers to Africans outside of the generally accepted boundaries of Mauritania.[34] Zurara's terminological inconsistency may demonstrate geographic confusion about the regions of Africa but it also suggests that in *Guiné* a new kind of Moor, the *mouro negro*, appears on the mental radar of the Portuguese as opposed to the northern Moor of Mauritania (Horta, "Primeiros olhares" 83). Devisse and Mollat incidentally observe that the "classic European view of Africa and Africans and the view held by the Portuguese did not overlap. . . . Yet the latter view contained certain basic factors which the former could not long ignore—namely, direct contact with the hitherto unknown continent and the importation of blacks reduced to slavery" (154). In addition to the *mouro negro*, Zurara documents the existence of yet another kind of Moor, the *azenegue* (Azanaghi, modern Sanhaja), a designation that usually means the lighter-skinned Berber Moors who live on the coast, as opposed to the populations living in the interior (Margarido 510, 533).

The narrative compilations of Valentim Fernandes (fl. 1494–1516) and Duarte Pacheco Pereira (ca. 1465–ca. 1533) are important syntheses of knowledge about Africa from the time of Prince Henry's sub-Saharan explorations through the mid-sixteenth century. Fernandes was a German printer who set up shop in Lisbon and was active in printing books related to expansion, such as the Portuguese translation of the book of Marco Polo (*Livro de Marco Paulo*) published in 1502, the same year Vasco da Gama made his second voyage to India. Fernandes also produced an early-sixteenth-century compilation of writings on expansion that focuses almost exclusively on Africa, known as the *Códice Valentim Fernandes* (Valentim Fernandes Codex). This manuscript contains, among other texts, geographic/ethnological descriptions of Africa and its inhabitants, portions of Zurara's *Guiné*, and the Latin *De prima inuentione Gujnee* of Diogo Gomes de Sintra. The codex contains numerous descriptions of Moors that reiterate skin color gradations according to geographic regions in that the more southernly Moors are darker. The geohumoral idea that dark skin is a climate-induced aberration of white skin appears in the early folios when Fernandes notes that the inhabitants of Arguim Island are "white men by nature" ("som homens aluos de naturaleza," 22) and become black by walking nude in the sun, an idea that will soon be refuted by Pereira. The Moors of Arguim (or "alarbes boons," good Arabs) are noteworthy because of their brown skin and because they are free from all vice, including sodomy (38). This is one of the only times in expansionist writings of the period that the "çugidade" (filthiness, 38) of Moors is linked to sexual sin and not to faith.

Duarte Pacheco Pereira's *Esmeraldo de situ orbis*, completed sometime in the very early sixteenth century, is a geographic treatise on the Portuguese explorations but it is also a compendium of knowledge on Africa. In its pages Pereira summarizes geographic information and lore, nautical sailing directions, and the characteristics of peoples beyond the borders of Portugal. Of interest here is Pereira's designation of two Ethiopias, upper and lower Ethiopia. Pereira's reiteration of this geographic divide solidifies certain notions about the distribution of Moors and the lands of the blacks for the sixteenth century, some of which notions originate in Zurara. Pereira identifies lower Ethiopia as the "Etiópias de Guiné" (Ethiopias of Guinea, 78)—that is, all African territories from the Senegal southward—and upper Ethiopia as "os opulentíssimos Reinos da Índia" (the most wealthy kingdoms of India, 84).[35] Pereira remarks that "na qual região so acharia tanta multidão de novos povos e homens negros, quanta do tempo deste descobrimento atégora temos sabido e praticado, cuja color e feição e modo de viver alguém poderia crer, se não os houvesse visto" (in this region a great multitude of new peoples and black men would be found; as, in fact, have been discovered from that time to our day; whose color and shape and way of life none who had not seen them could believe, 62). The insistence on the newness of the peoples of lower Ethiopia reinscribes the idea that Guinea marks an epistemological boundary and beyond it lies a new world, a slight relocation southward of Zurara's boundary in the form of Cape Bojador, the end point of knowledge and lore.

The alliance between land divisions and skin color means that Moors, black Africans, Ethiopians, or Guineans function like monsters in that they mark geographic boundaries and the limits of the known and the familiar. Perhaps one of the most dramatic and oft-cited instances of color differentiation occurs in Zurara's *Guiné* in what Lowe calls an "unprecedented spectacle of 'blackness'" (10). The scene is the first documented slave market, in August 1444, in the southern Portuguese town of Lagos:

> era hũa marauilhosa cousa de veer. Ca antre elles auya alguũs de razoada brancura fremosos e aspostos. outros menos brancos que queryam semelhar pardos. outros tam negros come tiopios tã desafeiçoados assy nas caras como nos corpos que casy parecia aos homeẽs que os esguardauam que vyã as jmageẽs do jmjsperyo mais baixo. (107–8)

> It was a marvelous thing to see. There were those among them of a reasonable whiteness, appealing and in good form; others were less white, and appeared brown; and there were others that were as black as Ethiopians, so ugly in face and body that they appeared, to those who looked on them, to be of the lowest hemisphere.

Lahon ("Black African Slaves" 262) notes the aesthetic judgment passed on the blackest African male here as derisive—a judgment, according to him, associated with the European fear of blackness. Sweet finds that Zurara's comments are shaped by a racial hierarchy (160); there can be little doubt of this given *Guiné*'s justificatory rhetoric of the enslavement of the sub-Saharan African. Yet, even if we accept the negative, racial valuation of blackness, it is important to note that this hierarchy is not a rigid stratification differentiating two poles of black and white but rather a continuum. What Zurara's description of the slave market makes clear is the connectedness between black and white, so that the presumed and authoritative white I/eye of the chronicler, and of the conquistatorial "we" that regularly appears throughout the text (defined mostly as Christian), belongs to an Iberian or Mediterranean inflection of white, even if, following Hulme, we allow "the term as accurate to describe the color of southern Europeans" ("Tales of Distinction" 162). Horta similarly notes that the categories of "Portuguese" or "white" are not clear ("Evidence" 114). The spectrum of skin colors, beginning with "reasonable whiteness" and ending in Ethiopian blackness, reflects the trajectory southward traced

by the Portuguese slavers that begins in northern Africa and ends in the
terra dos negros with each region's by now characteristic pigmentation.
Zurara's description aspires to geographic inclusiveness in that the color
continuum represents all of Portuguese Africa at the time of the chronicle. The colors of the bodies of the slaves visually demonstrate the reach
of Portuguese conquest along the west coast.

In this same chapter, Zurara reflects on the plight of the slaves:

> mas qual serya o coraçom por duro que seer podesse que nom fosse pungido
> de piedoso sentimēto veēdo assy aquella cōpanha Ca huūs tijnham as caras
> baixas e os rostros lauados com lagrimas oolhando huūs contra os outros.
> outros estauam gemendo muy doorosamente esguardando a altura dos ceeos
> firmando os olhos em elles braadando altamente como se pedissem acorro ao
> padre da natureza. . . . Mas pera seu doo seer mais acrecētado sobreueherom
> aquelles que tijnham carrego da partilha e começarom de os apartarem
> huūs dos outros . . . onde cōuijnha de necessydade de see apartarem os filhos
> dos padres e as molheres dos maridos e os huūs jrmaāos dos outros. (108)

> But what heart could be so hard that it would not be struck by painful
> sentiment to see that company? Some kept their heads low and their faces
> bathed in tears as they looked on one another; others moaned piteously and
> turned their faces to the heavens, crying loudly, as if asking for help from
> the father of nature. . . . But to augment their suffering even more, those
> in charge of dividing the captives began to separate them . . . and it was
> necessary to part children from their parents and husbands from their wives
> and brothers from brothers.

A certain skittishness can be glimpsed in the chronicler's commiserating
rhetoric. Margarido finds that Zurara's description of the slaves is an indication of the "surprise" manifested before somatic diversity (515). Yet it is
possible to read the passage as if the Portuguese (or the observational "I"
or "we") did not so much experience surprise at the range of pigmentation, but rather connection. Zurara's slave market presents the possibility
of a somatic link between slave traders and slaves, between conquistatorial explorers and human booty. African darkness, Zurara implies, is not
all that different from Portuguese whiteness, and in this his narrative voice

is sympathetic to the lamentations of the captives and to the genealogical violence the slave trade causes. Zurara's commiseration may well be a rhetorical move meant to distance himself and the proponents of expansion from the dangerously close darkness of Africa through a gesture of pitiful sympathy. This darkness becomes uncomfortably proximate through the racial intermediary, the brown (*pardo*) captive, who is neither entirely white nor entirely black. Brown is at once a color originating from Africa—such as the light-skinned *azenegue* Moors—as it is also one produced by expansion and the offspring of white Europeans and black Africans. Later, the most emblematic figure of this mixing in the culture of colonization is the child produced by the *lançado,* or the European who married indigenous women and lived in Africa, who "went completely native, stripping off their clothes, tattoing [*sic*] their bodies, and speaking in the local languages, and even joining in fetishistic rites and celebrations" (Boxer, *Race Relations* 9).[36] The children of such unions were often referred to as "mulattoes." Silva maintains that, as opposed to other European colonial practices, "Portuguese colonists did not forcefully exclude or condemn interracial sex" ("Raced Encounters" 27). *Mulato* as a designation for someone with brown skin may in itself be pejorative, if we accept the etymology of the word as a term originally used for a mule (Tinhorão 238). In Zurara, the brown-skinned African—either the mulatto or a light-skinned native—is a third racial term that upsets the black/white opposition and notionally connects explorers to their captives.

Zurara's description of the skin color of the captives admits this connection at the same time that it attempts to isolate brownness as a separate or discrete pigmentational category. Brownness in this taxonomic perspective functions as a buffer zone between white and black and allows a racial hierarchy to remain in place, however temporarily. The brown third term as a color that threatens to loosen the black/white distinction and construe southern European whiteness relationally rather than absolutely precipitates Zurara's recourse to aesthetics as an arbiter of moral categories. If the fact of whiteness in itself is not corroborated by the natural world as an innate marker of European superiority, then an aesthetico-moral reading of the hues of humankind revealed by Africa rescues the European's "natural" authority over the African. Pigmentational difference is, according to Haydara, one of the Western criteria of categorization that makes *Guiné* a founding text of imperialism (77). Those moments in which brownness (or lesser blackness) appears and inevitably links black to white activate taxonomic distinctions that maintain blackness as an aesthetically and morally "ugly" trait. If, for the crown-appointed chronicler and therefore curator of the ideological motives behind expansion, racialist difference serves as an easy way to maintain those motives in the encounters narrated, the slave market is an especially and intensely marked moment of this kind of difference and the value judgments it allows. That is, not all awareness of color differentials, either in Zurara or in other texts, acts in the same way or with the same force. Ann Laura Stoler summarizes, for later British colonialism, the dynamics of racism that have a precursor in Zurara; she notes that "studies of the colonial have only begun to recognize that the *quantity* and the *intensity* of racism have varied enormously in different contexts and at different moments in any particular colonial counter" (24, emphasis in original).

The innate or essentialist connection that expansionist writers attempt to establish between the lesser colors of black and brown and the gradually revealed peoples of Africa as a means of justifying conquest and of maintaining an aprioristic separation between "us" and "them" also surfaces in the description of geographic regions. Zurara establishes equations between space, its inhabitants, and the color(s) of inhabitants that will be repeated throughout the early-modern period; these associations metonymically transfer the color of inhabitants to the land itself.[37] Guinea is the "terra dos negros" (*Guiné* 116) much as Mauritania, up to the Senegal River, is the "terra dos mouros," the domain of the lighter-skinned *azenegues*. The tight association between the color of Africans (or Guineans) and the land itself creates specific regions of difference or otherness. In a study of geographic difference in Shakespeare, John Gillies notes a "complex and dynamic imaginative quality [to geography], with a characterological and symbolic agenda" (3), in which imperial expansion brought with it hosts of new others and the related need to differentiate, establish symbolic borders, and enact new rites of exclusion (6). Though Shakespeare's England and northern European experiences of imperial otherness (especially as it relates to Africa) are different from those of Portugal, Gillies's observation may be backdated to the fifteenth century and to the perceptions of African geography by Portuguese writers. The zones of Africa exist within both real and symbolic borders, borders that delineate geographic and cognitive newness and whose inhabitants unwittingly play a role in a European-centered, historico-imaginative gnosis of the continent. Once again Zurara's slave market is instructive. If the hues of the slaves' skin collectively gathered at the market symbolically represent Portuguese exploration through the territorial regions associated with those varying hues, the partitioning of the slaves is a symbolic appropriation of African space in absentia. Dividing the collected bodies is an analogue to the textual division and partitioning of Africa in Zurara, Leo Africanus, or Mármol Carvajal. In a study of the changing conceptualizations of Atlantic space from the Middle Ages to the discoveries, Luís Adão da Fonseca establishes that, in the later fifteenth century, the Portuguese had revised an idea of geography as dominated by places to one characterized by spaces, and that space was conceived of in terms of the bodies that occupied it (16). The slaves in Lagos are living markers and products of African space so that the tyranny of the slave market is yet one more act of control over Africa. In *Guiné*, Zurara's inconsistent use of *mouro* to refer to peoples outside of Mauritania frees the label from a geographically determined referentiality and allows for Moors to become the signifiers of African space. Moors are emanations of African space, in and outside of Mauritania, bodies that both conjure and mark Africa. In Fonseca's line of reasoning, Africa begins to exist in the fifteenth century in a fundamentally different way from previous eras: Africa now exists primarily because of the bodies it generates, and the capture and transportation of Guinean slaves captures space itself for the purposes of exploitation.

By metonymically racializing African land through the colors of its inhabitants, Zurara and others attempt to establish otherness as an inert fact of nature waiting to be revealed through the hermeneutic activity of writing. The natural world colludes with Zurara's Christian cosmos and its moral hierarchy by marking its inhabitants visibly and therefore placing those inhabitants in an order of being that it is up to interpreters like Zurara to read. In the early pages of *Guiné*, the chronicler summarizes geographic knowledge on Africa and writes:

Veio aqueles garamantes E aquelles tiopios que viuē sob a ssoõbra do monte Caucaso negros em collor por que Iazem de sob o posito do auge do sol o

qual sēedo na cabeça de capicornyo he a elles ē estranha quentura segūdo
se mostra pello mouimēto do centro de seu excentrico ou per outra maneira
por que vezinham cō a cinta queimada . . . (20)

I see those Garamantes and those Ethiopians who live under the shadow of
Mount Caucasus, black in color because they live opposite the full height
of the sun; and the sun, as it is in the head of Capricorn, shines a strange
heat on them that is demonstrated by the movements from the center of its
eccentric or by the proximity of these people to the Torrid Zone . . .

In a later chapter (borrowed from Alfonso X's *General estoria*), Zurara
again remarks on "o color meesmo daquelle pouoo de thiopya cujo sangue
he queimado da grande queētura do sol que ha ally o poder de todo seu
feruor" (the very color of the Ethiopian people, whose blood is burnt by
the immense heat of the sun which there commands the full power of its
heat, 239). The sun scorches the inhabitants of Ethiopia, and this blackness, in turn, is one of the signs of the natural world that expansionist
writers read authoritatively, like the color and run of the sea, the presence
of birds over water as indicative of the proximity of land, or the sign language of Africans. In this context, Zurara's locution "estranha quentura"
is notable—the "strange" or "wondrous" heat of the Torrid Zone traces
a line that, until the Portuguese expeditions, had not been crossed and had
therefore "naturally" prevented the passage of bodies and knowledge.[38]
Expansion abolishes this boundary and brings a corpus of knowledge
back from beyond the intense and strange heat of Africa; part of that
knowledge consists in the forms of African alterity and the beginnings
of a more comprehensive and verifiable African geography. By breaching
Cape Bojador and the storied Torrid Zone, Portuguese travelers-writers
create a geography of difference, if not strict otherness. This geography,
like the ontology of space studied by Syed Manzurul Islam in travel narratives, grounds otherness in spatial locations (5) and creates a sympathy
between spaces of dwelling and bodies that makes space a trope of essential differences (7). The expansionist texts on Africa create difference by
racializing space and the entire body and expanse of Africa as it gradually
revealed itself to expansionist eyes.

2

EXPANSION AND THE
CONTOURS OF AFRICA

THE CAMPAIGNS OF EXPLORATION AND CONQUEST begun with the capture of Ceuta in 1415 and that evolve into the expansive presence in Africa and India in the sixteenth century nurture a culture of writing that shapes Africa into a historiographic enterprise, one that includes traditional genres such as the chronicle as well as the kinds of texts that are a direct product of maritime voyaging such as the *roteiro* (rutter) or the personal account of nautical voyages. Numerous descriptions of expeditions into Africa exist in manuscript and printed form.[1] This cultivation of prose writings immediately precedes and informs *Os Lusíadas* and its formulation of Africa as a place of historical and imaginative experience and collective memory. In the writings of authors like Alvise Cadamosto, João de Barros, or Fernão Lopes de Castanheda, the spaces and contours of Africa are submitted to scrutiny and Africa is verbally mapped under several textual guises. Concomitant with explorations and travels through the new continent we also find assumptions about Africa as a historical continuity to a national past. This perceived continuity in part is what makes writings on Africa ideological in that, to varying degrees, they propose an inevitability of exploration, conquest, and colonization, an inevitability often expressed in the idiom of nautical travel and perception. The Portuguese discursive regime on Africa in the years leading up to Camões's epic as it is evidenced in representative texts is the subject of this chapter. This consideration, it should be noted, like P. E. H. Hair's survey of early documents on Guinea, is "necessarily Lusocentric" ("The Early Sources" 88) in that it focues on sources in Portuguese.

ROUTES, HISTORIES, AND CHRONICLES

No matter how one might choose to interpret the invasion and capture of Ceuta in general historical terms, either as the beginning of a new era of expansion or as the culmination of a medieval, chivalric, and crusading mentality, the fact remains that the incursion into Ceuta triggers a sustained textual productivity on Africa as one of the characteristic practices of empire. This textuality accompanies the exploration and conquest of Africa and the numerous slaving raids and trading ventures that were the backbone of the Portuguese Atlantic and Indian Ocean empire. "Colonialism . . . then, is an operation of discourse, and as an operation of discourse it interpellates colonial subjects by incorporating them in a system of representation" (3), write Chris Tiffin and Alan Lawson; the Portuguese discourse on and about Africa exemplifies the inextricability of textuality from imperial praxis.

This textual productivity, so far as we know, began with Gomes Eanes de Zurara's *Crónica da Tomada de Ceuta,* completed in 1450, thirty-five years after the capture of the Moroccan city. Although the kinds of writings produced on Africa will vary widely throughout the sixteenth century, Zurara formally initiates this discursivity with the chronicle, a genre that will remain a constant in the years of exploration and colonization as a preferred mode of historical writing. Zurara's chronicles are some of the few (extant) narrative texts from the fifteenth century on the Portuguese presence in West Africa.[2] The formation of Portugal as a seafaring, imperial nation emerges alongside this historiographic activity, so that what Richard Helgerson claims for Elizabethan England—that "[t]he discursive forms of nationhood and the nation's political forms were mutually self-constituting" (11)—holds true for Portugal as it moved from a land-bound, medieval past to a seafaring early-modern present and future. Zurara's works, together with the other kinds of texts I examine in this section, establish a practice of how European subjects write about foreign spaces and peoples, often under the authority (directly or indirectly) of the crown or its representatives. In their shared characteristics, these writings collectively manifest a loose code for writing and reading the world under early expansion. In order to characterize the culture of writing on Africa prior to Camões, I turn to a selection of texts of different types: the eyewitness narrative, the geographic description, the nautical *roteiro* or rutter, and the histories of the fifteenth and sixteenth centuries. The *Crónica da Tomada de Ceuta,* though technically the first Portuguese textual treatment of expansion into Africa, in reality deals less with the Portuguese invasion and occupation of the North African city than it does with the plans for the 1415 mission and the preparations leading up to it. This may be due to Zurara's own late coming to the project, because his predecessor Fernão Lopes had likely drafted parts of the chronicle before Zurara took over the post of *cronista-mor. Ceuta,* the third and final part of the *Crónica de D. João I,* shares a focus with the first two parts (which had been completed by Lopes) on João I's reign in Portugal and his political interactions with Spain. *Ceuta* is the foundational moment to the chronicler's ethics of expansionist historiography. Zurara links Ceuta and the Portuguese conquest of it by naturalizing Portuguese movement into African space; he begins the chronicle with the following claim:

> Concrusam he dAristoteles no segundo liuro da natural filosofia que a natureza he começo de mouimento e de folgança. E pera declaraçam desto aprendamos que cada huũa cousa tem calidade. per o qual se moue ao seu proprio lugar quando esta fora delle entendendo aly ser confirmada milhor. e por aquella mesma propriedade faz assessegamento depois que esta onde a natureza rrequere. (3)

> Aristotle concludes in the second book of natural philosophy that nature is the beginning of movement and rest. As proof of this let us realize that everything has a quality that compels it to return to its proper place when away from it, and in that place it is in its best state. And, by that same principle, it rests once in the place nature has deemed appropriate for it.

Following this, Zurara establishes João I's role as the "natural" lord of Ceuta by writing that

> [o] tempo e grandeza das obras nos constrangem fortemente que scpreuamos nos seguintes capitullos a gloriosa fama da muy notauel empresa tomada per este virtuoso e nunca vençido prínçipe senhor Rey Dom Joham. que seu preposito detreminou forçosamente per armas conquistar huũa tam

nobre e tam grande çidade como he Cepta. no qual feito consirando pode-
mos esguardar quatro sousas .ss. grande amor da fee. grandeza de coraçam.
marauilhosa ordenança. e proueitosa vitoria. a qual foy marauilhoso preço
de seu grande trabalho. (8)

Time and the greatness of certain deeds strongly compel us to write in the
following chapters the glorious fame of the remarkable enterprise under-
taken by this virtuous and undefeated King João. He resolved, with great
determination, to conquer by force of arms the noble and worthy city of
Ceuta. In considering this feat we may regard four things in relation to it,
namely, a great devotion to the faith, nobility of heart, a marvelous order,
and a worthy victory, which itself was a wondrous reward for this notable
effort.

Ordenança (order), Zurara's favored term for expressing the confluence of
a providential and cosmic ordering of the universe and the fulfilmment
of that order through *conquista* and subsequently through the considered
activity of the historiographer, is "maravilhosa" in the sense that it is the
revelation of a divine plan. In Zuraran discourse, this "order" is a naturalizing principle: anything that is a result of it has come about not by
human agency but by the operation of the celestial spheres that coordi-
nate historical action and its narrative expression. Within this scheme, the
chronicler historicizes Ceuta, not as a component of a more local or Iberian past but in terms that trace the city to the beginning of the world:

E conta della Abilabez que foy grande doutor antre os mouros que esta
çidade foy fundada depois da destruiçam do deluuio duzentos e trinta e tres
annos . . . E diz que o fundador della foy seu neto de Noe. e que esta foy a
primeira que elle fundou em toda aquella terra dAffrica. e que por tanto lhe
pos nome Cepta que quer dizer em lingua caldea começo de fermosura.
e diz que mandou escreuer huũas letras na primeira pedra que se pos no
aliçeçe. Esta he a minha çidade de Cepta a qual eu pouoei primeiramente
de companhas de minha geraçam. os seus çidadãos seram estremados de
toda a nobreza dAffrica. Dias viram que sobre o seu senhorio se espargera
sangue de diuersas naçoões e o seu nome durara ata o acabamento do der-
radeiro segre. (10)

Abilabez, a learned man highly respected by the Moors, tells that this city was founded two hundred and thirty-three years after the destruction wrought by the flood . . . He further relates that the city's founder was Noah's grandson and was the first city he founded in all the lands of Africa, and because of this he named it Ceuta, which means "beginning of beauty" in Chaldaic. And he ordered that letters be chiseled onto the first foundation stone. "This is my city of Ceuta which I have populated with people from my generation. Its citizens rank among the highest nobility of all Africa. There will come days when the blood of many peoples will be spilled here, and the name of Ceuta will last until the end of time."

Zurara appropriates Abilabez's narrative for the purposes of his chronicle in its presentation of the history of Ceuta as a narrative of beginnings. The story of Ceuta is literally a foundational story here since it is inscribed on the very foundation stone of the city. A crucial element of this narrative is the expression "começo de fermosura," which, as a moment in the flow of the chronicle itself, adumbrates the Portuguese campaigns of exploration and conquest as that which is *formoso* (beautiful) in the overall divine scheme Zurara persistently invokes. The beauty that Ceuta instantiates is therefore ethical in nature because it refers to the city's role as a primordial space of Portuguese expansion that combats the insidious cult and presence of "Mafamede" (Muhammad). Zurara's chronicle, by extension, participates in this ethical mandate by rendering the actions on Ceuta into text.

Within this history the rhetoric of a crusading Christianity and its violent manifestations become apparent as the Ceuta proposal undergoes deliberation. Crusade intersects with chivalric honor when Zurara dedicates two chapters at the beginning of the chronicle to João I's desire to find an appropriate occasion for knighting his sons. When the signing of a treaty with Castile (the monarch's initial choice) fails, João Afonso, a member of the royal household, approaches the princes and suggests the capture of Ceuta:

Vossos pensamentos disse elle sam assaz de grandes e boōs. e pois que vos taal vontade tendes eu vos posso assinar huūa cousa em que o podees bem e honrradamente executar. E esto he a çidade de Cepta que he em terra dAffriqua que he huūa muy notauel çidade e muy azada pera se tomar. (27)

Your ideas, he said [to the princes], are good and noble. Since you are inclined to such an enterprise, I can tell you of a deed that would be easily accomplished. And that is the city of Ceuta in Africa, a most famous city and quite propitious for capture.

This chivalric motive is one element of a larger historical justification. For Zurara, the importance of Ceuta prior to 1415 is not its function as an important trading center but as part of a centuries-long legend of betrayal that traces back to the Moorish invasion of the Iberian Peninsula in 711. Zurara refers to the story of Count Julián, governor of Ceuta, who took vengeance on Rodrigo, the last of the Visigothic kings, by prompting the Moors to invade Spain:

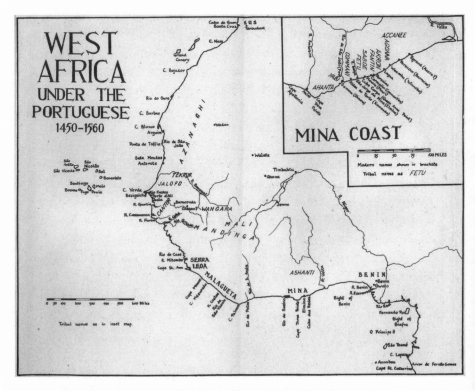

The Portuguese explorations and settlements in West Africa were coastal enterprises. The region south of the Senegal River was commonly referred to as "Guiné" (Guinea). From Blake, *Europeans in West Africa, 1450–1560.*

E assi devees de saber que depois que esta çidade primeiramente foy fundada ata o tempo que a elRey Dom Joham filhou. nunqua foy nenhum prinçipe nem senhor que cobrasse seu senhorio per força darmas. Por que ella foy primeiro de gentios como dito he. e depois foy conuertida aa fee de nosso Senhor Jehsu Christo. na qual durou ata o tempo que a o conde Juliam entregou aos mouros quando por vingança delRey Dom Rodrigo primeira-mente os mouros passarom em Espanha . . . (10)

So you should know that, since this city was founded and to the time that King João captured it, no prince or lord ever took its governance by force of arms. It first belonged to the gentiles, as we said, and was later converted to the faith of Our Lord Jesus Christ, and remained like this until Count Julián surrendered it to the Moors, who first came to Spain as vengeance on King Rodrigo . . .

The loss of Spain to the Moors is the first and authorizing incident of what Zurara repeatedly refers to as the "guerra dos mouros" (war against the Moors), an extension of the crusading enterprise. In chapter 11, titled "Como os letrados tornaram com rreposta a elRey dizendo que era seruiço de Deos de se tomar a çidade de Cepta" (How the learned men delivered a response to the king, which said that the capture of the city of Ceuta was in the service to God), the learned doctors who serve as João's coun-selors recapitulate the incentive to invade Ceuta in these terms:

abasta que nos que aqui somos presemtes per autoridade da samta escpri-tura, assy como homeẽs que ssem nosso mereçimento teemos graao na sacra theollesia, determinamos que uossa merçee pode mouer guerra comtra qua-aesquer jmfiees assy mouros como gemtios, ou quaaesquer outros que per alguũ modo negarem alguũ dos artijgos da samta ffe catholica, per cujo tra-balho mereçerees gramde gallardom do nosso Senhor Deos pera a uossa alma. (37)

It is sufficient that those of us who are present here by the authority of Holy Scripture, and who, though undeserving, hold degrees in sacred theology, do declare that your worship may incite war against any infidels be they Moor or gentile, or against whomever else denies any article of the holy

Catholic faith; for this work your worship will earn great reward for your
soul from Our Lord.

The rhetoric of subjugation of the infidel recalls the intractable rhetoric of the papal bulls (see below) that authorize the forceful capture of
Moors or "Saracens" in Africa in the name of the Catholic faith and, by
extension, condone whatever physical means might be necessary to effect
those captures. Zurara's retrospective gesture here to the mentality of the
holy war against the infidel and, in the previous citation, to Ceuta's "converted" status, importantly authorizes its capture as an act of reappropriation. The belief that Moors in (North) Africa were interlopers on lands
that by right belonged to Christians partly underlay the Portuguese understanding of conquest.

That the Moors themselves recognize and accept the imminence and
unavoidability of the Portuguese occupation of Ceuta is part of the chronicler's recounting of a secret reconnaisance mission with prophetic overtones, and is part of the self-justifying logic of Ceuta in terms of the
political and mercantile interests of the crown. In chapter 17, the captain
of this mission, Afonso Furtado, relates an anecdote to João I in his de-
briefing session on his return to Lisbon from Ceuta. He tells the king of
a "marauilhoso acomteçimento" (marvelous incident) during a trip he had
made to Ceuta as a child with his father who was in the service of João's
father, Pedro I. During that trip, he (Afonso) was approached by a venerable old Moor who asked him his origin. On learning Afonso was from
Lisbon, the Moor asked him who the Portuguese king was and if he
had any sons. Afonso told the Moor the names of Pedro's legitimate sons
and, after considerable effort, recalled that Pedro also had a bastard son,
João (who would become João I). On hearing this, the Moor let out a sigh
and entered into a state of mournful sadness. Afonso asked the reason for
this, and the Moor answered that João was destined to become king, and
that "sera o primeiro rrey dEspanha que teera posse em Africa, e sera o
primeiro começo da destruiçom dos mouros" (he will be the first king of
Spain to hold a possession in Africa, and he will mark the beginning of
the destruction of the Moors, 57).[3]

Later in the chronicle, Zurara relates the story of a wise and holy
Ceutan Moor who had a dream during Ramadan in which he saw Ceuta

covered in bees, and saw a lion coming across the Strait of Gibraltar accompanied by flocks of sparrows that devoured the bees. To interpret the dream, the Moors sought the aid of a renowned astrologer who read the stars, noted the presence of Orion and his sword (a sign of war), and predicted a terrible fate for the Moors of the city by observing that the bees of the holy man's dreams were Moors and the sparrows, Christians. The Christian symbolism becomes increasingly present as the chronicle nears its end, such as in chapter 96 in which a Mass, celebrated after the city's capture, includes a sermon that interprets the three syllables of "Ceuta" as a reflection of the Trinity and its five letters as mirroring the wounds of Christ.

The prophetic and oneiric visions of Ceuta and Moors as yielding to Portuguese power accomplish two main objectives, ones that will implicitly justify the campaigns of exploration of the uncharted west African coast in Zurara's next work, the *Crónica de Guiné*. Afonso Furtado's anecdote and the Moor's dream inscribe the capture of Ceuta within divine order and the workings of the cosmos. In this logic the crusade against the infidel is part of a cosmic directive that imposes a hermeneutic authority on Moorish science (astrology) and religion, one that corroborates the Christian holy war. The inscription of the Ceuta plan into the supernatural world legitimizes the authority of João I as king, arguably Fernão Lopes's main objective of the first two parts of the *Crónica de D. João I*. The prophesying of the destruction of Africa, in effect, naturalizes a bastard's claim to the throne.

With his next chronicle, the *Crónica dos feitos de Guiné* (1453), Zurara focuses squarely and exclusively on the Portuguese exploration of West Africa in the new geographic arena southwest of Morocco (generically termed "Guiné") in the three decades following the capture of Ceuta. In this period, exploration, trading missions, and slaving raids set the stage for Portugal's mercantile ambitions on the African continent—trade was the medium through which the Portuguese extended their influence, notes Blake (36)—and on the western Atlantic islands. *Guiné* narrates explorations along the west African coast to the mid-fifteenth century. The historical narrative proper begins with Gil Eanes's rounding of Cape Bojador in 1434, and includes chapters on the first capture of black Africans in 1441, Nuno Tristão's voyage to Cape Blanco in 1442, and his discovery of the island of "Gete" (Arguim),[4] and the first descriptions of non-Arabic *mouros* (Moors) or *negros* (blacks) living south of the Senegal River. The *Crónica dos feitos de Guiné* is the first text that details the experiences of European navigators in the until then unexplored lands south of Cape Bojador and that documents the initial moments of the Atlantic slave trade.[5] Zurara frames his narrative as a panegyric to the life and work of D. Henrique or Prince Henry. *Guiné* begins with an apostrophe to the prince:

An early pictorial representation of sub-Saharan black Africans in Guinea. The Guinean is one of the new kinds of Africans encountered by Portuguese explorers that appears in Portuguese writings on Africa beginning with Gomes Eanes de Zurara. From the book of Balthasar Springer (a German merchant who traveled to India with the fleet of Francisco de Almeida in 1505), 1508, in Walter Hirschberg, ed., *Monumenta ethnographica: Frühe völkerkundliche Bilddokumente,* vol. 1 (Graz: Akademische Druck- u. Verlagsanstalt, 1962).

Oo tu principe pouco menos que deuinal. Eu rogo aas tuas sagradas ver-
tudes que ellas soportem com toda paciēcia o fallecimēto de minha ousada
pena querendo tentar hūa tā alta materya como he a declaraçõ de tuas
vertuosas obras dignas de tāta glorya . . . (19)

O Prince, little less than divine! I beg your saintly virtues to withstand, with
all patience, the deficiencies of my bold pen, as it attempts such noble matter as the writing of your deeds, deeds worthy of high glory . . .

Jerome C. Branche, in a study of the rhetoric of *Guiné*, finds that the
chronicle espouses a "discourse of power" and a "triumphalist tenor" (33),
in which the eulogistic portrait of Henry informs a crusading ethic.[6] The
African Other, in Branche's analysis, is submitted to an us/them dichotomy
that rests on a power differential of domination and conquest, one that is
tantamount to a "figurative erasure" (37) of the (black) African in Zurara's
act of historical signification. Thus, in the "phenomenon of the manhunt"
(38), both people and the resources of the natural world are collapsed into
the category of "booty" (39). Branche concludes that *Guiné*, in its relegation of the African Other to a position of natural inferiority and the
violence such relegation promotes, stands as a "foundational document
for colonialism and transatlantic slavery" (44); it "labels blacks and other
colonized people as inferior, under various rubrics, and articulates a justification for their subjection, thereby setting a discursive precedent for
subsequent colonial writing" (35).[7]

Branche is correct in finding here a discursive precedent of construing
the non-Christian Other as an inferior being, part of the ideological infra-
structure of Portuguese expansion. This ideological posture alternately
moralizes (black) Africans (distinct, it is important to remember, from the
north African Moors who often acted as slave traders for the Portuguese)
in negative terms, while also absolving them for their lack of Christian
faith. Thus Zurara, in the apostrophe to Henry, writes: "[o]uço as prezes
das almas Inocētes daquellas barbaras naçõoes em numero casy Infijndo
cuia antiga Ieeraçõ des do começo do mūdo nūca vyo luz deuinal" (I hear
the prayers of the innocent souls of those barbarous nations, almost
infinite in number, whose ancient generations, since the beginning of the
world, never saw divine light, 19). Zurara is speaking specifically of the

non-Arabic black African who was considered to be pagan rather than an infidel or heretic. Much worse were the Moors who willfully followed the "sect of Muhammad" and for whom Zurara reserves the term *infiel* (infidel). Yet, even with such an ideologically charged language, the extent to which the capture of Ceuta and the explorations in Guinea are the products of a crusade mentality is open to critical debate. On the one hand, historians such as J. H. Parry argue against the idea of the fifteenth-century expeditions as a continuation of the Crusades, observing that crusades in earlier centuries had been costly failures (22). On the other hand, Sanjay Subrahmanyam notes the resurgence of the military orders in fifteenth-century Portugal and, through them, the retrospective establishment of a line of influence from the capture of Ceuta to the first Crusade (33–34). I do not intend to resolve this debate here, but wish simply to note that, whatever the historical praxis was in the fifteenth century, the survival of a crusading rhetoric is discernible in Zurara's chronicles and may stand in opposition to the practical demands of a unified effort against the infidel. *Ceuta* in this respect falls more comfortably into a crusading mold,[8] for by the time of the events narrated in *Guiné* the capitalist motives are ever more apparent as the search for goods, slaves, and booty intensifies. Zurara himself cannot entirely conceal the economic incentives of the incursions into Guinea no matter how much he might refer to saving African souls. The chronicler's repeated use of "guerra dos mouros" points also to a secular impetus. Whatever crusading mentality Zurara invokes in *Guiné* is a kind of performance, a remnant of a previous discursive tradition that seeks to justify the raw capitalist underpinnings of the Guinean expeditions with the hallowed veneer of militant Christianity. Zurara's successor to the post of *cronista-mor*, Rui de Pina (1440–1522), continues this vein of language in the *Crónica de D. Afonso V* (Chronicle of King Afonso V) by referring to Afonso V's incursions into Africa as "cruzadas," a reference to the continuing threat of the Ottoman Turks and a prelude to the intense ideological rhetoric of later historians such as João de Barros.[9]

The *Crónica dos feitos de Guiné* begins with Gil Eanes, the first known European to round Cape Bojador in 1434. The event bears significance in Zurara's writing enterprise and in the demarcation of conquistatorial, geographic space. Bojador for centuries had been the outer limit of Western knowledge about Africa. It was a "[psychological] barrier to the maritime exploration of the African coast" (Russell, *Prince Henry* 111; similarly, Barreto 84), a veil of fear separating Europe from sub-Saharan Africa beyond which lay the "Green Sea of Darkness," as ancient Arab geographers had called it. With Eanes's passage of Bojador in 1434, peoples living to the south of it came into the consciousness of Europeans, peoples distinct from the more familiar Moors and other African populations of the north. *Guiné*, reputedly the first book by a European on the lands beyond Bojador (Prestage, "The Life" 1), narrates an evolving encounter between Portuguese travelers and Africa and its inhabitants that is as much geographic as it is epistemological, since "Guiné" in Zurara's usage is at once a loosely defined coastal region and the idea of unknown, uncharted space. The toponym refers to an extensive region of the west African coast extending from Cape Blanco and Arguim Bay southward to Cape Catarina and beyond São Tomé and Annobom (Diffie and Winius 78). Bovill observes that "Guiné" was the term used by the Portuguese to refer to the land of the black Moors (*mouros negros*) in the Sudan as opposed to the brown-skinned Moors of the Sahara (116). Russell notes the vagueness of the term in the royal title "Senhor de Guiné" (Lord of Guinea) used by Portuguese monarchs, a title that referred to "a vast expansion of the territorial and and political possessions of the Portuguese crown . . . [that] included the whole of the Atlantic littoral of Black Africa as far south as the continent might prove to run" ("White Kings" 503).[10] Horta argues that the term ultimately carried political overtones in that

> African spaces were . . . perceived within wider political spaces that only made sense to outsiders, as spaces where European expansion and authority, in reality or in fiction, was projected. "Guinea" had a political meaning to the Portuguese crown, among other spaces that were part of a representation of overseas imperial power. ("Evidence" 115)

"Guiné," then, is both an arena of imperial action and a symbolic representation of expansionist power and the contested sphere of political advantage and prerogative, and as such is open to definition and redefinition. In its politically and ideologically motivated uses, "Guiné" functions much as Mauritania did in the Middle Ages as Barbour showed us in the preceding chapter as a space whose demarcation responded to shifting circumstances.

In contrast to Ceuta, a historically familiar city, Guinea initially emerges in the pages of *Guiné* as the region of the unknown so that its exploration and appropriation realize a process of coming-to-know, an entry into knowledge of a more expansive world space narrated by Zurara as the surpassing of both mental and physical borders. *Guiné* implicitly announces that a new way of writing and perceiving the world lies beyond Cape Bojador. Zurara first addresses this idea by identifying the reasons why Prince Henry sponsored expeditions to Guinea. These reasons are (1) to know once and for all what lay beyond Bojador, (2) to establish trade with whatever Christians might be found in those regions, (3) to discover the extent of the power and dominion of the Moorish infidel in such territories, (4) to locate a Christian prince or ruler in those lands as an ally in the war against the Moors, and (5) to bring lost souls forward for salvation. These reasons provide an access to knowledge: "[e]ntom maginamos que sabemos algũa cousa quando conhecemos o sseu fazedor e a fim pera que elle fez tal obra" (we imagine that we know a matter when we are familiar with its doer and the objective he had in doing it, 43). The identification of Henry's motivations for exploring Guinea inscribes ratiocination into the Guinean voyages as both motive and outcome. Zurara's chronicle completes the revelation or journeys of knowledge initiated by the prince. In another early chapter, the chronicler pauses to reflect on the place of Bojador in the history of Portuguese navigation, because for centuries Bojador was the southernmost point of Africa, an end-point of cognition. Its strong currents and storms prevented safe passage. When Gil Eanes successfully rounded the cape and returned to Portugal to tell his story, Zurara writes that

> elle [D. Henrique] tijnha voõtade de saber a terra que hija aallem das Ilhas de canarya e de huũ cabo que se chama do Boiador por que ataaquelle tempo nem per scriptura nẽ per memorya de nhuũs homeẽs nunca foe sabudo determinadamẽte a callidade da terra que hya aallem do dicto cabo. (43)

> [Prince Henry] wished to know of the lands beyond the Canary Islands and of a cape called Bojador, because until that time, the nature of the lands beyond said cape was not known, either in memory or in writing.

Bojador hence marks a geo-epistemological boundary. The territories beyond are a no-man's-land protected by fear. Zurara locates this fear in historical time by placing it in the collective, apprehensive voice of the mariners:

> Como passaremos . . . os termos que poserõ nossos padres ou que proueito pode trazer ao Iffante a perdiçom de nossas almas Iuntamẽte com os corpos. ca conhecidamente seremos omecidas de nos meesmos . . . Isto he claro . . . que despois deste cabo nom ha hi gente nẽ pouoraçõ algũa. a terra nom he menos areosa que os desertos de Libya. onde nom ha augua nem aruor nem herua verde . . . (47–48)

> How are we to pass the limits imposed by our forefathers, or what benefit can the loss of our souls and bodies bring to the Prince, since we will so manifestly become our own murderers . . . It is clear . . . that beyond this cape there is no human population and the land is not less sandy than the deserts of Libya, with no water, no trees, no green plant . . .

This passage—whose imagery recalls the forest of the suicides in canto XIII of the *Inferno* with its allusion to self-murder set in a landscape of negativity—melds a medieval sense of spiritual voyaging and its possible perils with the geographic voyaging of this chronicle of exploration. The land beyond stands as a border of spiritual and corporal danger that breaks with a genealogical heritage of landboundedness. This geographically inflected fear and sense of peril, a precursor to Camões's dramatic prosopopeia of Adamastor, is an affective correlate of the nautical limit or threshold. Briefly, but tellingly, Zurara links the structuring of the nautical/geographic world to the interiorized realm of perception. South of Bojador, uncharted Africa or Guiné comes into view through the navigational eye of science and the interior eye of cognition and affect. These twin perspectives, laboring under the weight of divine directive, construe Africa as an arena of blankness over which imperialism might be enacted and written. In order to write—or, indeed, rewrite—Africa within the authority of expansion, Africa must first be encountered within the frame of maritime practice and the knowledge of the world such practice makes possible. Africa is a space circumscribed by nautical experience that will soon expand dramatically as Portuguese ships double the Cape. It is a geographic and nautical reality and a metaphor through which an expansionist writing subject is brought into being.

Contemporaneous with Henry's explorations/exploitations of Guinea is a series of papal bulls that consolidate a campaign against inhabitants of Africa as objects of subjugation. Within a year of the capture of the first black slaves by Antão Gonçalves on the Saharan coast in 1441, these bulls began to be issued and ratified Portugal's rights (and not Spain's, Portugal's competitor for these rights) to African territories and resources.[11] The bulls demonstrate the importance of theology in the colonial enterprise (Raman 65). Branche notes that "such bulls would become the legitimizing instruments for future colonial (dis)possession" (45). The bull *Illius qui se pro divini* (1442) grants Henry a monopoly over Guinean territories. Subsequent to this document, the three other bulls considered to be the most important for Portuguese expansion in Africa are the *Dum diversas* (June 18, 1452), the *Romanus Pontifex* (January 8, 1455), and the *Inter caetera* (March 13, 1456). The *Dum diversas* authorizes the king of Portugal to conquer and subdue Saracens, reduce them to slavery, and confiscate their lands and goods. The *Inter caetera* grants perpetual spiritual jurisdiction to the Portuguese over the regions conquered or to be conquered from Cape Bojador to the Indies, and "gave religious sanction to Portugal to adopt an imperialist agenda toward the regions beyond Christendom" (Figueira 397n10).[12] Nicholas V's *Romanus Pontifex* stands out among these bulls and is considered to be the charter of Portuguese imperialism. The document reiterates the previous bulls and grants Portugal exclusive rights of conquest on the African coast beginning at Cape Bojador and extending southward. The bull reads, in part:

> Nos, premissa omnia et singula debita meditatione pensantes, ac attendentes quod cum olim prefato Alfonso Regi quoscunque Sarracenos et paganos aliosque Christi inimicos ubicunque constitutos, ac regna, ducatus, principatus, dominia, possessiones, et mobilia ac immobilia bona quecunque per eos detenta ac possessa invadendi, conquirendi, expugnandi, debellandi, et subjugandi, illorumque personas in perpetuam servitutem redigendi, ac regna, ducatus, comitatus, principatus, dominia, possessiones, et bona sibi et successoribus suis applicandi, appropriandi, ac in suos successorumque suorum usus et utilitatem convertendi . . .

We . . . weighing all and singular the premises with due meditation, and noting that since we had formerly by other letters of ours granted among other
things free and ample faculty to the aforesaid King Alfonso [Alfonso V]—
to invade, search out, capture, vanquish, and subdue all Saracens and pagans
whatsoever, and other enemies of Christ wheresoever placed, and the kingdoms, dukedoms, principalities, dominions, possessions, and all movable and
immovable goods whatsoever held and possessed by them and to reduce their
persons to perpetual slavery, and to apply and appropriate to himself and his
successors the kingdoms, dukedoms, counties, principalities, dominions, possessions, and goods, and to convert them to his and their use and profit . . .[13]

Mudimbe notes the "terrifying" (*Idea of Africa* 32) wording of this passage
in the powers it grants to the Portuguese king to subdue and conquer
Saracens and pagans; Branche finds a "sledgehammer legality" (46) to
the document. The language and implications are indeed sobering in the
wholesale authorization the bull grants to Portugal to confiscate (implicitly, by whatever means deemed necessary) African resources and peoples.[14]
Mudimbe argues that this (and other bulls) effectively empty Africa of any
native rights to land and resources, making Africa a *terra nullius* (no-man's-
land) and advocating a European right of sovereignty outside of Europe
and of colonization and the pursuit of slavery (*Idea of Africa* 37; *Invention
of Africa* 45). The bulls are important moments in the European discourse
on Africa because their rhetoric conflates the several distinct populations
of Africans into an undifferentiated mass, which is itself a strident ideological gesture. Not only is the difference between "Moor" and "black"
null in the *Romanus Pontifex,* as Randles notes (*L'Image* 121), they are not
operative categories at all. Africans are either "Saracens" or "pagans," all-
encompassing labels for the distant pontiff that do not recognize the demographic plurality of Africans as inchoately recorded in texts like *Guiné.*
From the outset of expansion, "Saracen" (in Latin or in Portuguese) is
always an ideologically charged term, unlike *mouro,* which can be neutral.
The bulls promulgate a way of speaking about Africa and Africans as much
as they authorize commercial interests under the cloak of evangelism. As
Lahon points out (*Os negros* 31), though the bulls do not specifically mention the slave trade, they end up legitimizing it nonetheless. By the time
we get to Camões and *Os Lusíadas, sarraceno* is in common usage as a

synonym for "Muslim," though the word's remote etymological origin is
Arabic *xaraqin*, which means "Oriental" or "Asiatic" (Machado, *Influência
arábica* 227).[15] If, as Machado claims (236), Portuguese *sarraceno* did not
come into use until the sixteenth century through Latin *sarracenus*, then
Camões participates in the early-modern fashioning of the term as a
counterpart to *Christian* in conquistatorial thought that is a rejuvenation
of the rhetoric of *reconquista*. Camões's terms for Muslims are either *mouro*
or *sarraceno*, and the poet shapes the entire course of the Portuguese past
as a seamless battle against the infidel.[16] For Camões, *mouro* has positive as
well as negative connotations (unlike the unilaterally negative *sarraceno*), as
the friendly relation between Vasco da Gama and the Moorish King of
Melinde proves, or the diplomatic facilitation of the Portuguese presence
in India through the Castilian-speaking Moor Monçaide in canto VII.

We continue our study of the textual matter of Africa by turning now
to an important non-Portuguese narrative on West Africa, Alvise Cadamosto's account titled *Navigazioni*.[17] Cadamosto was a Venetian merchant
who, during a trading voyage en route to Flanders in 1454, became interested in Prince Henry's expeditions to Guinea and West Africa and eventually rose to a position of trust and confidence with the Portuguese prince.
Cadamosto made two voyages to Africa under Portuguese colors in 1455
as a young man of twenty-three who sought "aquistar alguna facultade
etiam dē venir ad alguna perfecione de honore" (to acquire some measure of wealth and attain some degree of honor, 6).[18] Cadamosto's account
of his travels, redacted after he returned to Venice in the 1460s following Henry's death, includes information on a voyage made by Pedro de
Sintra in 1461 or 1462 to Sierra Leone. The *Navigazioni* is one of the important sources for Portuguese interests in Africa and the Henrican trade
in Saharan and black Africa subsequent to the information provided by
Zurara (Russell, *Prince Henry* 11).

Cadamosto's text initiates a tradition of eyewitness accounts on Africa,
even though, in this case, the narrative was not composed until almost
a decade after the actual voyages and therefore relies heavily on memory
and probably other written sources. As with other eyewitness writers after
him, Cadamosto relates his story according to the chronological or linear
progress of a nautical voyage. Hence the ship and the idea of the ship are
primary structuring principles in the text. Throughout the numerous

expeditions to shore and contacts with natives, the writer/traveler assumes a position of authoritative observation when confronted with the realities of Africa. Peter Hulme, in a study of later European travels to the Caribbean, has called this the "position of ethnographic authority." Hulme exposes "a process founded upon the distinction between 'self' and 'other,' that initial (and often implicit) splitting that constitutes the entity that sees itself (again often implicitly) as authorized to make distinctions" ("Tales of Distinction" 191). Not only does the position of ethnographic authority allow Cadamosto to make distinctions, but it allows him to codify those distinctions in writing as a detached, third-person observer, a narrative posture that creates a de facto separation between "us" and "them" which is a persistent trait of colonialist discourse. Cadamosto exercises this prerogative (and its systematic correlate, the creation of taxonomies) most notably in his descriptions of the African body. Like those in Zurara, Cadamosto's Africans are primarily distinguished from one another by geographic region and skin pigmentation. This geodemographic lens is purportedly the novelty of his narrative, for Cadamosto informs us that he is the first Venetian to cross the Strait of Gibraltar and plumb the "terre de negri" dela basa ethyopia" (lands of the blacks of lower Ethiopia, 3). He then systematically partitions Africa and its inhabitants into a grid that aligns skin color and geography: like Zurara, Cadamosto notes that the Senegal River "parte generation che se chiama azanegi dal primo regno de negri" (separates the Azenegues from the first kingdom of blacks, 18), or adds that the men of the kingdom of Meli (not mentioned by Zurara) "giera homini negrissimj e ben formadi de corpo" (were very black men with well-formed bodies, 23). Other observations record deviances from an assumed European cultural norm, such as the gender-transgressive behavior of men in the first kingdom of blacks in lower Ethiopia (the Wolofs), who "fano molti seruisi femenili como e de lauorar drapi e altre cosse e filar gottonj" (perform womanly tasks, such as working with cloth and other items, and spinning cotton, 31–32).

The imbrication of the land- and people-scapes of Africa occurs through the seemingly transparent or neutral discursive mode of description. But, as Ricardo Padrón advises us, although description appears to be the most mundane and purely referential way of utilizing language, it in fact "entails the encounter between data and expectations, between observations and culturally contingent assumptions about the production of meaning" (21). The alliance between African bodies (in their colors, shapes, and behaviors) and spaces through descriptive taxonomies exemplifies a nonneutral use of language in that Cadamosto's eyewitness observations submit Africa to European discursive control and reveal the strange, barbaric customs Europeans expected to find. These descriptions result from an authoritative optic over Africa that corporalizes its geographic expanses. Africa the geographic space becomes a body to be controlled and subjugated (like its human inhabitants) via the imposition of a grid that demarcates regions by the skin colors of its peoples.

Cadamosto's travels in Africa occur as a nautical voyage, which furnishes a cohesion to his narrative that is, in its particulars, anecdotal and episodic. The Italian navigator recounts numerous encounters with the "terre de diuerse generatione stranie" (lands of many strange peoples, 6) and uses "Africa" as a general toponym, a departure from Zurara's usual practice of referring to regions. With Cadamosto we find a fledgling perception of Africa as a discrete geographic whole, a perception that will not become standardized in Portuguese texts until the mid-sixteenth century. The ship with its controlled steerage displays cultural and political might and is the means, especially in texts that directly invoke the monarch (through dedications or prologues, for instance) by which the crown establishes its sovereignty outside the metropole. It is the presiding image that concatenates the diverse episodes of encounter and contact in Guinea, and it represents the shaping power of Western science and thought over undomesticated space and peoples. It is the vehicle of Western culture in all its political, linguistic, technological, and spiritual force. The ship is the medium, therefore, through which non-European or non-Portuguese space and resources become "domesticated," that is, annexed to and hence transformed into the Portuguese *domus* or home. The deep-sea ship (*nau, navio,* or *caravela*) lies at the heart of the arsenal deployed by travelers on journeys of exploration or conquest. The technological superiority of the ship differentiates the "civilized" mariner from "barbarous" peoples. Consider Cadamosto's observation:

Certificandouj quando costoro hebeno la prima vista de velle ne de nauili sopra el mare mai per auanti ne per loro ne per soi antecessori hauea piu

visto credeteno che quelli fosseno vxelli con ale bianche che uolasseno che
de algun stranio luogo fosseno li capitati . . . non intendo lo artificio del
nauilio Si chel tuto teniano che fosse fantasme . . . (19–20)

I declare to you that when these people witnessed sails or ships at sea for
the first time (for neither they nor their ancestors had ever seen such a thing
before), they thought they were seeing huge birds with white wings in flight
which had come there from some distant land . . . and not being familiar with
the structure of a ship, they were certain they were seeing phantasms . . .

It is not that the Africans are ignorant of sailing; Cadamosto frequently
refers to their dugout boats (*almadias*) and their practice of offshore
fishing. What supposedly arrests the Africans' attention is the design and
build of the deep-sea vessel, so wholly different from their own boats in
construction that it seems to come from the other world. Cadamosto indicates the presence of nautical science in Africa as an indisputable sign
of authority, because there is nothing given about such technology—it is
a construction, an "artifice," and hence the result of powers of rationality,
assessment, and calculation that outstrip the Africans' more naturalistic
seafaring knowledge as evidenced in the simplicity of dugout boats. This
seafaring technology, in turn, bestows a cohesion on Cadamosto's episodic narrative in that the forward-moving, controlled route of the ship
binds the several and often disparate episodes of the text into a discernible
whole or trajectory.

Cadamosto's indications of distances traveled and of time are typical of
the genre of nautical writing developed by Portuguese maritime travelers
known as the *roteiro* (rutter), a type of navigational guide. In this kind of
text, coasts and coastal waters are described, and natural signs or markers (e.g., rivers, trees, or gulfs) are mentioned in order to help pilots navigate and recognize certain stretches of land. Cadamosto's text displays
characteristics of the rutter that will be developed throughout the fifteenth
century, and it is in response to the realities of Africa that this nautical
mode of perceiving and writing the phenomenal world finds full expression. Some scholars have pointed out the inaccuracies of Cadamosto's
nautical information (such as his calculations of distances), but the accuracy of his nautical measurements or dating of events is secondary to the

habits of thought demonstrated in making such observations in which horizontal space and chronological or linear time are infixed into the *Navigazioni*. These habits of thought, to be repeated by all future authors of *roteiros* or similar writings in which encounters with indigenes and foreign lands are interpolated among observations of navigational information, overlay the navigational, linear progress along coasts or riverine waterways with the spatialization of chronological time; the directional progress of nautical voyages creates spaces of chronological time. Such spaces in part define Western imperial itinerancy. In *Ulysses' Sail*, Mary W. Helms explains how, in "traditional" societies, conceptions and constructions of geographic space and distance are "neither neutral nor homogeneous concepts" (8). What holds true for Helms's anthropologically based study of traditional societies finds an interesting correlate in early writings by Europeans on Africa because a similar practice obtains of construing geographic distance and space in nonneutral terms according to a vision of Africa and Africans as unmarked by history or technology and as therefore barbarous. Anne McClintock's comments on technologies of surveillance in the late-Victorian era encounter an important precursor in the textual matter of Africa; McClintock, in explaining the idea of "anachronistic space," a notion based on the premise that colonized lands are empty because "indigenous peoples are not supposed to be spatially there," argues that "colonized people . . . do not inhabit history proper but exist in a permanently anterior time within the geographic space of the modern empire as anachronistic humans, atavistic, irrational, bereft of human agency" (30). Space, distance, and time can therefore be ideological constructs. They relate Africa to a Western manner of measuring experience, space, and movement. Written discourse as the concrete instantiation of this manner is yet another technological advantage of the European. The perambulations of the deep-sea vessel write space, time, and historical consciousness onto the sands and waters of Africa.

Two other important texts continue the genre of the firsthand account and structure historical experience within the mold of a nautical voyage. These texts are Diogo Gomes de Sintra's *Descobrimento primeiro da Guiné* (First Discovery of Guinea) and Álvaro Velho's *Relação da viagem de Vasco da Gama* (Account of the Voyage of Vasco da Gama), both from the late fifteenth century.

Diogo Gomes (d. 1502) was *almoxarife* or royal tax collector of the town of Sintra on the Atlantic coast just west of Lisbon. Gomes became active in oceanic navigation in 1444 and made expeditions to Guinea. He was in the service of both Prince Henry and Afonso V. The narrative that bears Gomes's name is his recollection of Guinea expeditions as dictated to Martin Behaim (who would later become famous for his globe) while Behaim was in Portugal. Behaim composed the text in Latin. The accuracy of Gomes's technical information is open to question; as Russell notes, there are serious chronological errors and the narrative is often incoherent and contradictory (*Prince Henry* 327–28). The inaccuracies are likely the result of Gomes's recollection of events long past and the transmission of information from Gomes's spoken Portuguese to Behaim's written Latin, possibly through the mediation of an interpreter. The Latin version of the text (*De prima inuentione Gujnee*) appears in Valentim Fernandes's *Códice Valentim Fernandes*.

Despite Gomes's inaccuracies, Gomes's text, like Cadamosto's, is important for how it shapes and depicts Africa in narrative form. Although his memory may have been faulty, Gomes's memorialist structuring of his narrative implicates the individual memory into an evolving, collective memory that foreshadows Camões's act of poetic creation as a new "historical" memory, one that is the basis for the mythification of the Portuguese past. Gomes's sometimes desultory style, while frustrating for those seeking "historical" accuracy or coherence, foregrounds the *Descobrimento primeiro* as an act of memory, a valuation of memory making as part of the history of Portuguese presence in Africa. Gomes's first memorialist action is to begin his narrative in this manner:

> No ano do Senhor de 1415, um fidalgo do reino de Portugal, D. João de Castro . . . navegando pelo mar Atlântico, tomou pela força uma parte de uma ilha dita Grã-Canária . . . (51)

> In the year of Our Lord 1415, a nobleman of Portugal, D. João de Castro . . . navigating the Atlantic Ocean, took by force part of an island called Grand Canary . . .

Gomes identifies 1415 as a historical beginning of which his own narrative will be a continuation, yet surprisingly he identifies the importance of this year as being an expedition to the Canaries, not the capture of Ceuta. This may simply have been an error on Gomes's part, or a reference to a hitherto unknown fact about how the Ceuta expedition began, as Nascimento speculates in his edition of the text (132n12). Whatever the case, Gomes's citation of 1415 consolidates the year as the iconic beginning of Portuguese exploration and consequently of the textual tradition attending it.

Gomes's vision of Africans echoes the categorical generalizations of the infidel contained in the papal bulls. Accordingly, his preferred term for all Africans is *sarraceno*. He refers to the bull of Eugene V (incorrectly attributing it to Eugene IV, as Nascimento [148n85] notes) that grants Portugal a monopoly on the Guinea trade (65), and to the bull of Eugene IV permitting the Portuguese to enter into trade with the Moors so long as it is not a trade in arms (89). The crusading rhetoric of the bulls finds a ready, concrete counterpart in the sanctification the figure of Prince Henry. We noted earlier Zurara's eulogistic portrait of Henry in the opening pages of *Guiné;* Gomes elaborates on this by not only eulogizing the prince but by ascribing saintly attributes to his corpse:

> Eu . . . chegando junto ao cadáver, descobri-o e encontrei-o seco e íntegro, com excepção da ponta do nariz . . . Bem canta a Igreja: "Não consentirás que o teu santo veja a corrupção." (87)

> In approaching the cadaver, I found it dry and whole, with the exception of the tip of the nose . . . Well does the Church observe: "You will not allow your saints to suffer corruption."

The incorruptibility of Henry's body constitutes a de facto canonization of the prince and molds his Guinean projects and those of his successor as expressions of devotion and sanctity.

One of the most important fifteenth-century documents to combine the nautical rutter and historico-ethnographic description is Álvaro Velho's *Relação da Viagem de Vasco da Gama* (Account of the Voyage of Vasco da Gama), the record of Gama's journey from Lisbon to India (Calicut) and of the return voyage as far as the Rio Grande in Guinea in 1497–99. Velho was a scribe on board one of the four ships of the fleet, the *São Rafael,* captained by Gama's brother, Paulo da Gama.[19] This text is most typically identified as a *roteiro* or rutter, but its mixture of nautical observations with interpolations that provide realistic details and description, as Luís de Albuquerque observes (6) in his edition of the text, makes it difficult to fix Velho's text as a pure *roteiro* or *diário a bordo* (ship's diary). Nonetheless, the genre of the *roteiro* underlies Velho's narrative. These nautically motivated and structured texts were the products of a plurality of exigencies and circumstances, a fact reflected in the shifting and inconsistent mix of nautical detail and prose narrative. Velho's account was most likely used by Fernão Lopes de Castanheda in the redaction of the *História do descobrimento e da conquista da Índia pelos Portugueses* (History of the Discovery and Conquest of India by the Portuguese) and, probably through Castanheda, reached Camões. The voyage and route traced by Velho serves as the backbone of Camões's poetic rendering of Gama's trip in *Os Lusíadas.*

The enthusiasm for empirical description in Velho's account, together with Velho's regular observations on technical matters such as dates, distances traveled, or characteristics of the shoreline, might tempt one to conclude that these are "practical" texts, primarily meant to serve future pilots, captains, or explorers. While the practical side of documents like these is to some degree evident, to ascribe a pragmatism to them as their raison d'être is to ignore—or at the least, underestimate—their significance as manifestations of evolving habits of mind that perceive and shape the phenomenal world through nautical (including cartographic) modalities, as we noted earlier with Cadamosto's narrative. Since the notation of technical information is not systematic and frequently based on contingency (for example, as a result of an unexpected event or as linked to a specific moment of encounter with indigenes), it is difficult to see how these texts would have been able to guide the travels of subsequent mariners in any systematic fashion.[20]

The empirical observation, then, becomes part of a larger state of mind about how space is traversed nautically and the gestures of authority and the appropriation of space enacted by the writing of texts like Velho's *Relação.* For Luís Madureira, *roteiros* "are putatively the genre that most patently registers Portugal's contribution to Europe's empiricist 'revolution.'" In effect, the *roteiros* attempt to codify and stabilize both nautical knowledge and the boundaries of Portugal's maritime dominion. They are in a sense the textual indices of the triumph of Portuguese maritime technology" (34).[21] Consider Velho's opening observations:

> Em nome de Deus, ámen. Na era de mil quatrocentos e noventa e sete mandou El-Rei D. Manuel, o primeiro deste nome em Portugal, a descobrir, quatro navios, os quais iam em busca da especiaria, dos quais navios ia por capitão-mor Vasco da Gama, e dos outros: dum deles Paulo da Gama, seu irmão, e do outro Nicolau Coelho [e um Gonçalo Nunes, criado de Vasco da Gama, que ia por capitão da nau dos mantimentos].
>
> Partimos do Restelo um sábado, que eram oito dias do mês de Julho . . . [seguindo] nosso caminho, que Deus Nosso Senhor deixe acabar em seu serviço, ámen.
>
> Primeiramente chegámos ao sábado seguinte à vista das Canárias . . . (9)

In the name of God, Amen. In 1497 King Manuel, the first of that name in Portugal, sent four ships on a voyage of discovery, ships that went in search of spices. Vasco da Gama served as captain-major of all of these ships; Paulo da Gama, his brother, was captain of another; Nicolau Coelho, of another; and Gonçalo Nunes served as captain of the supply vessel.

We left Restelo on Saturday, July 8 . . . and pursued our course; God grant that it may be in His service, Amen.

First, we arrived in sight of the Canaries on the following Saturday . . .[22]

Velho takes care to note the royal mandate behind the voyage, its ultimate divine purpose, the constitution of the fleet, the date and place of departure, and the sequentiality of its various stages beginning with the sighting of the Canaries. There is a close coalition between royal/providential purpose, the fleet as a collective body (the itinerant subject of the *Relação*), and directionality; all these elements imbue Gama's trip with an authority and an objective, and with a predetermined way of traversing space sequentially and therefore in linear fashion which Velho terms *caminho* (course, way) or *rota* (route).

Velho records the journey according to a linearity created by the ship as it moves along the west and east coasts of Africa, on to India, and partially back again. When shorelines, dates, location, or depth of waters are noted, it is to establish location as part of a larger placement in geographic space, as a continuous act of orientation in a world being (re)revealed and experienced nautically. In a study of maritime orientation, Ulrich Kinzel notes how navigation itself was conceived as a "principle of connection" in that it connects two distant places (30) and that its object is a "route," or the recurrent passage which is directed to a place assigned (ibid.). Navigation seeks to track the trackless sea; it "conquers this powerful figure of oblivion by finding the routes that it does not seem to have" (Padrón 83). However, if we follow Kinzel's definitions, Velho's account technically describes more a journey of pilotage (sailing close to the shore) than navigation (sailing on the high seas), although it does exemplify the idea of (nautical) orientation in that "[o]rientation either implies that a *position* is fixed (on a map) or a *direction* is defined (in a route). These two modes have to be distinguished from a mode which is orientation-free and might be called *situation*, or . . . passage or way" (Kinzel 29; emphasis in original). Velho's *caminho* is analogous to Kinzel's definition of "situation," though it is not always possible to extract the idea of directionality out of it that Kinzel finds in English "orientation-free" writings. In Portuguese nautical narratives, *caminho* usually implies a general movement in a certain and predetermined direction. The *caminho* is a principle of spatial movement not only because of an implied and controlled directionality but also in its potential repeatability or recurrence. For Godinho, *descobrimento* (discovery) means to be able to understand space, move through it, and relate to its inhabitants, while the concept *descobrir* (to discover) is the ability to trace a route successfully back to a point of departure, return to a previous destination, and then return safely to the point of departure (633). This principle applies to journeys over both land and sea. Just after the incipit of Velho's account quoted above, we find a reference to the fleet's first storm in which Paulo da Gama's ship (on which Velho travels) is separated from the others and is lost to sight of the fleet.

E, depois que amanheceu, não houvemos vista dele nem dos outros navios; e nós fizemos o caminho das ilhas de Cabo Verde, porque tinham ordenado que quem se perdesse seguisse esta rota. (10)

And, once day had come, we could not find him [Vasco da Gama] or the other ships; we then made our way to the islands of Cape Verde, because it had been agreed that whoever might get lost should follow that route.

As the lost ship, Paulo da Gama makes his way or *caminho* to Cape Verde. The *caminho* occasioned by the storm stands in contradistinction to the general *caminho* of the India-bound fleet, and the *rota* is a specific path to reach Cape Verde that exists independently of the *caminho* to India— it would exist even if the storm had not occurred. Velho notes a similar interruption when some of the crew suffer from scurvy in southern Africa; afterwards, "fomos nosso caminho, e andámos seis dias pelo mar" (we went on our way, and we traveled for six days on the sea, 27). Here, as above, the "way" refers to the predetermined direction of the voyage and there-fore to the voyage itself as an exercise of inscribing Portuguese direction-ality, iterativeness, and knowledge on the coastlines and waters of Africa and Asia. The *caminho*, then, is the time-delimited instantiation of an organizing and orientational principle of which Velho's *Relação* is but one example. Notations of chronological, astronomical, or nautical data, in addition to whatever practical use such data might be put by future trav-elers, support this exercise of nautical cognition and experience. Africa is appropriated by moving, in a certain way and with a certain technology, through it.

In the first lines of his own narrative, Cadamosto refers to his journeys (and, implicitly, to the written account of those journeys) as "mio itiner-ario" (my itinerary, 3). With this term, Cadamosto locates his account in a tradition of medieval travel writing that also underlies the burgeon-ing culture of cartographic writing in the sixteenth century. The itinerary Cadamosto mentions undergirds Velho's narrative as well. These writers therefore manifest, in discourse, the visually oriented itinerary map. In a study of maps and verbal mapmaking in early-modern Spanish empire, Padrón notes that the itinerary defines a way of arriving at a destination, of delineating a way to get to a particular place or places; it represents a network of routes connecting travel destinations (54, 58). One of the dis-tinguishing characteristics of the itinerary is the perspective of the reader: while the map addresses a reader "who enjoys an abstract, idealized, and static point of view, the itinerary addresses a reader who is embodied, earthbound, and dynamic" (61). As a genre of cartographic writing, the itinerary or *itinerarium* is a "unilateral trajectory defined in terms of a succession of sites" (Conley 140). Cadamosto and Velho share character-istics with the itinerary insofar as they delineate (and therefore loosely connect) a succession of sites and present not an embedded reader but an embedded traveler/writer. They do not purport to be a vade mecum meant to get a future traveler from one place to the next, though there is information in these accounts that may be used in the ongoing business of navigation, travel, and information gathering. There is a certain privilege of abstraction enjoyed by the writers, like the reader of a map, in that a generalized view of geography and spatial distribution emerges from the itinerancy of the embedded subject who goes from point A to B to C. The rehearsal of technical information is significant in its iterative capacity. The embedded movement of the traveler/writer—that is, the movement through horizontal space—enacts a repetitiveness of encounter with the natural and human worlds that establishes *saber* or knowledge. The repetition of distances as expressed by leagues traveled, or soundings taken, is not simply practical but conceptual: the authority of imperial travel and writing rests in large part on the nonaccidental, on the deliberate scripting and repetition of the same experiences in the empirical realm. It is possible to find an analogue between the rehearsal of technical information in texts like Velho's and the monotonous, repetitive narratives of battles between Christians and Moors in chronicles like Zurara's *Crónica de D. Pedro de Meneses* (Chronicle of D. Pedro de Meneses) and *Crónica de D. Duarte de Meneses* (Chronicle of D. Duarte de Meneses). What is at stake in these historical texts is not so much the addition to historical memory of any one particular battle but the fact that such encounters are repeated. This repetition proves the providential inevitability of fighting the Moors. A series of victories over the infidel (or over "gentiles" or "pagans" like the sub-Saharan Africans), tirelessly and monotonously narrated, manifests the ineluctability of Christian imperialism. In like fashion, the iterative recording of information by an embedded traveler in an itinerary-like narrative through African space solidifies an evolving and cumulative corpus of knowledge. The validity of any one piece of information is secondary (or even irrelevant) to the overall assumption that nautical travel will always produce authority.

Velho does not fail to note the geographic distribution and color of native Africans and then of Indians as Gama's voyage progresses. In São Brás (Mossel Bay), for instance, he notes that the people are black and, during a trading excursion to shore, they begin to play pipes and dance;

Velho notes with some surprise that "não se espera música [de negros]" (one does not expect music from blacks, 17). In East Africa, Velho states that the *mouros* are "ruivos" (red-haired, 28), and later notes the presence of white Moors in Mozambique (33). The association between the color(s) of Africans and distinct geographic regions has become a constant in these texts ever since Zurara's descriptions of the various levels of darkness and whiteness among the sub-Saharans in *Guiné*. Like characteristics of the littoral or the ocean waters, Africans and their varying skin pigmentation act as geographic markers and delimiters of space. Moors, blacks, or Guineans mark and inhabit certain geographic regions and come to stand as emblems of those regions, much like the monsters of Pliny or Marco Polo. Native Africans are flesh-and-bone embodiments of spatial boundaries. They thus fulfill an orientational function, like the astrolabe, in that they can be used in the calculation of location. The realm of Prester John of the Indies acts in a very similar manner in Velho's account and in many histories of the sixteenth century. The legendary priest-king's elusive realm—"nos disseram que [o] Preste João estava ali perto, e que tinha muitas cidades ao longo do mar" (they told us that Prester John was close by, and that he had many cities along the coast, 29–30), Velho observes—acts as a principle of orientation. Like magnetic north, the kingdom of Prester John is a guiding beacon that influences both the overseas and overland *caminhos* of the travelers; unlike magnetic north, the realm of Prester John is nomadic, never fixed, always over the next hill or too distant into the interior to be conveniently verified.

Like the *padrões* left behind in Africa by Gama and his crew, Velho's text symbolically appropriates the lands and waters of coastal Africa on behalf of the imperial monarch.[23] In the progress of the voyage, Africa is an anticipation of, and obstacle to, India, something to be overcome and something that prepares for the arrival in Calicut. This sense of preparation becomes evident through the numerous stops or moorings the fleet makes along the African coast. At one point Velho relates an interaction with a Moor who informs the travelers that ships such as theirs have passed that way before: "e dizia que já vira navios grandes, como aqueles que nós levávamos; com os quais sinais nós folgávamos muito porque nos parecia que nos íamos chegando para onde desejávamos" (and he said that he had previously seen large ships such as ours; in this we took great pleasure, because it seemed that we were getting closer to our desired destination, 26). Africa is a transitional, albeit important, part of the *caminho* delineated by Gama's ships in the attainment of the East and as such functions as an intermediate space in the Portuguese realization of the Orient.

In the sixteenth century, historical writing on a large scale flourishes and historians take on the task of narrating the Portuguese presence in India. In this historiographic milieu prior to Camões there is no extant text dedicated exclusively to Africa. Africa appears either in the histories of Portuguese India or as part of the chronicles of the reigns of individual kings or colonial administrators. Generally speaking, expansion in Africa follows a rather pro forma recitation of military encounter, trade, the capture of slaves, or negotiations with African potentates, and chroniclers by and large do not engage in geographic descriptions of Africa. What is most important in these histories is the framing of Africa within a historical purview as part of expansionist activities and of the expansionist mind-set. The remainder of this section considers the work of three writers who best represent the sixteenth-century culture of historical writing that leads to the imagining of Africa in Camões. These writers are João de Barros, Fernão Lopes de Castanheda, and Damião de Góis.

The humanist João de Barros (ca. 1496–1570) worked during the reigns of Manuel I (1495–1521) and João III (1521–27), the monarchs whose respective rules encompass the most active and formative years of the establishment of Portuguese empire in India and in Brazil. Barros was treasurer of the India, Ceuta, and Mina (Guinea) customshouses and archives in Lisbon, important posts in the bureaucratic machine of empire. Like Zurara, he was official chronicler or *cronista-mor*. Manuel I encouraged Barros to write an epic history of the Portuguese in Asia, and in response the historian conceived an ambitious historiographic project that was meant to cover Portuguese expansion in all of its aspects and geographic reach across the globe. The completed history was to be divided into three major parts. The first, *Milícia* (Warfare), would document Portuguese conquest and military efforts in the four parts of the world (Europe, Africa, Asia, and Santa Cruz [Brazil]). Each of the sub-parts of *Milícia* would bear the generic title of *Décadas* (Decades), following Livy. The second part, *Navegação* (Navigation; alternately titled *Geografia* [Geography]), was to be a geographic treatise of the world and written in Latin. Barros conceived the third and final part, *Comércio* (Commerce), as a manual of natural and artificial products along with calculations of weights and measurements. Barros only lived to publish a small portion of his ambitious project—the first three *Décadas da Ásia* (Decades of Asia) published in 1552, 1553, and 1563— though his frequent references in the *Décadas* to other parts of the project (such as the *Geografia*) suggest that these other portions may have existed in draft form.[24] If so, they have since been lost.

It is unfortunate that we do not have Barros's *África* (one of the volumes of *Milícia*); however, the first three books (and a small portion of the fourth) of the first *Década da Ásia* deal with Africa, so we have an indication of how Barros conceived of the continent in the context of his larger enterprise.[25] In these books, the historian begins by narrating the history of Morocco, makes reference to the Moorish invasion of the Iberian Peninsula in 711, and then proceeds to the history of the Portuguese exploration of Guinea and the Cape of Good Hope. This history includes the voyages to Guinea ordered by Prince Henry, as well as the history of the factory of São Jorge da Mina (established in 1482), one of the mainstays of the Guinea trade. It also includes the discovery of Madeira, Cape Verde, the Canary Islands, and provides considerable detail about the search for the kingdom of Prester John. Barros tells us that his main source for the Henrican material is Zurara, though Barros's historiographic style and tone differ significantly from the fifteenth-century chronicler. Barros's discursive reshaping of the matter of Africa will have a significant influence on Camões. The end of the treatment of Africa proper comes at the beginning of Book Four of the first *Década* with Vasco da Gama's 1497 voyage to India. In these books, Barros does not inform us what his principle of selection is regarding the material included: that is, we do not know how these initial chapters supplement or repeat the material to have been narrated at more length in his *África*.

What we do know is that Barros sets his narrative in an ideological rhetoric and maintains it throughout his history. This is how chapter 1 of Book One of *Ásia* begins:

> Levantado em terra de Arábia aquêle grande antecristo Mafamede . . . assi
> lavrou a fúria de seu ferro e fogo de sua infernal seita, per meio de seus
> capitães e califas, que em espaço de cem anos, conquistaram em Ásia tôda

Arábia e parte da Síria e Pérsia, e em África todo Egipto àquém e àlém do Nilo. (7)

The great Antichrist Muhammad, arisen in the land of Arabia . . . so forged the fury, like iron and fire, of his infernal sect that, through his captains and caliphs, conquered all of Araby in Asia and part of Syria and Persia, and in Africa all of Egypt both on this side of the Nile and beyond, in the space of one hundred years.

Barros does not relinquish in the hundreds of succeeding pages the tenor of this ideological zealousness, a zealousness Camões will repeat throughout *Os Lusíadas* whenever the poet speaks of Moorishness as the antagonist to Christendom. In *Ásia*, Barros overlays this rhetoric onto the narrative of the voyages of African exploration traced and recorded by Zurara. In comparison to Barros, Zurara's narrative style in *Guiné* (or Álvaro Velho's in the *Relação*) appears flat or even pragmatic.

The historian's demonizing of Muhammad and Mauritania relies on a strategy that is as unrelenting as that found in the papal bulls of the fifteenth century. But unlike the papal edicts, Barros's view of Moors as a "praga" (plague, 7) from the east, as always and definitionally foreigners or strangers, is retrospective to medieval, pre-expansionist Portugal. Thus Barros speaks of military actions against the Moors as "cleaning house" (alimpar a casa, 11), actions that date back to before the reign of D. João I of Avis (1385–1433), the architect of the Ceuta invasion; by João I's time, Barros claims, "the house was clean" (assi estava limpa [a casa], 11). Barros ignores the presence of Moors and Moorish culture in Portugal during the time of João I and after. Expansionist activities in Africa and Asia will not so much "clean house" as continue the cleansing battle, initiated at home, in foreign lands. It is tempting to find in Barros a "Crusade doctrine against the infidel" (Rebelo 80), or a neo-Reconquest view of the Moor, a feasible assumption given Barros's initial emphasis on the 711 invasion as the "perdição de Espanha" (perdition of Spain, 11). If we are to apply the idea of a crusade to Barros's work, it must be understood to include aspects besides spirituality per se. Marques notes, in a discussion of the conquest of Ceuta, that a crusade involved several aspects and several goals, such as the defense of Christendom against non-Christians, attacking the infidel so he could not spread his error among others, securing economic bases for the prosperity of Christendom, and saving the souls of unbelievers (*History of Portugal* 141). It is clear here that "Christendom" is a label that can denote a collectivity of not just religious but also economic and political interests. The historical circumstances of Barros's sixteenth century were different, though, than those of the medieval crusades or the *reconquista*. Barros developed his historical project at a time when the bases of the Portuguese African, Asian, and American empires had already been laid; the initial years of Portuguese imperialism on three continents were over. Barros's history, unlike the texts of Zurara, were redacted after a significant period of time had elapsed since the earlier voyages of exploration. *Ásia* seeks to infix the history of expansion into a monolithic frame of spiritual militancy against Moors, Africa, and Araby in general. This is the aspect of Barros's work Camões found most apposite to his poetic project: in his historical vision, Barros establishes the war against the infidel for the sixteenth century as a defining trait of Portuguese maritime nationhood. This war not only is justification for conquistatorial action, but it has accompanied expansionist experience abroad long enough for it to be the defining trait of overseas expansion itself:

> É se ante da tomada de Ceita, não pôs em obra êste seu natural desejo, foi porque já em seu tempo neste reino não havia mouros que conquistar, porque os reis seus avós . . . a poder de ferro os tinham lançado além-mar em as partes de África. (14)

> And so it is that if before the capture of Ceuta, [Prince Henry] did not put into practice this natural desire [of war against the infidel], it was because in his time in this kingdom there were no more Moors to conquer, because [Henry's] ruling forefathers . . . by the force of iron had expelled them overseas to the various parts of Africa.

Barros implicates the medieval history of Christian–Moorish interaction in Portugal into the impetus of African expansion under Henry's initiative. He everywhere advocates for the religious and chivalric motives behind African expansion. While investing expansion with a religious mandate that makes possible the attainment of chivalric honor, the historian nonetheless denies any interest other than religious on the part of Henry for under-taking the Guinean voyages (32, 52); the prince captured blacks in West Africa solely for the purpose of conversion. Randles informs us that the Portuguese historian was the first to analyze systematically the legal impli-cations of the discoveries (*L'Image* 128). Such attention to the legal bases of *conquista* is apparent, for example, when Barros notes Manuel I's attempts to discover "terras habitadas de gentio idólatra e mouros heréticos, pera se poderem *conquistar* e tomar das mãos deles como de injustos possuï-dores" (lands inhabited by idolatrous pagans and heretical Moors, [so that] he could conquer them and take these lands away from their hands, as if they were unrightful owners, 228–29).[26] In a panegyric (1533) dedi-cated to D. João III, Barros draws a series of lessons for Portuguese empire from the example of Rome, and elaborates on what constitutes conquest and colonialism:[27]

> Os caminhos pera conquistar, são estes: aos vencidos não dar muita opres-são, mandar que os vassalos e naturais vão morar nas terras ganhadas, as quais povoações os romãos chamaram colónias; dos despojos fazer tesouro; afadigar ao imigo com cavalgadas, entradas e batalhas campais e não con-certos . . . (*Panegíricos* 113)

> The ways of conquest are these: do not overly oppress the vanquished, order vassals and subjects of the realm to live in the lands that were won—these populations were called colonies by the Romans; add booty to your wealth; exhaust the enemy with cavalcades, entrances, and field battles, and not har-mony and order . . .

By making Africa a prelude to the Portuguese colonial occupation of Asia, Barros casts Africa as part of a larger, "Orientalist" enterprise. In the *Ásia,* Africa emerges as an intermediate step in the equally ideological and "epic" Portuguese attainment of the East, an exemplification of Portuguese im-perial aggression and colonial exploration (Boxer, *João de Barros* 95). Africa is also, and perhaps just as importantly, a product of Christendom's competitor empire, Islam—recall that Barros opens the first *Década da Ásia* with a brief account of the history of Morocco. The work of João de Barros firmly locates Africa in a culture of writing and thinking that is best described, as we noted earlier, as the culture of Portuguese "Orientalness." The *Décadas da Ásia* make Africa part of a historiographic idiom of empire that is global rather than regional in its referentiality, an ideologically inflected narrative of beginnings. In this evolving, textual practice of Orientalness, Barros writes, like Zurara and unlike Cadamosto and Velho, from a bookish perspective in that his history is not the product of eyewitness experience. In this regard, Barros is thus an early Orientalist in the Saidian sense: his Africa and the Orient are part of a systematic or institutional discursive practice on the broadly defined East.

João de Barros's contemporary and rival, Fernão Lopes de Castanheda (d. 1559), published several books of his *História do descobrimento e conquista da Índia pelos Portugueses* (History of the Discovery and Conquest of India by the Portuguese) between 1551 and 1559; the final book was printed posthumously in 1561. Unlike Barros's treatment of Africa that includes the exploration of the Guinea coast from the time of Ceuta to Gama's voyage, Castanheda includes Africa only in the form of Gama's trip. For Castanheda, pre-Gaman African exploration does not relate to the Asian enterprise. The differences between Barros and Castanheda in how each writer implicates Africa into the larger historiographic narrative are pronounced. Whereas Barros writes—or better, rewrites—Africa as an object of imperial pursuit informed by an ideological mind-set, he nonetheless does so by recognizing the historical depth of Portuguese experience there (in his reliance on Zurara's work) and takes care to lay out rather detailed descriptions of African geography. Barros's narrative style is proto-novelistic with its invention of dialogues that foreground the chivalric and religious motives of African expansion, and indeed it is feasible to say that Barros composed the *Décadas* as if it were a chivalric novel (we should not forget that in his youth Barros also penned a chivalric narrative, the *Crónica do Imperador Clarimundo* [Chronicle of the Emperor Clarimundo]). Castanheda, on the other hand, eschews religious ideology in favor of mercantilism. Portuguese expansionist activity prior to India is only important for Castanheda in these terms:

> Antes que a India fosse descuberta pelos Portugueses, a mayor parte da
> especiaria, droga & pedraria dela se vazaua pelo mar roxo donde ya ter á
> cidade Dalexandria, & ali a comprauão os Venezianos que a espalhauão pela

Europa, de que ho reyno de Portugal auia seu quinhão, que os Venezianos
leuauão a Lisboa em galés . . . (5)

Before India was discovered by the Portuguese, most spices, drugs, and gems
were carried across the Red Sea to the city of Alexandria, where Venetians
bought them and distributed them throughout Europe. The kingdom of
Portugal was entitled to its share, which the Venetians brought to Lisbon by
boat . . .

For Castanheda, the Portuguese African enterprise only begins with João II
(reigned 1481–95), a date that relegates to the background all Guinean exploration conducted under Prince Henry. Castanheda writes that João II
"determinou de prosseguir ho descobrimento da costa de Guiné que seus
antecessores tinhão começado: porque por aquela costa lhe parecia que
descobriria ho senhorío do Preste Ioão das Indias de que tinha fama . . ."
(determined to continue the discovery of the coast of Guinea that his fore-
fathers had begun, since it was along that coast that it seemed likely he
would discover the realm of Prester John of the Indies, of which he had
often heard . . . , 5). Absent from Castanheda's comments are references
to the slave trade, to the various regions of sub-Saharan Africa mapped
by Zurara, or to religious difference (though the Moorish hatred of Christians is documented in chapter 8). Chivalric pursuits and providence also
receive no mention. Castanheda does not specify what aspects of Prester
John's realm informed João II's interests and efforts: Was it to establish
trade? To find the fabled communities of eastern Christians? To establish
diplomatic relations? One might argue (as some critics have done) that
there is a lack of zealous ideology in Castanheda's history—and that therefore Castanheda is more "objective"—as opposed to the religious rhetoric
of João de Barros, but such an argument overlooks the fact that the heavily mercantilist focus of Castanheda is just as ideological. Castanheda's
history of Africa in the first book offers no specifics as to the division of
lands or to the demographics of Guinea and southern Africa established
by the writers we studied above. Even with the caveat that Castanheda's
focus here is India and not Africa, there is a vision of Africa that subsumes
it into an undifferentiated sameness. Africa, in Castanheda, verges on an
abstraction. It is pushed into the background of Gama's India voyage, and

then only as a precursor to the importance of the *carreira da Índia* (India voyage) as a trade route that challenges the Venetian monopoly.

João II, known as the "Príncipe Perfeito" or Perfect Prince, was instrumental in continuing African exploration in the years following Henry's death. He resolved to penetrate the African interior, a further development of the coast-hugging expeditions carried out under Henry. The king sent Diogo de Azambuja to Mina in 1481 to build a trading factory, which Azambuja did in 1482, the same year Diogo Cão reached the Kongo. News of an inland priest-king by the name of Ogané was received sometime between 1485 and 1487 by João Afonso Aveiro, a factor at Benin; Ogané was thought to be Prester John. João II organized an expedition to search for this priest-king and to reach Ethiopia and India overland. The travelers sent on this expedition were Afonso de Paiva and Pero da Covilhã. Covilhã eventually reached India, but Paiva died somewhere in Africa. Under João II's orders, Bartolomeu Dias discovered the Cape of Good Hope in 1488.

João II's history is first recounted in a chronicle by Rui de Pina (1440–1522), Zurara's successor to the post of *cronista-mor*. Garcia de Resende, compiler of the famous *Cancioneiro Geral* (General Songbook, 1516), composed an anecdotal *Crónica de D. João II* (Chronicle of D. João II), published in 1545. The chronicle that is of most interest here, both because of its chronological proximity to Camões and its formulation of the African historiographic project, is the one completed by Damião de Góis (1502–74). Góis—a scholar, diplomat, and friend of Erasmus—spent two decades abroad and returned to Portugal in 1545 when he became the *guarda-mor* (royal keeper) of the Torre do Tombo archives in Lisbon. A defender of Erasmian orthodoxy, Góis was consequently imprisoned by the Inquisition and died while incarcerated. Góis penned his *Crónica do príncipe Dom João* (Chronicle of Prince João) while João was regent, and it was published in 1567. Like Barros, Góis was a humanist, well versed in Latin and classical learning, and his chronicle reflects his scholarly training and disposition.

The first portion of the chronicle narrates João's African ventures. Góis opens his narrative with a criticism of Zurara by implying that the chronicler stole material from his predecessor Fernão Lopes in his writings on Ceuta and Morocco, and he impugns Zurara's historiographic style as having "razoamentos prolixos, & cheos de metaphoras, ou figuras que no stylo historico não tẽ lugar" (long passages, filled with metaphors or other figures that have no place in historical style, 13). According to Góis, expansion was a capitalist enterprise and was what made Portugal famous abroad. Foreigners came to Portugal hoping to take part and cash in on these endeavors.[28] For Góis, the explorations along the west coast under Prince Henry were meant to find the sea route to India, a claim that makes Gama's journey the end result of a single, decades-long project:

[O Infante] determinou de mandar nauios aho longuo da costa Dafrica com tençam de chegar aho fim de seus pensamentos, que era descobrir destas partes ocçidentaes ha nauegação pera ha India oriental, ha qual sabia por çérto que fora jà em outros tempos achada. E esta çerteza que assi alcançou do trabalho de seu studo, lhe fez cometter tamanho negoçio, & nam per inspirações diuinas, quomo algũas pessoas dizem . . . (14–15)

[The Prince] resolved to send ships along the coast of Africa to achieve the objective of his thoughts, and that was to discover, through these wèstern parts, the maritime route to eastern India, which he was certain had been found in earlier times. And this knowledge he came to through the diligence of study, which was what led him to undertake such an enterprise, and not through divine inspiration, as some say . . .

Góis rejects a divinely inspired master plan for Henry's explorations in favor of a resolve that is the result of scholarly inquiry, and portrays Henry as a student of astrology and cosmography, as Russell points out (*Prince Henry* 6). The emphasis on cosmography (the book-based study of nature and the world) has important implications for the nature of African exploration, apart from the detail it adds to the biographical lore of the prince. To construe African exploration as a product of Henry's "pensamentos" (thoughts) and "studo" (study) is to make it an intellectual and epistemological enterprise, a pursuit informed by the creation of knowledge and a way of knowing the world. In postulating this impetus to Henry's maritime activities, Góis remobilizes Zurara's framing of sub-Saharan conquest as the initiation of a new knowledge of the world that is reflected in the "razões" or reasons behind Henry's exploration of Guinea, as we saw earlier.

Góis presents a summary of the "navegações" or maritime explorations carried out in Henry's time in chapter 8. He predictably begins the summary with the seizure of Ceuta. The recapitulation of navigational exploration here reaches to 1455, the year of João's birth. Events are presented in chronological order and, as in other chapters of the chronicle that detail the Portuguese voyages, receive little critical commentary by Góis. This summary, though, is significant because it establishes a genealogy or lineage of discovery, and Góis takes cognizance of previous writings so that new discoveries become part of an extant discursive regime on Africa, of a by now fairly long-standing tradition of expansionist *auctoritates*. The chronicler specifically mentions the "itinerario" of Cadamosto (21) among other, unnamed sources on the history of Guinea, and in so doing subsumes Cadamosto's individual experience into a larger historiographic enterprise, the more expansive history defined by João II's life and reign. This absorption invests Cadamosto's firsthand narrative account with a teleological ineluctability. The chronicler presents this "fim" (objective) early in the narrative so that all that follows, even those journeys made after Henry's death, originate in Henry's initial plan. Historical action (and this includes writing) moves toward a certain end; Góis's historical perspective makes individual actions part of a larger hermeneutic of empire. This is one of the lessons Góis will impart to Camões. One of the means the chronicler uses to construct this teleology is to identify the gaps in the history of expansion. At the close of his summary of discoveries made by Henry, for example, Góis states: "E deste tempo [1446] atté ho ano de M.cccclv. em que elRei dom Ioam nasçeo, nam achei cousa scripta, nem per memoria, de calidade pera se della fazer mēção" (And from this date [1446] to the year 1455 in which King João was born, I found nothing in writing or in memory worthy of mention, 23). After mentioning this gap, Góis fills it in with a short excursus on the discovery of the Azores. What is not clear is how Góis judges the "calidade" (quality or worthiness) of deeds written or remembered as appropriate for his historiographic standard, but it seems that Góis desires to foreground the power he has in overriding previous texts and perceptions of history. He thus brings to the forefront his role as a determiner of historical interpretation. The gaps in the historical narrative of Africa—if we understand, pace Góis, "narrative" to mean both the written form of history and individual or collective memories—are propitious moments for the individual writer to (re)direct historical interpretation, even if those gaps may be artificially created by rejecting any previous accounts as "unworthy of mention." Here we might find a narrative analogue to the "positive" empty spaces on grid maps, if we understand historiographic accounts of expansion as a mapping in verbal space. An empty space on a geometrically structured grid map is not a blankness or negative area produced by ignorance of an undiscovered geographic feature, but a "positive emptiness," an abstract space into which geographies are written, as Padrón (35) explains. Similarly, the genealogy and chronology of discovery traced by Góis invests the period between 1446 and 1455—"empty" in that nothing worthy of mention from this period can be found—with a positiveness, a receptivity and readiness for narrative. It is a positively charged, empty space in the overall map of history; it is empty precisely and only in relation to the other narrated events surrounding it, to the matrix of episodes and chapters constituting the chronicle. The discursive act of filling in the gaps establishes metonymy as an act of historiographic authority—the narrative part relates to the whole as a completion and fulfillment. "One of the ways in which ideologies work," Hulme writes, "is by passing off partial accounts as the whole story" (*Colonial Encounters* 15).

Strangeness under the Imperial Sun

In the texts we have just considered, writers on Africa make observations on geography, the customs and skin color of natives, and the new natural and human worlds that nautical travel reveals. These observations seek to taxonomize—and therefore contain and control—the spaces and peoples of Africa. The Western observer shapes the world and its inhabitants and infixes them into a schema of observation and knowledge; these writer-observers are the possessors of the "imperial eyes" that Pratt studies in texts of a similar nature in later centuries. The body of texts on Africa incrementally but surely creates a corpus of authority. The more texts, the more stable the practice of writing on Africa and the African and therefore, in imperialist thought, the more authority gained and wielded. The frequency and number of writings is in itself significant; taken collectively and over time, these texts constitute a systematic practice of writing. The discursive regime on Africa, independently of lived experience, is the basis of its own authority. The texts manifest a knowledgeable observer and writer while they also create an archive that serves to authorize further documents. The repetitiveness of taxonomic schemata similarly acts as an authorizing strategy in that, once the kind of information to be recorded about Africa has been established through practice, subsequent writings apprehend and shape Africa in the same manner. The writings we have been considering establish a frame through which Africa—and then Asia and America—will be textually rendered, known, and conquered. So it is that writing about Africa constitutes part of the Portuguese exercise of power known as *conquista*.

As an exercise of power, the creation of knowledge rests on both the empirical and imaginative realms. I wish now to turn to a concept that is notably present in the work of Zurara and Camões and that links these two authors who reside at distinct and distant points on the continuum of expansionist textuality. The concept I am referring to is the strange (*o estranho*), one of the ideas that allows us to place Zurara and Camões in dialogue as representatives of the historical and historico-imaginative rendering of Africa. Zurara envisions his activities as court chronicler as part of the cosmic structure of the universe, a clog in the "rodas celesti-ais" (celestial wheels) that move human action. As the vehicle that allows for Zurara's participation in the workings of the divine and human worlds through writing, Africa is historiographic in nature because, from its phys-ical and imaginative boundaries, a new writing of history unfolds. Camões's *Os Lusíadas* similarly places Africa at the center of its several narratives because the first five of the poem's ten cantos take place in African space. On Africa's sands and along its coastlines the actors of Camões's poem linger in order to narrate the history of Portugal and of Europe, to hear prophecies of the future, and to interact with gods of the Greco-Roman pantheon and participate in the governing energies of the cosmos. Camões's placement of this mix of history, myth, prophecy, knowledge, and action in Africa points back to a Portuguese writing subject and a Portuguese project of knowledge gathering. These African locales "suppose a non-African epistemological locus," as Mudimbe defines the European gnosis of Africa (*Invention of Africa* x).

Expansion is by definition a process of displacement, alienation, and outsiderness. To extend the boundaries of the *pátria* (country) outward is to create and inhabit foreignness. However ideologically cohesive the expansionist enterprise might be as rendered by its apologists, in practical terms its implementation is often disorienting, fraught with danger, and met with peril. Conquest voyagers confront the limits of knowledge and of supposed military or linguistic superiority in empirical terms that are as unexpected as they are dangerous. As itinerant conquerors, colonizers, traders, and missionaries become displaced from a grid of power and authority of the home country, they become out of place. The European (or those traveling under European organization) cannot help but become, to some degree, that which must "officially" be sought to be repressed, subdued, or controlled: a dislocated and vulnerable subject, largely dependent on the contingencies of time and place for survival. As the initial space of Portuguese expansion, Africa is therefore a vast contact zone between Europeans, Africans, Western knowledge, and the world "out there." Luso-African encounter—if we momentarily accept the viability of distinguishing "Portuguese" from "African" as stable categories of identity—generates the strange as a product of the encounter between spheres of experience and perception.

The Portuguese adjective *estranho* derives from Latin *extraneus* (external, extraneous, or foreign); something that is "strange" is therefore something that comes from outside. Africa itself is a locus of outsiderness, according to the possible etymological origins of the term explored by Miller. "Africa" may be an Arabic word, *Ifriqiyah,* that entered European languages through transliteration into Latin. Miller's etymological comments reveal sources that conceive of Africa as essentially separate or liminal, a void until brought into being by an outsider.[29] If, as Miller argues, "there is containment, subjugation, and negation of the object [i.e., Africa] at the same moment that the object is brought into being" (12), then Africa exists only as a place of strangers and strangeness because it is the outsider who calls Africa into existence. As a historical concept, outsiderness or foreignness carries political overtones, as Julia Kristeva explains:

If one goes back through time and social structures, the foreigner is the other of the family, the clan, the tribe. At first, he blends with the enemy. External to my religion, too, he could have been the heathen, the heretic. Not having made an oath of fealty to my lord, he was born on another land, foreign to the kingdom or the empire . . . With the establishment of nation-states we come to the only modern, acceptable, and clear definition of for-eignness: the foreigner is the one who does not belong to the state in which we are, the one who does not have the same nationality . . . The group to which the foreigner does not belong has to be a social group structured about a given kind of political power. (95–96)

The political nature of strangers and foreignness Kristeva identifies ex-plains in part the practice of imperialism as an imposed dynamic of out-siderness, of foreign genealogies and nonnative coalitions of power. Both conquerors and conquered constitute strangers because they do not belong to the same "social" group, although in the early-modern imperial con-text, instead of social groups it would be better to speak of racialized, religious, or linguistic groups. The mixing or dismantling of these group identities existed on a practical level in Portuguese empire with the infor-mal category of "stranger":

> [strangers were] the civilian Portuguese who for various reasons moved outside the areas of formal Portuguese jurisdiction and married into the local "native" population. These often formed distinct Luso-African or Luso-Asiatic communities, but sought neither to adopt Portuguese civilian institu-tions nor incorporation into the formal empire. Indeed these often formed a recognized category of "strangers" who enjoyed special privileges and pro-tection within African or Asiatic societies. (Newitt, "Formal and Informal Empire" 5)

Moreover, strangeness as a political concept does not necessarily acknowl-edge the process of integration or shifting power dynamics that obtain in the contact zone, or the fluidity of markers of identity negotiated between different ethnocultural groups that is the result of colonialism. Once a foreigner does not mean always a foreigner; the culture-crossing figure of the Moorish interpreter who is, linguistically speaking, both colonizer and colonized, and the *lançado* (a Portuguese who lives in colonized ter-ritory and who adopts indigenous habits of dress and language and fre-quently marries native women), are testimonies of the deliberate blurring of boundaries between groups of strangers.

This is not to say, however, that a political or politicized sense of strangeness does not appear in authors like Camões, if by "political" we mean interested relations of power in the appropriation and domination of foreign resources. Rather, as the texts of expansion continue to be written and expose the difficulties in any putative master narrative about the success of empire, the concept of the strange also expands to mark transitional moments in the European knowledge of the world and the imposition of Western culture as an ethical imperative. In a more general sense, Achille Mbembe reminds us that Africa has always been the locus of the strange with respect to the West's perception of itself:

> [Africa] the continent is the very figure of "the strange" . . . In this extremity of the Earth, reason is supposedly permanently at bay, and the unknown has supposedly attained its highest point. Africa, a headless figure threatened with madness and quite innocent of any notion of center, hierarchy, or stability, is portrayed as a vast dark cave where every benchmark and distinction come together in total confusion.[30] (3)

Mbembe is speaking of the West's configuration of Africa as a place of "absolute otherness" that has allowed the West to define itself and that "still constitutes one of the metaphors through which the West represents the origin of its own norms . . . [and asserts] what it supposes to be its identity" (2). Mbembe's formulation of African strangeness signals not so much any particular moment in the history of the West as it does a conceptualization of Africa as the other half of a binarism—West/Africa—throughout history. Mbembe identifies a process of making Africa an Other that has roots in classical antiquity and is intensified throughout the Middle Ages. As the dark counterpart to the West's construction of itself as rational and civilized, this formulation of African strangeness, though manifested at specific junctures in history, is predominantly ahistorical in that it is always more or less the same.

Zurara, Camões, and the expansionist writers in between only partially manifest an understanding of Africa as unsurmountably and persistently other, because, for instance, the North African enclaves of mercantilism (such as Ceuta) receive recognition as sites of culture and civilization with their own histories, laws, and spiritual practices, no less historically deep than their European counterparts. Zurara, for example, acknowledges the historical dimension of Islam and the sobriety of its rituals. While Arabic Moors adhere blindly to the precepts of their "sect," they also harbor a capacity for abstract and symbolic thought that the codified and ritualistic manners of religious observance make evident. This capacity demonstrates the existence of a kind of mental template that predisposes the Islamic Moor inherently or "naturally" to Christian conversion. The growing familiarity with Africa that the texts of the fifteenth and sixteenth centuries attest incrementally and increasingly banishes the possibility of Africa as diametrically Other. Familiarity allows for a nuanced comprehension of difference, if not even for moments of approximation or assimilation.

Let us consider specifically Camões and Zurara. The strange is a predominant conceit in the lexical and mental worlds of *Os Lusíadas*, a conceit that attends the dynamic of contact and expansion, a consequence of encounters with otherness that consolidates providential and hermeneutic imperatives. It is a principle of interaction that partially defines Portuguese *império* (empire). It signals the reformulation of knowledge and the arenas in which those reformulations occur. As such, the Camonian strange encompasses a variety of meanings that conjointly function as narrative and imperial principles, principles that are preliminarily sketched by Zurara.

In the chronicler's writings, as we might expect, strangeness is a concept related to the spatialization of Portuguese influence that will later come to be referred to as "empire," though the chronicler never uses this term. For Zurara, strangeness emerges mainly from the itinerant nature of the Portuguese cultural and political home. For instance, in the opening pages of *Ceuta*, as Zurara recounts the history of João I's decision to conquer the city, he presents a quasi-Edenic description of Portugal as a land of abundance, rich in resources and food. This image of the home country as a cornucopia implies that the plenitude found within its borders is a "natural" resource that can be carried abroad by ships, and that in such plenitude lies a power which is best expressed by conquest. "Temos muitos vinhos e de desuairadas nações. de que nam soomente a nossa terra he abastada mas ajnda se carregam muitas naaos e nauios pera socorrimento das terras estranhas" (We have many vineyards of various kinds which not only provide for our own land but which also allow many ships to be loaded and come to the aid of foreign lands, 20). The unspecified foreign or strange lands mentioned here to which Portuguese ships travel anticipate the specific land of Morocco in later chapters, except that, in that case, ships do not carry grapes or wine but a cargo of civilization. Once Ceuta has been captured, Zurara tells us, João I considers the possible and desirable role of the city as a place for the exercise of arms:

> com menos da quall despesa os eu posso . . . emuiar a esta çidade, homde me faram mujto mayor seruiço. E ajmda mujtos de meus naturaaes, que per alguũs negoçios ssam desterrados de meus rregnos, milhor estaram aqui fazemdo seruiço a Deos, e comprimdo sua justiça, que sse hirem pollas terras estranhas e desnaturaremsse pera todo sempre . . . (258–59)

> With less expense can I . . . send [those who wish to serve me in arms] to this city, where the service would be better rendered. And even many of my subjects, who on account of a number of matters are away from my realm, would render much better service if they were here, serving God and administering His justice, than to wander through foreign lands and become exiles forever . . .

Zurara's term for subjects is *naturaaes* (literally, "naturals") and, for "to be exiled," *desnaturar-se*. These ideas stand in opposition to "terras estranhas" (foreign lands). There is a demarcation of "natural" as opposed to "foreign" territories, and Zurara includes Ceuta in the first of these categories. Ceuta no longer constitutes a strange land after its conquest, and has been appended to Portuguese soil.

As a spatial notion, foreignness partitions and reconfigures the globe as expansion progresses. The Moorish lament on the loss of Ceuta acknowledges the Moors' forced dispossession of the city that occasions a dislocation of Moorish populations as the Portuguese traveling political home literally gains new ground. The conquest of Ceuta decenters Moorish trade, so that Portuguese occupation has created a new economic orientation to eastern trade routes. "[A]uia hy tal que numqua com tamanha femença esguardara onde viam os seus muros cheos de gentes estranhas" (No [Moor] there had ever contemplated with such great anxiety the walls of Ceuta, filled with foreign peoples, 247), Zurara writes. Then we hear a

collective plaint by Moorish voices as they address the loss of the flower
of all African cities:

> onde acharam daqui adiante os mouros estranhos que vinham de Ethiopia
> e de Alexandria e de terra de Siria e de Barbaria e de terra de Assiria que
> he o rregno de Turcos. e os do oriente que uiuem aalem do rrio de Eufrates
> e das Indias. e doutras muitas terras que sam aalem do exo que estaa ante
> os nossos olhos todos estes vinham a ti carregados de tantas e tam rricas
> mercadorias. (248)

> Where will [its inhabitants] find the foreign Moors who came from Ethi-
> opia, Syria, Barbary, and Assyria, in the realm of the Turks? Or those of the
> Orient who live beyond the Euphrates River and India? Or those who live
> in any other lands beyond this center we see before us, who come to you,
> Ceuta, laden with such plentiful and valuable goods?

There is a geographic relativism here in that this passage demonstrates a
non-Western perspective of the foreign or the strange, and this permits
the redrawing of the map of the world to be regarded as an activity that
is universally comprehensible by Europe and its various Others and therefore "natural," as objective as the fact, say, that Africa lies south of Europe.
If the Moors, spiritually blind because of their adherence to the law of
Muhammad, are unable to grasp Christianity as the organizing principle
of the division of the globe, their awareness (as Zurara writes it) of Africa
as a center ("exo") that has now been supplanted by the West draws them
complicitously into the colonialist enterprise. Zurara's attribution of the
foreign to both Portuguese and Moorish perspectives is a discursive move
that creates a single optic determining geographic space. The foreign oper-
ates as a marker of positionalities which, in turn, attest to the inevitability of expansion. The labeling of the Portuguese as "foreign peoples" on
the walls of Ceuta identifies not just the invader but also marks a recon-
figuration, an estrangement, of the history of Portuguese–Moorish contact
within the land borders of Portugal prior to 1415. Only in a presentist sense
are the Portuguese strangers or foreigners in Ceuta, because long before
the date of its capture the city had been frequented by Iberian traders and
merchants. Zurara estranges the deep-rooted, historical familiarity between

"Portuguese" and "Moors" by implicitly claiming that there is a new kind of contact here, one that exemplifies the cognitive conceit of the "shock of newness" (espanto da novidade) Zurara repeatedly invokes in *Guiné*. The foreignness evident in Ceuta marks a new paradigm of contact, a first encounter that is meant to be prophetic of the later history of Portuguese exploration along the Guinean coast.

More than a century after Zurara, Camões likewise infixes the idea of the strange into the ideological discourse of *Os Lusíadas*, though the poet relates it to writing as well as to expansion itself. In the introduction, Camões invokes foreign Muses in a pronounced intertmingling of the historical and the mythological:

Ouvi: que não vereis com vãs façanhas,
Fantásticas, fingidas, mentirosas,
Louvar os vossos, como nas estranhas
Musas, de engrandecer-te desejosas. (I.11.i–iv)

Hark! Thou shalt never see, for empty deed
Fantastical and feigned and full of lies,
Thy people praised, as with the foreign breed
Of muses that still vaunt them to the skies.[31]

The "foreign breed / Of muses"—that is, those Muses responsible for inspiring the epics of Boiardo and Ariosto—opposes Camões's "my nymphs of Tagus" (Tágides minhas) identified in stanza 4 before the lines cited above, the Muses of the Tagus River to whom Camões appeals for his voice, decorum, and stamina. Camões's invocation of homegrown Muses acts as an apologia of Portuguese history and his own text in that the deeds and epics of antiquity have been surpassed by the events about to be related. The banishing of the foreign Muses in favor of domestic ones shapes expansion as an epic act and Portugal as a site of literary and mythological genesis: it creates a center or home that is at once Portugal and Camões's poem. This unprecedented literary/historical/mythological home entails, in Camonian logic, the creation of an equally unprecedented archive in the form of national memory, a national and collective historical awareness in which expansion figures in all of its providential and prophetic dimensions. When Jupiter foretells the success the Portuguese will have in attaining the East, for instance, Bacchus resents the proclamation because it confirms what the Fates had prophesied, that

> . . . viria
> Hūa gente fortíssima de Espanha,
> Pelo mar alto, a qual sujeitaria
> Da Índia tudo quanto Dóris banha,
> E com novas vitórias venceria
> A fama antiga, ou sua ou fosse estranha.
> Altamente lhe dói perder a glória
> De que Nisa celebra inda a memória. (I.31)

> There would come . . .
> From Spain a people, terrible in war
> O'er the high seas, and they would subjugate
> As much as Doris bathes of India's shore,
> And with new victories they would make less great
> Old fame of his or other conqueror.
> Sorely it irked him thus to lose the fame
> For which yet Nysa venerates his name.

In Camões's pantheon Bacchus is the antagonist of Portugal because, as the mythic conqueror of India, he stands to be eclipsed by the actions of Vasco da Gama. In these lines—and what the translation cited here does not make entirely clear—foreign fame ("fama estranha") and memory ("memória," translated loosely as "name") are a conceptual dyad, a definitional pairing since the India enterprise works against a presumed bacchic privilege in the form of the god's fame or historical memory as the conqueror of India. The Portuguese navigators sail against Bacchus, the deity who in the world of heroic and unheroic passions is dangerously brooding and melancholic, like Adamastor. Camões creates a historiographic home and authority that legitimizes Portugal's foreign enterprise and resides at the heart of a new memory, one that supplants the pagan, melancholic memory of Bacchus and his dominion over the East.

Following the initial presentation of foreignness or the strange as underlying a new authority, Camões then unfolds *o estranho* into a plurality of meanings throughout his poem. The first five cantos (those in which the poetic narrative is situated in Africa) contain the widest semantic range. Africa is a Camonian locus of the strange. The Portuguese acquire new knowledge of the world and new ways to acquire that knowledge in the form of maritime experience; the strange is a marker of these epistemological shifts as well as of the conversion of indigenous peoples to Christianity and therefore to the ideologies (including the Christian geographic optic, as Zurara formulated it) of empire. Cantos III and IV, for instance, contain the long narrative of Portuguese and European history delivered by Vasco da Gama to the King of Melinde during the fleet's stay in East Africa after rounding the Cape of Good Hope and before crossing the Indian Ocean to reach the subcontinent. Gama's historical peroration is itself a symbolic act of conquest in that to produce narrative in the space of expansion is to appropriate that space, more so when the peroration is in answer to the king's request to tell that story:

> Mas antes, valeroso Capitão,
> Nos conta (lhe dezia) diligente,
> Da terra tua o clima e região
> Do mundo onde morais, distintamente;
> E assi de vossa antiga gèração,
> E o princípio do Reino tão potente,
> Cos sucessos das guerras do começo,
> Que, sem sabê-las, sei que são de preço. (II.109)

> "But, first," he said, "courageous Chief, make plain
> To us distinctly and in order due
> The climate of your land, the region main
> As of this world that it pertains untó,
> There where you dwell. Tell what your ancient strain,
> Whence its beginnings your strong kingdom drew.
> And from the first your deeds of war relate,
> Which, knowing not, I yet must know are great."

The king listens in attentive, if symbolically subjugated, silence. Gama's narrative ranges chronologically from the pre-Roman history of the Iberian

Peninsula to the safe passage of Good Hope just prior to Gama's arrival in Melinde. In the opening stanza of canto III Camões calls on Calliope to provide him with the wherewithal to renarrate Gama's history (thus fusing poetic and historiographic authority) and observes:

> Pronto estavam todos escuitando
> O que o sublime Gama contaria,
> Quando, despois de um pouco estar cuidando,
> Alevantando o rosto, assi dizia:
> 'Mandas-me, ó Rei, que conte declarando
> De minha gente a grão geanalosia;
> Não me mandas contar estranha história,
> Mas mandas-me louvar dos meus a glória.' (III.3)

> Now eagerly all men stood listening by
> To hear what noble Gama might relate,
> Who, after giving thought to his reply,
> Looked up again and made his answer straight:
> "Thou hast commanded, O great King, that I
> My nation's splendid lineage should narrate.
> Thou dost not ask me for some foreign story,
> But plainly bidst me speak of my people's glory."

Gama's "estranha história" (foreign story) is crucial. The narrative project of nationhood, conceived of as a lineage or genealogy, takes place on African soil and thus makes a historiographic home of Africa. The multilayered refraction of voices we find in this stanza—the King of Melinde asks Gama to tell his story as Gama responds to the request through the narrative voice of Camões—is compounded when we consider the positional perspectives implicit in the adjective *estranha:* the king, a foreigner to Gama, asks the foreigner Gama to tell a story that is both foreign (to Melinde) and domestic (to the Portuguese traveler). Gama's story makes the implicit claim that Portuguese expansion and its narratives, while definitionally a project of strangeness or foreignness, creates "homes" throughout the world.

Gama identifies the allure of reaching strange lands and strange peoples as an underlying motive of expansion, doing so in a manner that invests imperialism with a heavy epistemological charge. As he details the years immediately prior to his own expedition, Gama singles out the reigns of João II (1481–95) and Manuel I (1495–1521) as the most decisive ones in terms of the Portuguese arrival and presence in India and of expansion as a "strange" enterprise. The pivotal role that Manuel I plays in expansionist voyaging and knowledge (since it was under his orders that Gama was appointed to the India fleet) transcends the immediately temporal or historically circumstantial and is raised to a quasi-mythic status by Gama's narrative of Manuel's prophetic dream of Portuguese expansion (canto II, stanzas 65 to 70). In that dream, the king learns of the imminent, worldwide reach of Portugal through the medium of the Ganges River, anthropomorphized as an old man. In Manuel's dream, the monarch is transported to a celestial height from which he views the globe beneath:

Aqui se lhe apresenta que subia
Tão alto, que tocava à prima Esfera,
Donde diante vários mundos via,
Nações de muita gente, estranha e fera . . . (IV.69.i–iv)

It seemed to him that he had climbed so high
He must have touched on the first sphere at last,
Whence many various worlds he could descry
And, of strange folk and savage, nations vast . . .

Manuel I apprehends the eventual spaces of empire through elevated sight as he views the globe as he would a map. In this the view is tantamount to completed expansionist action: "Maps reflect a desire for completeness, a dream of universality, a yearning for power in which seeing from a point of view forbidden to all others [i.e., from a zenith] . . . is equivalent to possession" (Jacob 1). Strangeness implicates itself into the visual sphere that is a proclamation of power and of an imminent appropriation of other spaces, peoples, and nations, and of the knowledge acquired through that appropriation. The strange indicates a temporal disjunction between the world as it is when Manuel views it and its inevitable future incorporation into the Portuguese ideological *oikoumene*. The lands and peoples are "strange" insofar as they have not yet been reached by Portuguese travelers, so this strangeness is equivalent to futurity; yet Manuel's visual cognizance of the globe is an act of appropriation, and his imperialist eyes, at the moment of seeing from above, make the strange familiar or "natural," as Zurara might have termed it. Manuel's zenithal optic thus conflates the future and the present in an instant, and so refutes chronological time. His perception carries a mythic charge as an experience of time and destiny not available to the earthbound traveler.

In a consideration of the "strangeness of experience" in *Os Lusíadas*, Fernando Gil ("O efeito-*Lusíadas*") argues that strangeness is premised on the idea of the absolutely new (37) and of the extraordinary (38), and this premise links strangeness to the marvelous. For Gil, "[o]ntologically . . . the strangeness of experience is perhaps a result of the voyage as a kind of unavoidable compromise between different experiences—all of them disquieting, both in and of themselves and in their confluence" (40). I concur, though in my view Camonian strangeness also reflects the epistemological challenges posed by expansionist voyaging and the specific moments of unknowability regularly marked by Camões with the adjective *estranho*. This is distinct from a more passive understanding of the marvelous as a kind of surrender to the inscrutability of the phenomenal world, an aporia of rational thought. In fact, the Portuguese negotiation and triumph over the strange in *Os Lusíadas* is one of the victories the poem records. Camões implies strangeness into an expansionist telos by linking it to a continuum and development of knowledge; only after empire has achieved these peoples and places will they cease to be strange, and only then will empire have reached its plenitude as an exercise of power.

Manuel's beholding of the Ganges River and the Indian landscape in his prophetic dream is a precursor to the vision of the globe, of the "máquina do mundo" (model of the world) that will be afforded to Gama during the return voyage to Portugal in canto X. There, the full geographic reach of Portuguese expansion is laid out and the future deeds of conquerors are narrated in detail as Gama contemplates a crystalline model of the earth suspended in the air. It is the goddess Tethys who shows Gama the globe:

"Faz-te mercê, barão, a Sapiência
Suprema de, cos olhos corporais,

Veres o que não pode a vã ciência
Dos errados e míseros mortais.
Sigue-me firme e forte, com prudência,
Por este monte espesso, tu cos mais."

. . . .

Não andam muito, que no erguido cume
Se acharam, onde um campo se esmaltava
De esmeraldas, rubis, tais que presume
A vista que divino chão pisava.
Aqui um globo vem no ar, que o lume
Claríssimo por ele penetrava,
De modo que o seu centro está evidente,
Como a sua superfície, claramente. (X.76.i–iv; 77)

"Wisdom supreme, O hero, shows you grace,
In that you shall behold with corporal eye
What the vain science of the erring race
Of wretched mortal men cannot descry.
Firm, strong, and prudent, follow me apace
Up this wild crag, with all your fellows by."

. . . .

Not far they went, ere on the towering height
Within a field themselves they shortly found,
With ruby and emerald so thick sown the sight
Conceived that they were treading holy ground.
There, high in air, they saw a globe, for light,
Piercing right through it, shed such glory round
That to the eye the center was as clear
As ever was the surface of the sphere.

Tethys then describes each part of the globe in detail, noting where the Portuguese have already arrived and their deeds yet to come.

In this passage, Camões continues the conceit of the viewing of the world through a cartographic eye, an eye that beholds the Portuguese occupation of foreign or strange space and is the first agent by which that space is mapped and appropriated before the arrival of ships. The surveying of the arena of empire and colonialism, those realms of strangeness that are literally "supervised" (in the etymological sense of "to see from above") by a Portuguese, scopic agency and therefore symbolically subjugated, formalizes the authority of the expansionist *pátria*. Camões grants primacy to the eye, a common valuing of the hierarchy of the bodily senses in the medieval and early-modern periods. The eye is the medium of moral distinction and judgment. The owners of this superior sense are European, or at least are so within the symbolic play of Christian seeing, pagan blindness, and the power of cartographic perception. The poet takes pains to clarify that it is to Vasco da Gama's "corporeal eye" (or "eyes," "olhos corporais") that the expansionist world is revealed. Tethys declares: "aqui te dou / Do Mundo aòs olhos teus, pera que vejas / Por onde vas e irás e o que desejas" (I have conveyed / Hither before your eyes, that you may know / Your heart's desire, and where you come and go, X.79.vii–viii). The verb translated as "know" is, in the original Portuguese, "to see." Camões establishes a causal connection between seeing and knowing. In a parallel fashion, earlier in canto IV, the anthropomorphic figures of the Ganges and Indus rivers present themselves in Manuel's dream as manifestations before oneiric eyes: "Das águas se lhe antolha que saíam, / . . . / Dous homens" (from the waters issued [or so fancy told] / Two beings, IV.71.i–iii). There is a prevalence of sight, a visual conjuration; the impersonal verb "se lhe antolha" (perhaps translated better as "it became apparent to [his] eyes") insists on the eye (*ante* [before] + *olho* [eye]) because it is the mode of both oneiric and waking cognition. The inextricability of dreams and sight also appears in the prelude to Manuel's dream where Camões states that sleep is an activity primarily affecting the eyes: "Os olhos lhe ocupou o sono aceito" (sleep o'er his eyes accustomed influence shed, IV.68.v). Again the Portuguese original reveals a shade of meaning not apparent in the translation, because Camões employs the verb *ocupar* (to occupy) to describe the action of sleeping and dreaming. Sleep not only closes the eyes but actively engages them.

The authoritative, cartographic gaze wielded by Gama and Manuel that enacts expansionist power and confirms a Christian privilege over the spaces of the globe contrasts with an African gaze as Gama narrates his fleet's approach to the Cape of Good Hope just prior to the encounter with Adamastor. Here, the crew encounters and captures a native honey-gatherer:

Eis, de meus companheiros rodeado,
Vejo um estranho vir, de pele preta,
Que tomaram per força, enquanto apanha
De mel os doces favos na montanha.

Torvado vem na vista, como aquele
Que não se vira nunca em tal extremo;
Nem ele entende a nós, nem nós a ele,
Selvagem mais que o bruto Polifemo. (V.27.v–viii–28.i–iv)

And lo, a black-skinned man of aspect dire [lit., "strange man"]
I saw, by my companions hemmed around,
Whom, without more ado, by force they caught,
While on the hill sweet honeycomb he sought.

The man's whole countenance was full of woe,
As one who ne'er was in such dread extreme.
His speech we knew not, ours he could not know
A savage worse than brutish Polypheme.

The sighting of this black African is noteworthy in the demographic logic of Camões's poem because the honey-gatherer is not a *mouro,* the blanket term used to cast Africans and natives of India as inimical to expansion as practitioners of Islam.[32] This African is a *preto* (black), a sub-Saharan African without culture, religion, or intelligible language. The comparison of this "savage" to Polyphemus not only anticipates Adamastor a few stanzas later but construes indigenous or pagan brutishness as a kind of blindness. Camões writes that the honey-gatherer is "torvado na vista," or "twisted in sight" (Bacon translates this as "with a countenance full of woe"), comparing Polyphemus's monstrous and restricted sight to the strangeness of the sub-Saharan who stands as a figure of utter inscrutability, not decipherable by a Portuguese, Christian viewer. The strange man from a realm of geographic unfamiliarity speaks a language foreign to both Portuguese traveler and Moor and experiences the world through a deformed perception. All that is recognizable in him, Camões seems to suggest, is an instinct for survival demonstrated by his fear and his harvesting of honeycomb. This African embodies strangeness or the possibility of the lack of knowledge as a kind of force or product of the natural world. He is stripped of the signs of culture, civilization, and history, so his brutally twisted, uncomprehending view of the Portuguese travelers corroborates his baser nature and therefore justifies his abduction. The "estranho vir" is the untamed, geographically bound cipher that must be forced into subjugation because even the supposed universality of the appeal of precious metals and exotic goods is unknown to him:

> Selvagem mais que o bruto Polifemo.
> Começo-lhe a mostrar da rica pele
> De Colcos o gentil metal supremo,
> A prata fina, a quente especiaria:
> A nada disto o bruto se movia. (V.28.iv–viii)

> A savage worse than brutish Polypheme.
> To him rich fleece of Colchis did I show,
> The gentle metal, above all ores supreme,
> And silver fine and the hot burning spice,
> But all to move the brute could not suffice.

The honey-gatherer is representative of a brutish, African blindness to the products of culture, and over this blindness Gama's enticements hold no power. Gama's expansionist embrace of the world, present here by the listing of products foreign to Portugal, trumps the unenlightened vision of the hapless African.

AFRICA AND THE IMAGINATION

Sight and seeing are part of the expansionist ethos of Os Lusíadas, a dynamic of appropriation of foreign space and the inscription of that space into a Portuguese, maritime gnosis of the world. Gama and his company encounter the world that reveals itself before the prows of his imperial ships by seeing it first; the ship becomes a metaphor for cartographic seeing. Fernando Gil interprets the reading of maps as an activity that relates to Os Lusíadas as the "victory of the gaze over distance and the inaccessible" ("Viagens do olhar" 91), in which ships, in their traversal of oceanic space, perform a "first-person effect" (91). A visually oriented means of knowing dovetails not only with a cartographic gaze but with the Portuguese preeminence in the ocularcentric science of celestial navigation, so that the Gaman method of traversing the world and the manner in which he comes to know it are seamlessly overlapped. Camões first dramatizes the primacy of sight as the basis of an expansionist epistemology by having Gama corroborate the legend of Saint Elmo's fire and report on the existence of waterspouts off the coast of Africa:

Os casos vi que os rudos marinheiros,
Que tem por mestra a longa experiência,
Contam por certos sempre e verdadeiros,
Julgando as cousas só pola aparência,
E que os que tem juízos mais inteiros,
Que só por puro engenho e por ciência
Vem do Mundo os segredos escondidos,
Julgam por falsos ou mal entendidos.

Vi, claramente visto, o lume vivo
Que a marítima gente tem por Santo,
Em tempo de tormenta e vento esquivo,
De tempestade escura e triste pranto.
Não menos foi a todos excessivo
Milagre, e cousa, certo, de alto espanto,
Ver as nuvens, do mar com largo cano,
Sorver as altas águas do Oceano.

Eu o vi certamente (e não presumo
Que a vista me enganava): levantar-se
No ar um vaporzinho e sutil fumo . . . (V.17–18, 19.i–iii)

But I beheld those things, which sailors rude,
Who long experience for their mistress own,
Count ever truth and perfect certitude,
Judging things by appearances alone.
But they with more intelligence endued,
Who see world mysteries, only to be known

By science or pure genius, reason still
Such things are false or else conceived of ill.

And I have clearly seen that living light,
A holy thing, as mariners consent,
In time of storm with wicked winds at height
And dark tornado making sad lament.
Nor was it less miraculous in our sight,
And surely 'tis a terrible event,
As in a pipe, the sea-mists to descry
Drawing up to Heaven Ocean's waters high.

I do not think that my sight cheated me,
For certainly I saw rise up in air
A smoke of fine and vaporous subtilty . . .

Gama promotes an equation between vision and certitude, but a vision buttressed by the workings of reason and deliberation, as opposed to the uneducated reliance on appearances by "sailors rude." This kind of informed seeing is a veridic discourse on the phenomenal/maritime world, one that corroborates the folkloric legends of unlettered sailors and records novelties of the natural world.

Sight, then, is implicated into the many journeys of *Os Lusíadas:* journeys through geographic space, through history, affect, knowledge, and the very imaginary of Portuguese Renaissance culture. The landscapes charted by Camões are as much exterior as they are interior; the voyages of the poem trace inner cartographies of memory, knowing, and writing as much as they do the land- and seascapes of Africa and India. Sight is part of a larger dynamic of perception and cognition inherited by early-modern artists and thinkers from medieval expositions of the topic, especially those relating to "faculty psychology," a complex theory of cognition based on the interaction of the exterior world and the human brain and soul. In postulations of faculty psychology, the external world enters the body through the five external senses, which then create images or impressions to be processed by the internal senses, or "inward wits," the human powers that occupy the area between the body and the soul (Harvey, *Inward*

Wits 2). The term "faculties" refers to the several areas or "ventricles" of the brain and to their functions involved in the processing of images and the subsequent deliberations and judgments made on these images. The theories of the interior or inward wits constitute an early speculative elaboration of the relation between the sensorial world and the powers of the soul to process data and then deliberate on that data.[33] This process happens in the "sensitive" soul, one of the two souls resident in the human body (the other is the "vegetative" soul). One of the internal senses connected with sight is the imagination or *imaginatio,* a concept we find in the Portuguese textual matter of Africa as informing both the writing of Africa and, in Camões's case, the creation of a "memory" or collective, mental archive of history that is gradually charted in *Os Lusíadas.* The imagination appears in some of these texts on Africa as one of the mechanisms of visual and mental perception—Clark reminds us that in this time period perception was a visual process (5)—and is related to judgment, assessment, and the (un)reliability of the seen and empirically experienced world.

Generally speaking, the *imaginatio* is the interior wit that acts as the "image-making power" (Carruthers 54) of the brain. This faculty receives and stores images received through the eyes before further deliberation of the images by the intellect causes them to enter into memory. Robert Folger, in discussing a sixteenth-century Spanish treatise on the interior wits, summarizes the process by which the faculties interact:

> The common sense receives the first "impression" . . . of the "debuxos" which the external senses generate when stimulated by an object. The "forms" of the objects perceived are also imprinted in the fantasy . . . In contrast to the common sense, which is only capable of representing objects while excited by the external senses, fantasy represents its object . . . "segun que es absente" . . . [I]t is, then, a retentive power that stores the sense impression temporarily after the object is no longer sensed by contact. The third interior wit, the "ymaginatiua" . . . is the power to transform sense impressions and create new images on the basis of previous experience and sense data. (29–30)[34]

Both humans and animals possess this capacity for processing data but, according to Thomas Aquinas, humans also possess a "cogitative" power that allows them to deliberate on the images stored in the imagination (Carruthers 51). Aquinas posits that humans have an "intellectual memory," a theory that

> arose in part to resolve the problem of how one could remember conceptions, since one's memory stored only phantasms of particular sense objects or composite images derived from particular sense objects. The type of memory which recalls abstractions, things created in thought rather than sensorily perceived, is a part of the intellect. (Ibid.)

The Persian physician and philosopher Ibn Sīnā or Avicenna proposes the existence of a "deliberative" imagination, "which has a composing function, joining images together . . . This power of composing an image in both humans and animals is joined to a power of judgment, whereby we form an opinion of the image we have composed" (Carruthers 53). In Iberia, one of the most available and influential explanations of the interior wits and the imagination is Alfonso X's *Siete partidas,* though here Alfonso avoids the physiologically based idiom typical of other treatments of the topic.[35] Moreover, Alfonso discusses the interior wits in the laws devoted to how people must serve their king to the best of their abilities; this context of moral and civic responsibility to the crown maps well, for example, onto Zurara's chronistic enterprise as a service to his patron D. Afonso V. Alfonso's laws lay out a code of ethical behavior that, in Zurara's pen, becomes implicated into historiographic discourse as an ethos of expansion.

These basic tenets of faculty psychology help us to understand the allusions made to the imagination and the visually oriented world we find in Zurara, Barros, and Camões. References by these writers to faculty psychology are only general and do not engage in detailed allusion, but by context and use we can discern a familiarity with the basic concepts that is brought into the specific writing projects at hand. Let us begin again with Zurara. In both *Ceuta* and *Guiné* the chronicler regularly invokes the *imaginaçom* as a mechanism of perception of the world related to conquest in Africa. Zurara's use of "imagination" at first might seem to be nothing more than the chronicler's term for intellectual capacity or the power of mental abstraction or speculation, but the term's use as a method of perception of a visual nature allies it with a general understanding of faculty psychology. Zurara ascribes perceptual powers to both Christians and Moors, but takes care to specify the failure of the Moorish imagination and implies that this is what relegates Moors to a naturally inferior status and elevates Portuguese perception to a level of uncontested authority.

In the early pages of *Ceuta*, as the numerous deliberations by members of the Portuguese court on the viability and desirability of seizing the Moroccan city are narrated, there is an evolving conviction among João I's sons that the invasion of Ceuta is urgent, a conviction that is not so much a result of any one reason or argument but the product of a spiritual imperative. Here is how Zurara depicts the princes' preoccupation with Ceuta:

> ca os seus pemssamentos numca podiam seer liures nem apartados daquella maginaçom, e tamto corriam per ella em diamte, que passauam per todallas duuidas, e começauam e proseguiam o feito per tall guisa que sse esqueçiam do pomto em que estauam, e uiamsse no meyo daquella çidade emuolltos antre os mouros allegramdosse com o espalhamento do seu samgue. E tamta duçura semtiam em taaes maginaçoões, que lhes pesaua quamdo see lhe offereçia cousa per que sse tirauam dellas. E porque assi como naturallmente os feitos em que a maginaçam do homem he ocupada de dia, esses se lhe rrepresemtam depois que o sono tem ocupado seus semtidos . . . (34)

> for since their thoughts could never be freed from that image that was so consistently before them it alleviated their doubts; so they took action and persevered, so much so that they forgot everything else. They saw themselves in the middle of that city surrounded by Moors and rejoicing in the spilling of their blood. Such a delight they took from these images that they became irritated when anything distracted them from such images. And so it is that, naturally, the things which occupy man's imagination by day are also present after sleep has taken over the senses . . .

Here, the image (*maginaçom*) of the princes amid the Moors spilling blood is an image received directly from the divine sphere because the vision of Ceuta and its Moors would not have entered the mind through the bodily senses yet; the contemplation of this image affords pleasantness or *duçura*. The image is so strong that it persists into the dream state and overcomes the waking senses—much like Manuel's prophetic dream in *Os Lusíadas*. The resilience of the imagination in retaining the victorious image over the Moors in Ceuta suggests its inevitable realization as actual experience and divine approval of the invasion. In sleep, the intellect may contemplate celestial things (Harvey, *Inward Wits* 49) and "[t]rue dreams of the future come about through the soul's kinship with the intelligences of the spheres" (ibid.). The prophetic certainty of the princes' imaginations contrasts, some chapters later, with the imperfect *entendimentos* of the Moors. *Entendimento* may be translated as "understanding," though in the idiom of faculty psychology it can also be a rough equivalent to "intellect," the power of the soul that creates abstractions and deliberates on them. So it is that some Moors, after the capture of Ceuta, "comsijraram sobre a uimda destas gallees, mal diziam a ssy e a fraqueza de seus emtemdimentos" (reflected on the arrival of the galleys, and cursed themselves and the weakness of their intellect, 53). The power of Moorish reflection is faulty, a general deficit of the *entendimento* or intellect. Zurara juxtaposes the Christian and Moorish powers of the soul in a predictably derogatory fashion for the Ceutan Moors. He indicts the functioning of the Moorish mind by ventriloquizing the Moors' recognition of their own deficient *entendimentos* since they failed to assess the image of the invading fleet "correctly" as the certain sign of the city's defeat. The Moorish imagination fails because, while it possesses the ability to process and store images, it lacks a properly functioning deliberative imagination or power to form correct judgment.

In *Guiné*, Zurara remarks briefly, as we saw earlier, on the scorching heat ("estranha quentura" or "strange heat") of the Torrid Zone as the cause for the black skin of Ethiopians. A plausible precursor to Zurara's geo-humoral formulation of African corporality is Alfonso X's translation into Castilian of an Arabic astrological treatise by 'Ubayd Allâh al-Istiji, the *Libro de las cruzes* (Book of Astrological Influences), completed in 1259. In one passage the book postulates a correspondence between climate and the specifics of regional character (in this case, the realms of India, Babylon, and the Middle East) in that variations in climate produce such factors as a temperate complexion, certain physical characteristics, and the "civilized" trait of the rule of law.[36] The *Libro de las cruzes* notes apropos of the Ethiopians who inhabit the "southern" region that la gran calentura non se tempra en aquel logar, et pareçe en ellos, que an su color et sos queros negros et crespos cabellos. Et por esto non se estienden sus espiritos por la grant sequedat et por la grant calentura que los quema, et por esto non an sotil entendemento, ni an sennorio, ni leyes, nin decretos, nin se entremeten de sciencias nin de saberes . . . et esto es por que semeian a las bestias en sus mannas. (8)

the immense heat is not tempered in that region and it is evident in them [i.e., Ethiopians] in their color and their black skin and woolly hair. Because of it their spirits do not circulate due to the great dryness and heat that burns them, and that is why they do not possess a subtle intellect, and have no state, or laws, or decrees, and do not pursue sciences or knowledge . . . and this is why in their manners and customs they are like beasts.[37]

Zurara's comment on the "strange heat" of the Torrid Zone as the cause for blackness of skin stops short of the moralization of blackness as inferior in the *Libro de las cruzes,* though in other passages of his chronicle Zurara notes the bestial manners of Africans and thereby justifies enslavement (Branche 42). The *espiritos* of Alfonso's book refer to the physiological basis of the inward wits and the effect on the "entendemento." The "spirits" here refer to the bodily spirits (Latin *spiritus,* Greek *pneuma*), the form of refined blood thought to cause the body's operation by emanating from the heart and communicating with all the body's members. The heat of Africa prevents the spirits from reaching all members of the body (thus causing a slowness of movement) and adversely affects the intellect (*entendemento*) so that Ethiopians—and indeed all black Africans—are like beasts.[38] Alfonso invokes medieval physiology and psychology to explain the inferior nature of Ethiopians and in so doing makes Africanness an interior, physiological quality, an organic and therefore natural disposition that is created and conditioned by the sun's heat. The Learned Monarch also addresses the intellectual inferiority of Africans in the first part of the *General estoria* in a discussion of Genesis and Noah's son Ham, the primogenitor of Africans. For having scoffed at his father, Alfonso writes that "Cam [era] de menor entendimiento que los otros [hermanos]" (Ham was not as astute as his brothers, 85). The lesser intellectual capacity of Ham would justify the presumed right of Europeans to invade and conquer Africa.

We are now in a position to understand better Zurara's use of the *imaginaçom* in *Guiné* as it relates to the chronicler and the hermeneutic authority of the state and the monarch and to the perceptual/intellectual capacities of Portuguese sailors and *negros* or *mouros*. Zurara establishes his own position in an opening chapter by noting of Prince Henry's historical example that "[t]ua glorya teus louuores tua fama ẽche assy as minhas orelhas e ocupã minha vista que nõ sey a qual parte acuda primeiro" (your glory, praises, and fame so fill my ears and eyes that I do not know where it is best to begin, 19). The eyes and ears, in the hierarchy of the senses in faculty psychology, are the highest senses. Zurara speaks of a sensorial plenitude when faced with his subject matter and in so doing tacitly privileges his imagination as that which will render this historical matter into a collective, "authorized memory." This authorized memory is also, in part, a function of Zurara's position as official chronicler of the realm. In another passage of the chronicle Zurara praises the virtues of Henry and appeals to the Portuguese monarchy by asking that these virtues and worthy deeds be kept "enteiros e saãos em vossa maginaçom" (whole and sound in your imagination, 41). The *maginaçom* refers to the storage of the deeds of Henry in the mind of the chronicler's first reader, Afonso V, while the episodes and deeds of the chronicle itself might also be an image to be contemplated by any of Zurara's readers. There is a moral responsibility imputed to these readers in that they are to contemplate Zurara's chronicles as if they were images or concepts received by the imagination to then be subjected to deliberation:

> Todos estes segredos e marauilhas trouue o engenho do nosso principe ante os olhos dos naturaaes do nosso Regno. Ca posto que todallas cousas de que falley das marauilhas do nillo per seus olhos nõ podessẽ seer vistas o que fora impossiuel grande cousa foe chegarem ally os seus nauyos onde nũca he achado per scriptura que outro alguũ nauyo destas partes chegasse . . .
> (241)

> All of these secrets and marvels did the genius of our prince bring before the eyes of the subjects of his realm, for although all the marvels of the Nile I spoke of could not be witnessed by him with his own eyes, because that would be impossible, it was a great feat indeed that his ships arrived there,

since it is not recorded in any written source that any other ship from these
parts had ever come . . .

Zurara juxtaposes the sensory or physiological eye to interior sight, the
creation of an image that has not been witnessed by his readers' bodily
eyes and is therefore a product of the imagination. His chronicle brings
the experiences of Prince Henry to the readerly eyes of the subjects of the
realm. In the absence of the sensory (or empirical) eye of direct experience, the chronicler creates images through his own imagination for contemplation and judgment.

In narrating the many contacts and encounters between the Portuguese
and *mouros* or *negros,* Zurara frequently speculates about how any one
encounter might have been (mis)perceived. For example, in considering
the strategy for capturing Moors, the Portuguese mariners concur that a
retreat to their boats at night might be a way to deceive the Moorish
inhabitants of the coast:

> Ca podera seer disserã elles que os mouros vista nossa tornada pensarom
> que nos viemos como homeẽs desesperados de os podermos cobrar E com
> tal maginaçõ faram a uolta pera seu alloiamento. E nom soomente nos
> aproueitara sua tornada ally mas ajnda a ssegurança com que se podem
> lançar em repouso. (97)

> For it is likely, they said, that the Moors, having witnessed our retreat,
> will think we fled like men in despair of not being able to capture them,
> and with such a sight before them, will return to their lodgings. And not
> only would that retreat profit us, but also would their sense of security as
> they rest.

The Moors are ascribed an imagination because one of the points of this
passage is the meaning the Moors will make of the sight of the Portuguese returning to the ships. That the Moors will interpret this image
incorrectly is assumed, and the weaker or more deficient Moorish imagination—that is, the incapacity of the Moors to apply a reliable faculty of
judgment and deliberation on the images received by their eyes—gives
the Portuguese the advantage. Zurara speculates about the visual capacity

of another population of Africans (now called *negros*) when narrating the expedition of Dinis Dias to the *terra dos negros* for the purpose of capturing slaves:

> E hindo fazendo sua vyagē ao longo daquelle mar virō a carauella os que estauã na terra da qual cousa forom muyto marauilhados. ca segundo parece nunca viram nē ouuyrã fallar de semelhante ca huūs presumyã que era peixe outros entendyã que era fãtasma. outros diziã que podya seer algūa aue que corrya assy andando por aquelle mar E rrazoandosse assy sobre esta nouidade filharō quatro daquelles atriuimento de sse certificar de tamanha duuida . . . (127–28)

> And as the caravel was tacking along that sea, those who were on land saw it and marveled at the sight, because it seemed they had never seen or heard of such a thing. Some thought it was a fish, while others believed it was a phantom, and yet others said it could be a bird that traveled in that manner across the water. After deliberating on this, four of them were captured who were bold enough to investigate their considerable doubt . . .

Although Zurara does not use the term *imaginaçom,* the point of this passage is nonetheless the capacity to deliberate reliably on the images received by the eye. The chronicler ascribes a naive imaginative capacity to the *negros* the Portuguese intend to capture—in fact, it is this capacity that causes them to board boats and investigate the strange and unfamiliar caravels, an action that ends in their abduction. A similar instance occurs in a reconnaissance expedition by two Portuguese horsemen away from the coastal zone and of their consequent contact with the Africans: "qual maginaçom serya no pensamēto daquelles homeēs tal nouidade .s. dous moços assy atreuidos de coor e feiçoōes tã stranhas a elles" (what would the image be in the minds of those men, seeing two brave youths of a color and features so strange to them? 56). While Zurara interestingly allows the African natives a capacity for marvel—as does Cadamosto, who supposes that to black Africans whiteness must seem strange and monstrous—and in so doing makes the marvelous or the *maravilha* not exclusively an experience of the European mind, it is a marvel that functions, in the end, naturally to native detriment because it causes fear and therefore subservience. It is feasible to posit that Zurara's Moorish imagination allows Africans a notional subjectivity, but one uninformed and stunted by a lack of Christian faith. The powers of the soul, as medieval theorists of the imagination such as Aquinas tell us, are geared toward the divine. By bringing the imagination to the writing of history, and indeed by claiming that perceptions of the empirical world through the workings of the imagination are part of the history being narrated, Zurara recontextualizes the theory of the imagination from its medical and patristic sources into historiography and the encounter with Africa. The conquest of Africa enacts a cognitive process of experiencing and writing history, and becomes a site for a renewed attention to the mechanisms of truthful deliberation and judgment.

Zurara's inscription of the imagination into the historiographic enterprise will be repeated by João de Barros and then by Camões. In the prologue to his *Décadas da Ásia*, addressed to João III (reigned 1521–57), Barros comments on the creation of letters and writing as the preserver of national history. In summarizing his own historical writing, Barros initially compares the task of the historian to that of the architect:

[o]s quais, primeiro que ponham mão na obra, a traçam e debuxam, e desi apresentam êstes diliniamentos de sua imaginação ao senhor de cujo há de ser o edifício. Porque, como esta matéria de que eu queria tratar era dos triunfos dêste reino, dos quais não se podia falar sem licença do autor dêles, que naquele tempo dêste meu propósito era El-Rei vosso padre ... lhe apresentei um debuxo feito em nome de Vossa Alteza ... O qual debuxo ... foi ũa pintura metafórica de exércitos e vitórias humanas ... A qual pintura, por ser em nome de Vossa Alteza, assi contentou a El-Rei vosso padre depois que soube ser imagem desta que ora trato ... (5)

such people [architects], before they begin building, first trace and make an image and then present these designs of the imagination to the patron whose building it is to be. And since the matter I wish to treat of here is the triumphs of this realm, about which one cannot speak without the approval of their maker, which in the era I speak of was your father the king ... I presented a sketch to him made in your own name ..., and this sketch was a metaphoric painting of armies and human victories ... Said painting, by having been done in Your Majesty's name, pleased the king your father once he found out it was the image of that which I now write ...

Barros compares the construction of buildings to the task of the historian through the vocabulary of images and the imagination. For him, historiography is a process of creating (textual) images or paintings— some of them "metaphoric" or "figural"—that are then approved of by the monarch whose victories such images depict. Like Zurara, Barros's historiographic writing creates images for contemplation and deliberation as part of what might be called an ethics of historiography. The mimetic nature of the visual image as received through the senses and passed on to the brain was often assumed in early modern contemplations on the topic, but, as Stuart Clark argues in *Vanities of the Eye*, the imagination in the early-modern period was also suspect and distrusted in its processing of sensory images; its mimetic capacity was frequently brought into question. Barros circumvents the problem of mimetic representation with his "pintura metafórica," a synecdochic reference to the entirety of his *Ásia* and one that, because of its metaphoric qualities, does not challenge the authority of the writer who composes at a temporal and spatial remove from the events narrated. We might find a loose correspondence to both this trust and distrust of the imagination between Barros and Zurara because both writers present their texts to readers for final judgment. The care with which these chroniclers detail the presence of images and the imagination in their histories suggests a certain skepticism about the imagination if not properly supervised or engaged; in fact, Zurara's Moorish imagination may be as much a caveat against, or a parable of, the "incorrect" contemplation of images as it may be suggestive of a Moorish perceptual capacity or subjectivity.

Camões also incorporates the concepts and vocabulary of the inward wits into *Os Lusíadas*. The poet emphasizes the *imaginação* and the *fantasia* (or *phantasia*, often synonymous with imagination as the image or mental picture that was the final product of the process of sense perception to be viewed by the eye of the mind [Clark 11]), most likely because of the primacy accorded to firsthand experience and sight in the empirically oriented world of the poem. Consider a first instance, the harangue of the Velho do Restelo (Old Man of Restelo) in canto IV who censures Gama's enterprise at the moment of departure of the fleet, a harangue that has often been interpreted as a warning against avarice in the heavily mercantilist motives for expansion. The Old Man remarks "[j]á que nesta gostosa vaïdade / Tanto enlevas a leve fantasia" (thou who now into pleasant vanity / Are swept away by fantasy so light, IV.99.i–ii). *Fantasia* suggests not so much a passing "fancy" but a conceptual image that the intellect must consider and regulate with discipline. The Old Man accuses the mariners of harboring memory images of wealth that are in danger of steering their course irresponsibly if the mediating, ethical operation of the intellect does not ponder them with sufficient gravity. This initial admonition by the Old Man of Restelo prefigures the encounter with Adamastor in canto V, another reckoning with the imagination, as we will see in the next chapter. In both episodes, the imagination as the seat of an ethical capacity of judgment is implicated into the imperialist venture.

Bacchus, one of the many gods of the classical pantheon populating the stanzas of *Os Lusíadas* and enemy of the Portuguese, encarnates a Christian–Moorish divide in the workings of the imagination. In the episode of the false Moorish pilot in canto I, Bacchus descends to Earth disguised as a Moor in order to incite the Moors in Mozambique to sabotage the Portuguese by providing them with a treacherous pilot in hopes of destroying the India voyage. The governor of Mozambique regards Gama and his fleet suspiciously:

> Porém disto que o Mouro aqui notou
> E de tudo o que viu, com olho atento,
> Um ódio certo na alma lhe ficou,
> Hūa vontade má de pensamento.
> Nas mostras e no gesto não o mostrou,
> Mas, com risonho e ledo fingimento,
> Tratá-los brandamente determina,
> Até que mostrar possa o que imagina.
> . . . .
> Do claro Assento etéreo, o grão Tebano
> . . . .
> No pensamento cuida um falso engano,
> Com que seja de todo destruído.
> E, enquanto isto só na alma imaginava,
> Consigo estas palvras praticava (I.69, 73.i; v–viii)

> Because of what he noted there displayed,
> And the Moor watched everything with eye intent,

Sincerest hatred in his spirit stayed,
And will toward us wholly on evil bent,
Which neither bearing nor his face betrayed.
Rather, with laughter and feigned merriment,
He had in mind gently to cheat us, till
He might at length unveil what he might will.

. . . .

The mighty Theban from his ethereal seat

. . . .

In thought he conjured up a treacherous cheat
By which he trusted that they all might die.
And the thing mulling in his soul the while,
Unto himself he spake after this style

Camões's choice of words is revealing: the poet gestures to the idiom of faculty psychology (*alma* [soul], *pensamento* [intellect], *imagina* [imagines]) to narrate the attempted bacchic deception, brought about by credulous Moors who follow his ruse. This treachery is located in the soul, the location of the interior wits. There is a twisted intellect (*pensamento*) that "imagines" the treachery—that is, deliberates perniciously on a speculative image of the destruction of the fleet. Bacchus's malevolent use of the imagination is actualized by Moors, who by association participate in the perverted use of the powers of the sensitive soul—this heretical antagonism to Gama's Christian protagonism is one of the battles enacted through Bacchus, the dark god. Once the Portuguese are in India, the imagination will again be misdirected by Moors in canto VIII. The Catual, or potentate of Calicut, suspects a malicious plot on the part of the Portuguese and refuses to meet them, and Gama senses this: "antes, revolvendo / Na fantasia algum sutil e astuto / Engano, diabólico e estupendo" (rather he [the Catual] designed / In fancy an ingenious subtle net, / A fearful trap of diabolic kind, VIII.83.ii–iv). Gama perceives the danger here because he deliberates on the words and actions of the Catual as they are presented to his deliberative judgment by the *fantasia*. In so doing, he avoids an ambush; his correct functioning of the inward wits has saved his crew from destruction.

3

The Monster of
Melancholy

HALFWAY THROUGH *Os Lusíadas* and halfway through the voyage from
Portugal to India that serves as the historical basis of Camões's poem,
Vasco da Gama and his fleet approach the southern tip of Africa. Known
initially by the Portuguese as the *Cabo Tormentório* (Cape of Storms) it
was later renamed the *Cabo de Boa Esperança* or Cape of Good Hope. As
Gama's eastward-bound sailors draw near, a cloud appears and roils in the
darkening sky, out of which an apparition takes shape—suddenly, thun-
derously, and terrifyingly, like a storm at sea. This apparition, whose name
we soon learn is Adamastor, towers above the ships and berates the mariners: how dare they violate the ancient geographic and nautical boundary
at which he stands guard, how dare they presume to uncover secrets of
nature and the sea. Adamastor, the "eclipsing menace" as Herman Melville would call him three centuries later in *Billy Budd*, delivers a series of
prophecies to Vasco da Gama about the fate of Portuguese explorers to
follow in his footsteps that are as historically true as they are disastrous.
On interrogation by Gama, Adamastor relates his own tragic story, one of
military and amorous defeat. A Titan of the earth, Adamastor rose in rebellion against Neptune and fell in love with the sea nymph Thetis, only
then to be deceived at the moment of a promised tryst with the nymph
and punitively transformed, eternally, into the inhospitable and rocky terrain of the cape.

The Adamastor episode, at the center of Camões's text (in the middle
of canto V of the ten-canto poem), comprises stanzas 37–60 and is part
of the long narrative delivered to the King of Melinde by Vasco da Gama

on the history of Portugal and its imperial enterprise during his stay in East Africa. When Gama is recounting the episode of Adamastor, his fleet has already rounded the Cape of Good Hope and has therefore conquered the geographic danger and fear represented by the phantasmal giant.[1] It is Gama's voice we hear in dialogue with Adamastor. Here is the episode:

Porém já cinco Sóis eram passados
Que dali nos partíramos, cortando
Os mares nunca de outrem navegados,
Prosperamente os ventos assoprando,
Quando hũa noite, estando descuidados
Na cortadora proa vigiando,
Hũa nuvem, que os ares escurece,
Sobre nossas cabeças aparece.

Tão temerosa vinha e carregada,
Que pôs nos corações um grande medo;
Bramindo, o negro mar de longe brada,
Como se desse em vão nalgum rochedo.
"Ó Potestade (disse) sublimada:
Que ameaço divino ou que segredo
Este clima e este mar nos apresenta,
Que mor cousa parece que tormenta?"

Não acabava, quando hũa figura
Se nos mostra no ar, robusta e válida,
De disforme e grandíssima estatura;
O rosto carregado, a barba esquálida,
Os olhos encovados, e a postura
Medonha e má, e a cor terrena e pálida;
Cheios de terra e crespos os cabelos,
A boca negra, os dentes amarelos.

Tão grande era de membros, que bem posso
Certificar-te que este era o segundo
De Rodes estranhíssimo Colosso,

Que um dos sete milagres foi do mundo.
Cum tom de voz nos fala, horrendo e grosso,
Que pareceu sair do mar profundo.
Arrepiam-se as carnes e o cabelo,
A mi e a todos, só de ouvi-lo e vê-lo!

E disse: "Ó gente ousada, mais que quantas
No mundo cometeram grandes cousas,
Tu, que por guerras cruas, tais e tantas,
E por trabalhos vãos nunca repousas,
Pois os vedados términos quebrantas
E navegar meus longos mares ousas,
Que eu tanto tempo há já que guardo e tenho,
Nunca arados de estranho ou próprio lenho:

Pois vens ver os segredos escondidos
Da natureza e do húmido elemento,
A nenhum grande humano concedidos
De nobre ou de imortal merecimento,
Ouve os danos de mi que apercebidos
Estão a teu sobejo atrevimento,
Por todo o largo mar e pola terra
Que inda hás-de sojugar com dura guerra.

Sabe que quantas naus esta viagem
Que tu fazes, fizerem, de atrevidas,
Inimiga terão esta paragem,
Com ventos e tormentas desmedidas!
E da primeira armada, que passagem
Fizer por estas ondas insofridas,
Eu farei de improviso tal castigo,
Que seja mor o dano que o perigo!

Aqui espero tomar, se não me engano,
De quem me descobriu suma vingança.
E não se acabará só nisto o dano

De vossa pertinace confiança:
Antes, em vossas naus vereis, cada ano,
Se é verdade o que meu juízo alcança,
Naufrágios, perdições de toda sorte,
Que o menor mal de todos seja a morte!

E do primeiro Ilustre, que a ventura
Com fama alta fizer tocar os Céus,
Serei eterna e nova sepultura,
Por juízos incógnitos de Deus.
Aqui porá da Turca armada dura
Os soberbos e prósperos troféus;
Comigo de seus danos o ameaça
A destruída Quíloa com Mombaça.

Outro também virá, de honrada fama,
Liberal, cavaleiro, enamorado,
E consigo trará a fermosa dama
Que Amor por grão mercê lhe terá dado.
Triste ventura e negro fado os chama
Neste terreno meu, que, duro e irado,
Os deixará dum cru naufrágio vivos,
Pera verem trabalhos excessivos.

Verão morrer com fome os filhos caros,
Em tanto amor gèrados e nacidos;
Verão os Cafres, ásperos e avaros,
Tirar à linda dama seus vestidos;
Os cristalinos membros e perclaros
À calma, ao frio, ao ar verão despidos,
Despois de ter pisada, longamente,
Cos delicados pés a areia ardente.

E verão mais os olhos que escaparem
De tanto mal, de tanta desventura,
Os dous amantes míseros ficarem

Na férvida e implacabil espessura.
Ali, despois que as pedras abrandarem
Com lágrimas de dor, de mágoa pura,
Abraçados, as almas soltarão
Da fermosa e misérrima prisão."

Mais ia por diante o monstro horrendo,
Dizendo nossos Fados, quando, alçado,
Lhe disse eu: "Quem és tu? Que esse estupendo
Corpo, certo, me tem maravilhado!"
A boca e os olhos negros retorcendo
E, dando um espantoso e grande brado,
Me respondeu, com voz pesada e amara,
Como quem da pergunta lhe pesara:

"Eu sou aquele oculto e grande Cabo
A quem chamais vós outros Tormentório,
Que nunca a Ptolomeu, Pompónio, Estrabo,
Plínio, e quantos passaram, fui notório.
Aqui toda a Africana costa acabo
Neste meu nunca visto Promontório,
Que pera o Pólo Antárctico se estende,
A quem vossa ousadia tanto ofende!

Fui dos filhos aspérrimos da Terra,
Qual Encélado, Egeu e o Centimano;
Chamei-me Adamastor, e fui na guerra
Contra o que vibra os raios de Vulcano;
Não que pusesse serra sobre serra,
Mas, conquistando as ondas do Oceano,
Fui capitão do mar, por onde andava
A armada de Neptuno, que eu buscava.

Amores da alta esposa de Peleu
Me fizeram tomar tamanha empresa.
Todas as Deusas desprezei do Céu,

Só por amar das Águas a Princesa.
Um dia a vi, co as filhas de Nereu,
Sair nua na praia: e logo presa
A vontade sinti, de tal maneira,
Que inda não sinto cousa que mais queira.

Como fosse impossibil alcançá-la,
Pola grandeza feia de meu gesto,
Determinei por armas de tomá-la,
E a Dóris este caso manifesto.
De medo a Deusa então por mi lhe fala;
Mas ela, cum fermoso riso honesto,
Respondeu: "Qual será o amor bastante
De Ninfa, que sustente o dum Gigante?

Contudo, por livrarmos o Oceano
De tanta guerra, eu buscarei maneira
Com que, com minha honra, escuse o dano."
Tal resposta me torna a mensageira.
Eu, que cair não pude neste engano
(Que é grande dos amantes a cegueira),
Encheram-me, com grandes abondanças,
O peito de desejos e esperanças.

Já néscio, já da guerra desistindo,
Hūa noite, de Dóris prometida,
Me aparece de longe o gesto lindo
Da branca Thetis, única, despida.
Como doudo corri, de longe abrindo
Os braços pera aquela que era vida
Deste corpo, e começo os olhos belos
A lhe beijar, as faces e os cabelos.

Oh! Que não sei de nojo como o conte!
Que, crendo ter nos braços quem amava,
Abraçado me achei cum duro monte

De áspero mato e de espessura brava.
Estando cum penedo fronte a fronte,
Que eu polo rosto angélico apertava,
Não fiquei homem, não, mas mudo e quedo
E, junto dum penedo, outro penedo!

Ó Ninfa, a mais fermosa do Oceano,
Já que minha presença não te agrada,
Que te custava ter-me neste engano,
Ou fosse monte, nuvem, sonho ou nada?
Daqui me parto, irado e quase insano
Da mágoa e da desonra ali passada,
A buscar outro mundo, onde não visse
Quem de meu pranto e de meu mal se risse.

Eram já neste tempo meus Irmãos
Vencidos e em miséria extrema postos,
E, por mais segurar-se os Deuses vãos,
Alguns a vários montes sotopostos.
E, como contra o Céu não valem mãos,
Eu, que chorando andava meus desgostos,
Comecei a sentir do Fado immigo,
Por meus atrevimentos, o castigo.

Converte-se-me a carne em terra dura;
Em penedos os ossos se fizeram;
Estes membros, que vês, e esta figura
Por estas longas águas se estenderam.
Enfim, minha grandíssima estatura
Neste remoto Cabo converteram
Os Deuses; e, por mais dobradas mágoas,
Me anda Thetis cercando destas águas."

Assi contava; e, cum medonho choro,
Súbito de ante os olhos se apartou.
Desfez-se a nuvem negra, e cum sonoro

Bramido muito longe o mar soou.
Eu, levantando as mãos ao santo coro
Dos Anjos, que tão longe nos guiou,
A Deus pedi que removesse os duros
Casos, que Adamastor contou futuros. (V.37–60)

But now five suns had gone upon their way
Since we had parted thence, those seas to plow,
None save our brethren sailed before our day.
And the winds for us blew prosperously now,
Until one night as at our ease we lay,
Keeping our watch above the cutting prow,
A cloud that darkened all the atmosphere
Above our heads did suddenly appear,

So terrible and with such darkness stored
That in our hearts woke terror overgrown.
And bellowing afar the black sea roared,
As if it broke in vain on reefs of stone.
"O Power," I cried, "exalted and adored,
What divine menace, mystery unknown,
Will the new sea and region now make plain,
For it looms larger than the hurricane?"

I had not finished when a form appeared,
High in the air, filled with prevailing might.
The face was heavy, with a squalid beard.
Misshaped he was but of enormous height.
Hollow the eyes, and bad and to be feared
The gesture, and the color earthen-white,
And, thick with clay, the lank hair twisted hangs.
And the mouth was black and full of yellow fangs.

So huge of limb he was, I swear to thee,
That the thing's equal only could be found
In the Rhodian's colossal prodigy,

One of the Seven Wonders world-renowned.
And the voice seemed to thunder from the sea,
As he spoke thickly with a ghastly sound.
Our hair stood up on end, our flesh went cold,
Only to hear the monster, and behold.

"O braver race than all who undertake
Throughout the world whatever great affair,"
He cried, "Who from those cruel wars you make
Rest never, nor from travail, nor from care;
Since now through my forbidden bounds you break
And to sail through my vast oceans dare,
Which long while I have guarded nor allowed
By strange or native shipping to be plowed;

"Since you would pierce mystery inviolate
Of Mother Nature and the Ocean Sea,
Permitted unto none, however great,
Worthy of ageless fame though he may be,
The penalty of your inordinate
And arrogant insolence, now learn from me:
Everywhere, every sea and every shore,
You are to subjugate in desperate war.

"Know that henceforth whatever ships shall track
With reckless courage on the course you sail
Will deem this region the demoniac
Home of the tempest and unmeasured gale.
And for the first fleet standing on this tack,
That seeks o'er seas forbidden to prevail,
I'll impose penalty foreseen by none,
Till grief looms greater than the risks they run.

"Here I shall take, if hope prove not a cheat,
From him who found me fearful recompense.
Nor even so will vengeance be complete,

That punishes your stubborn insolence.
If what I think be true, each year your fleet
Shall look on many a shipwreck, and immense
Variety of ruin shall befall,
Till death itself shall be least ill of all.

"As for that foremost great adventurer,
Whose fame and luck shall lift him to the sky,
In this my strange, eternal sepulchre
God's viewless purposes will have him lie.
His Turkish naval spoils, proud though they were,
And prosperous, the conqueror shall lay by.
Nor I, for wrong done, threaten him, alone,
But Mombassa and Quilóa overthrown.

"Here will another come, of fairest fame,
A knight, a lover, and of liberal mind,
Bringing with him that most delicious dame,
Love, of his mercy, for his love designed,
Whom their sad fortune and dark fate shall claim
Here in my country, angry and unkind,
Which, though it let them through rough shipwreck live,
'Tis but the sight of greater ills to give.

"Starving to death, they shall see children dear,
Begot and born in love beyond compare,
And the fierce Caffirs, envious of her gear,
From the sweet lady all her vesture tear,
And limbs, so beautiful and crystal clear,
Naked in the sun and frost and windy air,
After the long march when her delicate feet
Have suffered the beach sands' ferocious heat.

"Their eyes shall see, such as escape again
From so much misadventure and distress,
The lovers in their misery remain

Deep in the hot implacable wilderness.
There, when for bitter tears of grief and pain
The very stones seem not so merciless,
Those two, in close embrace, their souls shall free
From the fair prison of their agony."

Yet more the ghastly monster would have said,
Touching our fate. But I rose up before
And asked him: "Who art thou, whose shape of dread
Has filled me with astonishment so sore?"
Twisting his mouth and the black eyes in his head,
With a bellow and a horrifying roar,
Heavily, harshly his reply he made,
As one on whom the answer gravely weighed:

"I am that vast cape locked in secrecy,
That Cape of Hurricanes your people call,
Of whom Pomponius, Strabo, Ptolemy,
Pliny, the whole Past, lacked memorial.
I round out Africa's extremity
In my hid headland, where the shore lines fall
Away, toward the Antarctic Pole prolonged,
Which your audacity has deeply wronged.

"I was Earth's child, like those of ruthless might,
Egeus, Enceladus, and Hundred Hands.
I am Adamastor, and I fought the fight
With him who rattles Vulcan's thunder brands.
I piled not mountain height on mountain height,
But, to make Ocean bow to my commands,
Captain by sea was I, and thither went
To come to grips with Neptune's armament.

"The love it was of Peleus' consort high
That made me such a venture undertake,
Misprizing every goddess of the Sky

Only for the Lady of the Waves' sweet sake.
Her, 'mid her Nereids, once I happed to spy
Coming naked up the beach, and felt awake
Desire within with such prevailing power
I know no greater yearning to this hour.

"And since there was no way to have her charms,
With my huge ugliness and look unmeet,
I thought to take her by main force of arms
And before Doris laid my case complete.
Doris spoke for me, troubled by alarms,
But my love answered with chaste laughter sweet:
'How shall sufficient her affection prove,
A nymph who must sustain a giant's love?

"'But that we may deliver all the sea
From such a war, devices I shall find,
Mine honor saved, to 'scape the penalty.'
My go-between brought answer in this kind.
I, who could never fall by treachery,
For lovers are magnificently blind,
Now found my inmost heart filled up and thronging
With the abundance of my hope and longing.

"Like a poor fool the battle I gave o'er.
And lo! as Doris promised, on a night
Appeared to me a long, long way before,
Naked, alone, sweet grace of Thetis white.
From afar I ran, like one in madness sore,
With arms outstretched to clasp the life's delight
Of this my body, and those eyes so fair
I fell a-kissing, and her cheek and hair.

"What grief do I not know, who this recount!
I deemed my love was in my arms, no less,
But found I had embraced a rugged mount,

Full of rough woods and thickset wilderness?
And with the high crag standing front to front,
When I thought that face angelical to press,
I was unmanned and, dumb, still as a stock,
Became a rock joined to another rock.

"O nymph, the loveliest in all the sea,
Although my presence ne'er thy pleasure wrought,
Why labor in that gin to capture me,
Whether it were mount or cloud or dream or naught?
Thence half-way mad in fury did I flee,
Because of hurt and shame upon me brought,
To seek another world she could not know,
Who made such mockery of my grief and woe.

"And in that hour, all of my brethren's band
Sank beaten in the extremity of ill,
And the false gods, in safer state to stand,
Buried them, each under some mighty hill.
Against high Heaven can avail no hand.
And I, for my own sorrows weeping still,
Began to feel at last what punishments
The hateful Fates kept for my insolence.

"This flesh of mine was changed into hard clay.
My bones, of crags and rocks, took on the cast.
These limbs you see, this form and body, lay
Stretched out in the great waters. And at last
Into this promontory faraway
The gods transmuted all my stature vast.
And, that I might endure redoubled ill,
The seas of Thetis circle round me still."

He told his tale, and, weeping wild, before us
In a twinkling he had vanished from our view.
The black cloud broke, and, moaning and sonorous,

Far-ranging sound over the ocean flew.
Raising my hands to the angelic chorus,
Who this long while had given guidance true,
I prayed God in his mercy to withhold
Those evils Adamastor had foretold.

Adamastor is arguably Camões's most famous poetic creation, a feat of literary invention rivaling the composition of *Os Lusíadas* itself. In a dramatic exercise of *imitatio*, Camões supersedes the classical models available to him in the startling immanence of Adamastor and in the apparition's pronounced and arresting proclamation of selfhood. Manuel Correa, an early editor (1613) and commentator of the poem, remarked apropos of the appearance of Adamastor that "[n]ão tenho palauras para encarecer a linguagẽ, propriedade, & eloquentia desta octaua, que realmente faz este fingimento & Metamorphosi que vay tratando deste Cabo de Boa Esperança, vẽtagem as de Ouidio" (I have no words to do justice to the language, decorum, and eloquence of this stanza; these qualities here supersede anything in Ovid and so vividly portray this fabled creation and metamorphosis of the Cape of Good Hope, 153r). Two centuries later, in a defense of Camões's originality another editor of the poem will go so far as to claim that "[in this episode] Camões had no model to imitate" (Amorim 1:492). Voltaire includes Camões's poem in his "Essay on Epic Poetry," published in London in 1727, and though the author of *Candide* is harshly critical of Camões, he does say of Adamastor that "I believe . . . such a Fiction would be thought noble and proper, in all Ages, and in all Nations" (342).[2] Over time, the Adamastor episode has generated a mixture of awe and interpretive grappling that might be said to reflect Adamastor's own enigmatic nature. The giant at the ends of the earth is polysemous, an exegetical conundrum. The specter is simultaneously many things. He is, for instance, the anthropomorphic manifestation of the Cape of Good Hope and a nebulous, airy phantom, a joining of the empirical and phantasmal worlds; he is an earthbound body and an end point of geographic and cartographic knowledge, a numinous glimpse of the secrets of the earth and the Ocean, of "mystery inviolate / Of Mother Nature and the Ocean Sea" (V.42.i–ii).[3] The range of interpretations Adamastor invites understandably prompted Lawrence Lipking to observe that Adamastor "might be taken rhetorically for the figure of undecidability" (217), and that

> [g]eographically, Adamastor stands for the place where maps lose their potency—here be monsters; historically, for an unknown part of the past, a legend and reality concealed from the ancients and yet to be explored; epistemologically, for a point beyond which human perceptions fail; theologically, for the forbidden. (215)

Moreover, the interpretive possibilities attending Adamastor stem in part from the dual nature of his voice.[4] First he declaims prophecies in an epic register, then relates autobiographically and lyrically his own story of impossible love and enduring anguish. Adamastor's characteristic tone of speaking is an explosive rage and sorrow: he speaks to Gama "with a bellow and horrifying roar" (V.49.vi) that is "heavy and bitter" (V.49.vii); he cries that his deception by Thetis left him "ireful" and "half-mad" (V.57.v). The end of his encounter with the Portuguese is punctuated by a "weeping wild," a "moaning and sonorous" cry (V.60.i, iii).

Much of Adamastor's poetic and critical appeal derives from the apparently disparate aspects of his shape and comportment. I want to argue for a reading that interlaces many of those aspects, a reading that is grounded in the giant's status as the emblematic, expansionist encounter with Africa at the end of the sixteenth century. A constellation of attributes—Adamastor's Africanness, his monstrous body, his disposition that is fearful, ireful, and vengeful, and his two distinctive modes of speech—form an integrated whole if we consider Adamastor through the lens of medieval and early-modern conceptualizations of melancholy. The culture of melancholy and monsters invests the phantasmal giant with a wide-ranging hermeneutic currency. In fashioning Adamastor as a melancholic, Camões shifts melancholy from its primarily lyrical and philosophical antecedents in medieval and early Renaissance Portuguese culture to the imperialist imaginary and the narrative of movement through spaces of expansion. Adamastor hence emerges as a distinctly Camonian composite of the ideologies of maritime empire in which Africa is initially and necessarily implicated.

Africa, therefore, must shape the understanding of Adamastor as a component of the journey of knowledge and authority represented by Vasco da Gama and his fleet. In *Epic and Empire,* David Quint studies Adamastor in an analysis of the tradition of the epic curse in *Os Lusíadas* and finds the origins of the spectral giant in Polyphemus in the *Odyssey* and the *Aeneid.*[5] For Quint, "the burden of Camões' episode—and the basis of its alleged superiority to classical epic—is to show how such poetic inventions can be historical" (114). Quint argues that Camões chose the Portuguese experience in Africa to demonstrate the conflation of poetic inventiveness and historical experience. In this discussion, Quint considers the possibility of hearing in Adamastor's curse an indigenous, African voice of rebellion and resistance that becomes melded into a "blind fury of nature, a resistance that is not particularly directed at [the Portuguese] or the result of their own acts of violence" (118). Any such African voice of resistance is ultimately silenced, whereby "the figure of Adamastor is both substituted for the Africans and simultaneously emptied of their presence and made to point instead to their Portuguese masters" (123).[6] Van Wyk Smith builds on Quint's discussion of the *Odyssey* by finding in Polyphemus's curse on Ulysses a model of colonization: "his [Polyphemus's] island and the Greeks' covetous view of it encapsulate a veritable paradigm of the colonial process . . . it is . . . only one of many legitimising paradigms of the colonial imperative that the Portuguese would have garnered from classical and biblical sources" ("Ptolemy, Paradise and Purgatory" 88–89). Yet Adamastor as a possible "representation" of the indigenous—or, in postcolonial terminology, "subaltern"—voice is not an easily resolved issue, nor is the relationship between the African specter and Gama in the schema of standard binaries that oppose Europeans and their Others. Camões deliberately erodes the boundaries between Adamastor and his imperialist onlookers; if Adamastor's obstreperous body and vengeful speech are eventually subsumed and overcome by Portuguese expansion, we can also read behind his rageful plaint a sober acknowledgment, from the perspective of the indigene, of the sacrifice of African land and bodies to the machine of conquest. André Brink proposes that Adamastor does not so much evoke disgust as awe (which is, presumably, a more deferential attitude toward Adamastor the African than a rote brutalization of the imperial Other), and in so doing comes to the conclusion—correctly, in my view—that "even in setting up the Other as hideous and terrifying, [Camões] suggests a subjectivity which transcends easy categorisation" ("A Myth of Origin" 45).[7]

Adamastor, as Filgueira Valverde (339) points out, is not part of the classical pantheon of gods. In a bold act of mythogenesis, Camões creates Adamastor as on a par with Greco-Roman mythology.[8] Camões's Adamastor myth may indeed have classical or Renaissance sources, but to consider those sources exclusively is to ignore another, more local mythification of giants and Africa in the pages of two major historiographic texts of the Iberian Middle Ages, Alfonso X's *General estoria* (General History) and *Primera crónica general de España* (First General Chronicle of Spain). The early pages of the *Primera crónica general* narrate Hercules' arrival in Spain from Africa as he crosses the sea with a fleet of ten ships and bringing with him an Arabic astronomer, Allas, named after Mount Allant in Ceuta (8). The mythic hero demarcates the beginning of the West by erecting a tower, one of the Pillars of Hercules. In this brief story, the founding of Spanish cities such as Cádiz and Seville occurs as a result of maritime travel from Africa, linked to Ceuta through the Moorish astronomer. The second part of the *General estoria* traces the lineages of biblical and classical giants (chapter 21) who are telluric figures because of their commemoration in the names of the world's mountains. Of interest here is the legend of Atlas, king of Africa ("Libya") who "era gigant e uno de los mayores onbres de cuerpo que en aquella sazon eran en aquella tierra" (was a giant and who had one of the largest bodies among men of the time in that land, 280). A mountain was named for Atlas and the narrative tells us that Atlas was the son of Japeth, who himself was son of Titan, "el gigant" (the giant, 281); it is repeated that "era Athlas mayor de cuerpo que todos los otros omnes que eran a aquella sazon" (Atlas had the largest body of any man living during that time, 281). These two histories incorporate Africa and Ceuta into a foundational myth of Spain and Iberia, dominated by two legendary figures of great size and strength. In the *Crónica da Tomada de Ceuta,* as we noted earlier, Zurara dubs Ceuta the "começo de formosura" (beginning of beauty), a beauty that is ethical in nature because Ceuta adumbrates the Portuguese campaigns of exploration and conquest that are part of a divine scheme that combats the insidious "sect" of Muhammad.[9] In *Os Lusíadas,* it can be argued that Camões relocates Zurara's ethical Ceuta southward to the Cape of Good Hope, the locale where the eastern enterprise begins. In so doing, Camões makes Adamastor, the earthbound giant and Titan (like Atlas), the guard of the

entrance to the Indian Ocean, which, in the history of nautical exploration as Camões recounts it, had not been breached until the voyage of
Gama.[10] Like the Pillars of Hercules, Adamastor represents the *ne plus
ultra* of knowledge and travel, now placed in southern, rather than northern, Africa. Adamastor's threats and rage echo the boundary of the oceanic
forbidden associated with the Pillars of Hercules as that which, in medieval times, had "symbolized . . . the interdiction for man to penetrate into
the Atlantic" (Randles, "The Atlantic" 2).[11]

If Quint argues for Adamastor as a kind of literary exemplum through
which Camões demonstrates the historical basis of myth, then it can be
concluded that the relationship between Africa and Adamastor is not
much more than a convenience, a circumstantial appropriateness. On the
one hand, Africa is an apt historical stage on which to demonstrate a his-
toricizing underpinning to poetic invention, and, on the other, the paradigm of colonization embodied in Polyphemus's curse, and therefore in
Adamastor's voice, could easily apply to any colonized peoples. Such ideas
situate Adamastor within the ideological frame of expansion and imperialism suffusing the narrative of *Os Lusíadas*. However, the relation between
Africa and Adamastor moves beyond the apposite to the essential when
we consider the connection between expansion, monstrosity, and melancholy, between the imperialist imperative and the particular and metaphoric expression of it in the monster at the end of the world. Adamastor
the monstrous melancholic could never be anything but African—quite
apart from the fact that he is the very soil of Africa in his metamorphosed
limbs—because Africa gives birth to melancholy in Camões's poem as
both an ethical and a worldly phenomenon.

Our own critical encounter with Adamastor begins by noting the metamorphosis of the apparition and his identities, which are variously navigational, meteorological, mythological, and oneiric. In the relatively short
space of the twenty-three stanzas of the episode, Camões enlists a number
of descriptors: Adamastor emerges from the nocturnal storm cloud first
as a "figure" (*figura*), then as a strange, second Colossus of Rhodes that
causes a frisson of fear to ripple through the Portuguese onlookers, a
"horrifying monster" (*monstro horrendo*), a "stupendous body" (*estupendo
corpo*), a captain of the sea, a giant and Titan, and finally, the cape itself.

The kaleidoscopic forms and identities of Adamastor, not to mention the pronounced affective response he generates, advocate for a Camonian objective of making the Adamastor a momentous episode in the voyage; in Camões's sources (such as Barros's *Décadas*), the rounding of Good Hope is accomplished easily and without hindrance, almost incidentally. Terry Cochran has argued for Camões's use of *figura* as an abstraction that marks Adamastor as a decisive moment in the poem in which "the disjuncture between the historical and the figural, between experience and its realization, comes to a head" (139).[12] Cochran's analysis helps us understand the Adamastor episode in the broader context of discourse, figuration, and "the relationship between culture and state that literary and national history presuppose" (121), yet we need to be wary about making Adamastor too much of an abstraction, because there is such a pronounced, physical imminence to Adamastor in his sudden, gigantic, and obstreperously fear-inducing body. Adamastor's corporality must therefore inform attempts to come to exegetical terms with this key figure of Camonian *poiēsis*. And it is this corporality that motivates an important lexical shift in the terms used to describe Adamastor: after Adamastor has materialized as a defined body (and once he has delivered his prophecies on the fate that will meet Portuguese explorers after Gama in Africa), he is no longer a *figura* (stanza 39) but a *monstro* (stanza 49). Interestingly, this is only one of three times that Camões uses *monstro* in a poem teeming with strange beings and penned when the fascination with monstrous bodies, both remote and domestic, was firmly part of the European imaginary. Vasco da Gama registers Adamastor's monstrous nature as partly residing in his extraordinary body. He remarks, "Yet more the ghastly monster [monstro horrendo] would have said, / Touching our fate" (V.49.i–ii), an echo of Virgil's description of Polyphemus as a "monstrum horrendum, informe, ingens" (a monster, awful, shapeless, huge) (*Aeneid*, bk. III, 657); Gama then addresses Adamastor directly and exclaims "that stupendous body, for certain, has caused me great wonder!" (V.49.iii–iv).[13] Gama's pronouncement intertwines monstrousness, corporeality, and wonder (or marvel), and in so doing establishes Adamastor as *Os Lusíadas*'s preeminent monster, which in turn allows us to read him as a creation that is especially dense with signification. In his essay on monster culture, Jeffrey Jerome Cohen argues that

[t]he monstrous body is pure culture. A construct and a projection, the monster exists only to be read: the *monstrum* is etymologically "that which reveals," "that which warns," a glyph that seeks a hierophant. Like a letter on the page, the monster signifies something other than itself: it is always a displacement, always inhabits the gap between the time of upheaval that created it and the moment into which it is received, to be born again . . . Monsters must be examined within the intricate mix of relations (social, cultural, and literary-historical) that generate them. ("Monster Culture" 4–5)[14]

In Cohen's formulation, a monster is always and necesssarily a metaphor, a symbol, an allegory, a deflection away from literalness. Cohen proposes that a monster's meaning (or existence) cannot exist independently of a reader or interpreter. The monster's hermeneutic function hence lies at the core of its nature and is its raison d'être. The monster enjoys a privileged position as a marker and representative of the literary, philosophical, historical, theological, or scientific values of the cultures and societies that generate it. As heir to the monsters of classical epic, according to Quint, Adamastor performs the literary function of the epic curse; others read the giant as the voice of fate, a hostile force of nature, or the fear of the unknown that Gama's voyage finally and definitively dispels.[15]

Gama's use of the verb *maravilhar* (to wonder or marvel [at]) places Adamastor in the tradition of *mirabilia* that is a constant presence in the genre of medieval and early-modern travel narrative and which took shape in travel narratives such as the books of Marco Polo or John Mandeville with their hosts of Plinian monsters. The marvel or wonder that Gama records is that Adamastor occasions a momentary suspension of the authority and epistemological certainty that otherwise define Gama's voyage and privileged position as explorer and knower of the world *além-mar* (overseas). Adamastor shares the trait of geographic frontierdom typical of Plinian monsters who reside at the edges of the known world. Such monsters, in their remarkable bodies, suggest new epistemologies or ways of knowing the world, or the limit of knowledge. A number of Plinian monsters appear throughout the poem's stanzas, which attest to Camões's familiarity with this kind of liminal being.[16] But unlike the earlier writers who included Plinian monsters in their tales, usually located in "India" (a generic term for eastern lands) or "Ethiopia," Portuguese travelers revealed that no such monsters existed in these places or in Africa, though occasional references in Portuguese texts to sub-Saharan Africans as having the faces of dogs (a vestige of the *cynocephali* or dog-headed people) can be found.[17]

The kind of monster I would like to focus on, though, is the kind that is created in the imagination as part of the psychosomatic theory of seeing and knowing, briefly explored in chapter 2. As opposed to the faraway, legendary monsters of the Middle Ages, the Renaissance monster, while still retaining its etyomological nature as something that is portentous or that warns, exists more within the scientific realms of medicine and physiology and the preoccupation with the teratological body. Such monsters were seminally studied by French physician Ambroise Paré whose *Des monstres et prodiges* appeared in 1573. As Huet's *Monstrous Imagination* lays out in considerable detail, one of Paré's fundamental objectives was to understand the etiology of monstrosity by seeking out the monster's biological causes. Paré locates monstrous causation in the imagination, and monsters are born when, at the moment of conception, a woman looks on, say, a dog or frog. This image transmits itself to the fetus, which then bears traits of the animal. We find similar monsters in the *Jardín de flores curiosas* (Garden of Curious Flowers) of Antonio de Torquemada, a Spanish humanist. Torquemada's book was published in 1570; the first treatise is dedicated to nature and what is outside of nature. Monsters appear here and, like Paré's book three years later, are essentially monstrous births. The power of the imagination receives considerable discussion by the interlocutors of the dialogue, since it is capable of changing the external, sensory world. "[L]a imaginación intensa tiene tan gran fuerça y poder que no solamente puede imprimir diversos efectos en aquél que está ymaginando, pero también puede hazer efecto en las mesmas cosas que ymagina" (the intense imagination has such a great force and power that it can not only imprint numerous characteristics on he who is imagining, but it can also affect the very things that it imagines, 533). This formulation of the imagination attributes an agentive, transformative power of the imagination on the objects perceived by the eye in the outside world, much like the rays that emanate from the eyes and could potentially cause damage, such as the *mal de ojo* or evil eye.[18] The interlocutors in the *Jardín* go on to note that once the Portuguese had arrived

in India, no monsters such as those contained in old books were encountered. The monsters, they reason, must have fled into the mountains.

Torquemada's claim that the monsters of India flee to the mountains
and for that reason are unverifiable, and that monsters still exist in Africa,
suggests a migration that is not entirely geographic in nature or dependent
on the authority of eyewitnesses. Monsters by the mid-sixteenth century
have entered once more into the realm of the symbolic and the "psychological," a realm supervised by the imagination. They not only live in the
mountains but also in the recesses of the mind and the working of the
senses. They are no longer allegories of the margin; monsters now pose a
relationship between the world and the perceiver, between empirical realities and the mind's eye of knowing and deliberation. They are, as we will
now see, products of the melancholic imagination.

ADAMASTOR *MELANCHOLICUS*

Adamastor's gigantic body erupts into the middle of Camões's regulated
progression of *ottava rima* stanzas with huge, misshaped limbs that offend
the Renaissance aesthetic value of proportion and harmony. Adamastor is
an aggregate of the legends and reports of monsters said to be dwelling
in Africa and at the outer limits of experience that accrued over the centuries in the European mind; he is, in J. L. Hilton's words, a "new paradigm of the unknown" ("Adamastor"). Yet his monstrous form in the
details of Camões's description manifests certain traits of melancholy, as
do his discursive registers that are first prophetic and historiographic,
then autobiographical. The reaction of Gama and his crew that is simultaneously fearful and darkly fascinated by the specter implicates the imperial onlookers into Adamastor's monstrous nature. Camões's anatomical
itemization of the monster in the description of his mouth, hair, limbs,
face, and pallor construes the giant as a melancholic corporeality that
dominates the minds and affects of the India-bound travelers. Melancholy
is part of the terrain charted and traversed by Gama's ships as it appears
in Adamastor's affective repercussions on his onlookers and in his physicality that is one and the same with the rocks and soil of the Cape of Good
Hope. As Jennifer Radden notes, "[f]or most of western European history,
melancholy was a central cultural idea, focusing, explaining, and organizing the way people saw the world and one another" (vii). Lyons likewise

The dramatic confrontation between Adamastor and Vasco da Gama. From *Os Lusiadas: poema epico* (Paris: Firmin Didot, 1817), with engravings by Jean-Honoré Fragonard.

attests to the general importance of melancholy by noting that "[the] diverse traditions about melancholy expressed, implicitly, the idea of its social importance—it was a physical and psychological condition that expressed an orientation towards the world and society—and this made it particularly susceptible to literary treatment" (1), and studies such as the one by Marion Wells advocates for melancholy as part of the formation of the early-modern subject.

In the writings of its theorists, melancholy was always a relational principle in that it codified a series of equivalences, parallels, and analogies between the human body, the four elements, the cosmos, and the forces of nature. Melancholy was, in short, a multivalent and constantly evolving way of seeing the multifarious dependences between the spheres of human physicality, perception, action, and the cosmic and divine structuring of existence. With its proposition of ineluctable connections between the worldly and celestial realms, melancholy theory in some respects locks tightly into place with the science of celestial navigation as a deliberate reading of the heavens and the stars to direct the larger negotiation of the human agents of maritime expansion. In this regard, navigation might be considered the melancholic science par excellence, and its originating practitioners, the Portuguese, as influential proponents of this negotiation of the waterways of the world.[19]

Although Camões never uses the word *melancholic* to describe Adamastor, traces of this theory of body, temperament, and intellect infuse the episode and the dynamics of the giant's personality and tense exchange with Gama. The shudder of fear that creeps over the mariners unites them to Adamastor, a connection of bodies to a body, an acute reminder of the corporalities at the center of the episode. For this reason let us consider Adamastor as a melancholic body first. Adamastor's physicality bears the marks of melancholy as it was explained in humoral physiology. This medical understanding of melancholy, originating in classical antiquity and surviving throughout the Middle Ages and Renaissance, was based on the work of Greek physicians such as Galen and Hippocrates. It was developed and elaborated by numerous authors over time.[20] Humoral theory proposed a direct cause-and-effect relation between somatic constitution and psychology by seeking to explain behavioral types, called "temperaments" or "complexions," according to the qualities and quantities of the body's four constituent humors. These humors are blood, black bile (melancholy), yellow bile (choler), and phlegm. An ideal proportion of the four humors would dictate perfect health of body and mind (Babb 9), while a preponderance or excess of one or another would create a characteristic temperament. If the humor in abundance is blood (the most desirable humor), the temperament would be sanguine; if black bile, melancholic; if yellow bile, choleric; and if phlegm, phlegmatic. Each humor possessed greater or lesser degrees of moisture and heat. If the humor in excess was black bile, the resulting melancholic would usually favor solitude, night, and darkness, and would be given to fits of sorrow and fear; the melancholic's characteristic color was black. "Of all the four complexions . . . the most miserable is the melancholic," Babb notes (10). Humoral doctrine also presupposed a set of equivalences between the humors and the structure of the world: each humor corresponded to one of the four basic elements and to seasons of the year and the life span of humans. By nature cold and dry, black bile is earthy and autumnal. Choler, on the other hand, is hot and dry, an equivalent of fire and summer. The choleric's natural disposition is angry, proud, revengeful, bold, or ambitious (Babb 9). At immediate glance, Adamastor's climatological situation, comportment, and body suggest a correspondence to these precepts of humoralism. He emerges at night from a black cloud, and his complexion is dark; his mouth is black, and his teeth yellow—the colors, respectively, of black and yellow bile.[21] His body that is the land of the cape, washed by the ocean's waters, suggests the cold dryness typical of black bile. Adamastor's rageful, vengeful, and hubristic behavior, tinctured by his overwhelming sorrow and grief at the loss of Thetis, contains elements of both the melancholic and choleric temperaments. We might also find in Adamastor's dirt-encrusted hair or in his limbs ("crags") that stretch into the sea an allusion to the earthy nature of black bile and, with his beard, of the choleric's and melancholic's tendency to hirsuteness (Babb 9, 33). These basic traits of the melancholic are stereotypical and do no more than suggest a general shaping of Adamastor as a melancholic according to ideas that were in wide circulation in the Renaissance.[22] On their own, the physical characteristics of the melancholic do not help us particularly in understanding why Camões would have conflated Africanness and melancholy as part of the poetic rendering of expansion or as part of the geographic landscape traversed by Gama. To that end, we must consider other ideas about melancholy and its philosophical implications.

Adamastor spatializes melancholy through the connection between his body and the landmass of Africa, and in his partial identification with the sub-Saharan black African. That Camões means to associate Adamastor with Africa is clear, though it is important to remember that the giant does not have one, single identity—as a Titan, he originates elsewhere so is a foreigner to the shore of Africa, but his love obsession with Thetis, in the Ovidian metamorphoses that generate his shapes, has converted him into the land of Africa. Much as he is the anthropomorphic conjuration of the Cape of Good Hope, he is also a synecdoche for the entire African coast: "Aqui toda a Africana costa acabo" (I round out Africa's extremity, V.50.v). Camões tacitly imbues Adamastor with blackness through the description of his hair as "crespos os cabelos" (woolly [or curly] hair, V.39.vii), a trope so commonly used in expansionist writing to describe sub-Saharan black Africans that, by Camões's time, it has become a stereotype.[23] The association between melancholy and Africa is an old one, as Mary Floyd-Wilson demonstrates in her study of geohumoralism. Floyd-Wilson notes that one vein of geohumoral thought held that African heat burned the humors and thus made African bodies cold and dry (2). In other geohumoral texts, the extreme heat of Africa is thought to cause madness, sexual licentiousness, and effeminacy in men. Juan Huarte de San Juan (1529?–88), a contemporary of Camões, is perhaps the most well known Iberian theorist of (geo)humoralism and the psychological states and intricacies of the mind associated with it; his *Examen de ingenios para las ciencias* (Examination of Men's Wits) was published in 1575. Huarte de San Juan, as Floyd-Wilson points out, subscribes to the idea that "there is a reliable correspondence between the external 'complexion' of one's skin and one's humoral complexion" (Floyd-Wilson 69), so that black skin could be an indicator of melancholia. The correlation between physiognomy and disposition is not restricted to comparisons that juxtapose peoples separated by large-scale geographic distances, such as that separating Spaniards from Africans; Huarte de San Juan finds differences between the various inhabitants of Iberia itself—such as the Catalonians, Portuguese, Galicians, Andalusians, Valencians, or Aragonese—and asks "¿Quién no ve y conoce lo que estos difieren entre sí, no sólo en la figura del rostro

THE MONSTER OF MELANCHOLY

y compostura del cuerpo, pero también en las virtudes y vicios del ánima?" (Who does not see and recognize the differences these people exhibit, not only in the shape of the face and the stature of the body, but also in the virtues and vices of the soul itself? 247). If Adamastor's body is melancholically constituted and is therefore cool and dry (it is composed of soil and bathed by the sea) and his rageful, sorrowful temperament is evidence of black and yellow bile, his prophetic pronouncements suggest another form of melancholy, genial melancholy, a widespread idea throughout Renaissance Europe that began to dissociate melancholy from a purely somatic condition.

Genial melancholy is based on Aristotle's *Problem* XXX, 1, in which melancholy no longer simply denotes a humoral disposition or disease but is rather a state of being responsible for creativity, genius, or exalted intellection. Aristotle combines humoral theory with the Platonic notion of divine frenzy (*furor*) or inspiration, so that melancholy becomes a desirable, rather than pathological, condition.[24] The theory of genial melancholy was disseminated throughout Europe by the writings of Italian humanist Marsilio Ficino, especially in his treatise *De vita triplici* (Three Books on Life).[25] It is a "unique and divine gift" in Ficino's words, bestowed by Saturn (Silva, "Songs of Melancholy" 32). The genial melancholic is noted for his gift of prophecy or soothsaying, often considered typical of melancholics in southern regions. "[F]or Ficino . . . the melancholic's outstanding abilities are characterized by their orientation towards the future" (Schleiner 26). So it is that the first half of Adamastor's peroration in which he describes the future events of Portuguese explorers can be understood as the gift of divination possessed by genial melancholics. The epic curse hence meets Ficinan humanism and Aristotelian melancholy, but it is important nonetheless to separate the epic curse from the melancholic lament. For Camões, melancholic rage is prophecy. Adamastor as a "genius of the shore," then, is not only a guardian spirit of a coastal locale, as Lipking calls him following the coinage in Milton's *Lycidas*, but is a genial prophet since "prophesying is part of the melancholic experience" (Schleiner 319).[26]

The prophecies Adamastor delivers are, as we have been noting, the first part of his discourse to Gama. Disturbed by such predictions, and by the specter's boastful claim that the tragedies to befall Portuguese explorers are a vengeance for Gama's audacity in entering into previously unknown topographies of space and knowledge, Gama interrogates the apparition with a terse "Quem és tu?" (Who art thou? V.49.iii). Adamastor writhes under the weight of a question we sense he would prefer not to answer but must, like the shades who reluctantly and in anguish respond to Dante's queries throughout the *Inferno*. With a moan and a bitter and heavy voice Adamastor identifies himself as the cape and gives his name. Here the second, autobiographical part of Adamastor's discourse commences. We learn of Adamastor's passion for Thetis, ignited when he glimpsed the nymph bathing nude. Adamastor's will became imprisoned, and, because of this desire for Peleu's wife, he waged war on Neptune. Doris, Thetis's mother, tricks Adamastor into thinking he might possess Thetis in order to end the war, and, as a result of his audacious desire, the giant is punitively metamorphosed into the cape with the waters of Thetis forever and agonizingly lapping against him. Adamastor, with his suffering and wailing, "halfway mad in fury," exhibits the acute symptoms of lovesickness or passionate love as postulated by medical writers of the Middle Ages as one of the deleterious states of affect caused by melancholy.[27] This "morbid love" (also known as *amor hereos*) is an unrequited love that causes suffering based on a fixation on the love object, originally apprehended through sight and transformed into an image or phantasm in the imagination. Lovesickness becomes a significant presence in the medical tradition for the first time in the writings of the humoralist Galen (Wack 7). Babb notes that although lovesickness is not a melancholic affliction per se it can become so if love remains unsatisfied (134) because the phantasm in the imaginative faculty has become unhealthily tenacious (Wells 10). The lover's skin can manifest a discoloration or pallor (Babb 136), and this may well explain Camões's description of Adamastor's appearance as, improbably, both "earthy" and "pallid" (V.39.vi).[28] Central to the dissemination of ideas on lovesickness throughout the European Middle Ages was the work of Constantinus Africanus or Constantine the African (d. 1087), a native of Carthage who traveled to Italy, converted to Christianity, entered the abbey of Montecassino, and worked in the shadow of the medical school at Salerno. Constantine introduced much Arabic learning into Europe through his translations of Arabic medical texts into Latin.[29] The chapter devoted to lovesickness in his *Viaticum* became one of the authoritative treatments of the malady in its many editions, translations, and commentaries, in addition to other works such as the *Canon medicinae* of Ibn Sīnā (Avicenna). In the *Viaticum*, as Wack (40) informs us, love is a forerunner of melancholy while in another Constantinian translation, love is a type of melancholy. Portuguese translations of Constantine's *Viaticum* and the works of Avicenna appear in catalogs of royal library holdings in Portugal prior to Camões's time.[30] Of interest here is the Constantinian assertion that love is caused by the sight or contemplation of a beautiful form, which itself can spark a Platonic furor (Folger 36).[31] Once the beautiful form is glimpsed, the phantasy (a faculty of the mind that stores sense impressions) retains it (Folger 30), and the lover may cogitate obsessively over the absent form itself and thus enter into a state of "morbid" love and melancholy.[32] Such a state is pathological, in need of a cure. In Adamastor, Camões has mythified the lover who suffers from love-melancholy by transforming him eternally into the landscape of the cape surrounded by Thetis's waters.[33] Adamastor's embodiment as earth and rock symbolizes an eternal, restless, and morbid contemplation of the seen and lost Thetis, maddeningly close and forever distant. Perhaps Adamastor's lovesick lament and petrified form echo the plaint of the lover in Petrarch's poem 23, "il suon de'miei gravi sospiri, / ch'acquistan fede a la penosa vita" (the sound of my heavy sighs which prove how painful my life is, 60), who feels as if transformed into "un quasi vivo et sbigottito sasso" (an almost living and terrified stone, 62).[34] The natural elements of Camões's world, of geography itself, become invested with a melancholic memory of the past.

Adamastor's bifurcated address to the explorers, then, reveals the giant's melancholia as both humoral temperament and mantic ability. Yet such melancholy would be little more than a literary topos were it not implicated into Vasco da Gama's journey as a defining moment in the voyage to India. It is this aspect of the presence of melancholy in Camões's text that makes the Portuguese reaction to Adamastor in the form of fear or *medo* so central to melancholy's valuation as a concept imbricated into the expansionist imagination. The boundary separating European explorer from a dark, threatening, and monstrous African Other becomes blurred because Gama, as the representative of an itinerant Portuguese culture, not only confronts Adamastor but becomes problematically identified with him. Adamastor is a figure of melancholy because the Portuguese

travelers themselves have experienced a precipitous fall into melancholy—
the darkness of the cape with its night phantom reflects a traumatic and
troubling experience of melancholy that dramatizes the authoritative relationship between Gama and the empirical world, an authority based on
the primacy of the eye and sight, as we noted earlier. This melancholic or
humorally inflected trip is reflected in the language of other texts that
document Gama's voyage. Álvaro Velho, for example, fleetingly establishes
a distinction between Gama who experiences "merencoria" (melancholy, 62)
and the disrespectful, inattentive attitudes of the natives who are "homens
fleumáticos" (phlegmatic men, 63). In the memorialist-style history of Gaspar Correia (ca. 1495–ca. 1565), the *Lendas da Índia* (Legends of India),
Correia makes the observation that Gama was an "homem colérico" (choleric man, 17). In this humoral landscape, Adamastor is a reification of a
troubled, melancholic state of mind that provides an opportunity for a
determined, heroic act of will. To round the cape successfully is to conquer the fear of Adamastor, to conquer the danger to Gama's authority as
a reliable seer and interpreter of the world. Adamastor, then, in his status
as a fear-inducing African, may, to some degree, be a "figure of radical
otherness" (Cochran 147), but he is also, as a melancholic, a figure of a
problematic and uncanny familiarity. Navigating the turning point of Africa
triggers a kind of psychomachia in which fear and phantasms threaten to
disrupt the imperialist venture; melancholy, as Judith Butler reminds us,
"returns us to the figure of the 'turn' as a founding trope in the discourse
of the psyche" (168). Camões scripts the passing of the cape as a deliberate act of daring when confronted with a psychological underworld, a cata-
basis that Gama and his company must undergo. Adamastor occasions a
passage through a troubling interiority.

The Portuguese approach to the cape rehearses some generally accepted
postulates about the melancholic state. Nocturnal hours are typically
potent hours for melancholy and thoughts of fear and evil, evident in the
Portuguese encounter with Adamastor at night.[35] Closely associated with
night is the wakefulness of the sailors ("vigiando," V.37.vi) which corroborates the Aristotelian notion that "melancholics were not lovers of sleep"
(Agamben 14n2).[36] Such a melancholic insomnia, notes Babb (31), could
produce hallucinations, and indeed we may well consider the specter of
Adamastor as a kind of oneiric, nightmarish phantasm. The passage of the

cape in the autumn coincides with the commonly held notion that fall is the melancholic time of year, not to mention the association of the melancholic with long sea journeys or the susceptibility to stellar influences.

In faculty psychology and theories of melancholy, the imagination is often adversely affected by melancholy—recall that the imagination is where images received by the eye are stored after they pass through the common sense. The *imaginatio* (sometimes called *phantasia*) receives images in the form of impressions, but, unlike the common sense, the imagination can recall impressions of objects to the mind even in the absence of the object itself (Wells 41). The imagination wields the power to create combinations of previously received and stored images never actually seen by the eye. The imagination, then, is the locus where monsters and chimeras are born; the combinatory power of the imagination can create composite images. For this reason, the imagination is unreliable and prone to error (Clark 45) and can be afflicted by melancholy. In a discussion of this process, Pedro Mexía in his *Silva de varia lección* (Forest of Many Lessons, 1540) notes the "estrañas ymaginaciones" (strange imaginations, 586) produced by this creative and often uncontrollable ventricle of the mind. Adamastor is a monster created in the melancholically afflicted imaginations of Gama and his crew, and as such stands as a critical moment when the European gaze as the basis for epistemological authority falters. The monster represents a lapse in Gama's ability to relate to the world authoritatively as the bearer and guarantor of cognitive superiority.[37] Adamastor as an experience of marvel ("esse estupendo / Corpo, certo, me tem maravilhado!" V.49.iii–iv) recalls more Wells's proposition, apropos of Italian epic, that the marvelous might be thought of as a "phantasm-effect" as a moment of ontological ambiguity (144). This understanding of the marvelous coincides more with the tenor of the encounter with Adamastor than does, say, Greenblatt's discussion of the imagination and the marvelous or wonder in New World colonial textuality in which it is argued that "Renaisssance wonder [is] an agent of appropriation" (24). If anything, at this moment in *Os Lusíadas* Gama is momentarily disempowered as an agent of imperial appropriation; he enters Africa as much as Africa enters him.

The fear of Gama and his company that results from Adamastor's fatal prophecies and his monstrous form does not, then, signal a distancing between the explorers and the spectral-telluric African, but rather an approximation, a vexed rapprochement. Camões further establishes this equivalence through the concept of daring or boldness (*ousadia* or *atrevimento*), so central to Camonian, heroic voyaging and the pursuit of conquest. The positive, heroic quality of boldness is mirrored darkly in Adamastor, who is punished for his own intrepid pursuit of Thetis and for waging war on the Olympians. It is the Portuguese incarnation of boldness or daring that Adamastor initially identifies in his locution "gente ousada" as that which offends him and the boundary he both guards and instantiates. That there exists a slippage between practices of boldness— it can be either positive or negative, as in the Portuguese exercise of it or in Adamastor's version of the same trait—inflects this crucial requisite to epic action with an ethically murky undercurrent.[38] Adamastor's narrative of his failed quest for Thetis functions as an imperialist parable embedded into the heart of *Os Lusíadas,* a negative exemplum in that Adamastor's story as a "captain of the sea" is a story of attempted conquest and failure. The failure of his boldness is the basis for his melancholy, and this implicates him into the epic logic of the poem. Gama and Adamastor are two sides of a Portuguese seafaring identity, the positive and negative inflections of heroic passion. If, as Philip Fisher argues in *The Vehement Passions,* "passionate" connotes a positive state of being (a legacy of Homeric epic) and is "the very essence of an aroused and dynamic spirit" (5), and if anger and fear are themselves virtues in the classical formulations of these affects, then Gama's fear of Adamastor and his indignation at the monster's audacity on one level manifest his epic exemplarity.[39] Although Gama does not exhibit an overt anger—there is no rage of Achilles driving the imperialist's voyage—his spirit of *ousadia* might be understood as the expansionist equivalent of this classical, passionate state. Camonian boldness or daring is a principle of movement, of iteration and expansiveness; it is geographic, epistemological, spiritual, and cultural; it is what propels Camonian ships through the seas as they fertilize the world with culture and Christianity. As a fearless, outward-projecting state of spirit and mind, *ousadia* in Adamastor metamorphoses into a perpetual, melancholic inwardness that confronts the Portuguese sailors as a symbolic death, a stasis.[40] Surely this is one reason Camões's giant grieves so fiercely, confronted with a form of *ousadia* that is familiar yet ultimately antithetical to his own. Adamastor's melancholy is the opposite of adventurous daring.[41] Perhaps Adamastor's melancholia reflects the distinction Silva finds between Ficinan and Mannerist melancholy—this latter form, "unlike the 'generous' and 'heroic' melancholy of Renaissance Humanism, is a disease, a pathology of the body and soul, a morbid state of mind in which genius and the exceptionality of the creative faculties are allied to suffering, anguish and insanity" ("Songs of Melancholy" 34). In Vasco da Gama, the passion of *ousadia*, of *atrevimento*, permits itinerancy, conquest, accomplishment, and the sensual delights (themselves an allegory of fame and ethical plenitude) on the Isle of Love. Adamastor's thwarted and ill-fated daring locks him in one place, a counterpoint to the Portuguese success that comes with its own inevitable and disturbing consequences. "[Adamastor's] situation is in fact a perpetual mocking of him for his abortive efforts to conquer the sea by force and to conquer the Nereid by love. [The sea is] both the realm he tried to conquer and the abode of his beloved, but in his immobile state he is unable to reach out and attempt another conquest of either," Ronald de Sousa observes (544).

The double nature of daring or boldness that is both positive and negative underlies the dilemma that confronts Gama at the cape: does he push past Adamastor or succumb to the fear of the monster's prophecies and return home? There is, of course, only one possible answer to this question, but the fact that Camões makes the passage of Good Hope a fearful and dangerous undertaking in his narrative is significant. Gama's dilemma is an ethical one because he must make a choice to heed (or not) Adamastor's fatalistic words. There is an ontological charge to the confrontation between monster and mariner since, notionally speaking, Adamastor is Gama's equal. The giant exercises the right of extended historiographic narrative, a form of discourse that is elsewhere in the poem reserved for Camões, Gama, or deities.[42] Adding to the drama of the encounter and to the equivalence between Adamastor and Gama is Adamastor's response to Gama's question "Quem és tu?" (Who are you?) with "Eu sou aquele oculto e grande Cabo" (I am that vast cape locked in secrecy, V.50.i). At first the response may seem expected enough, but it gains critical weight when we realize that it is one of only three instances in Camões's poem in which the verb *ser* (to be) is conjugated in the first-person singular, "sou." At one level, the use of the first-person singular marks a significant departure from the narratives of Ovid's *Metamorphoses* as one of the structural models of the episode. The Latin poet presents his metamorphosing world through third-person narratives; Adamastor narrates his own metamorphosis, and on his own initiative, unlike, for example, the passive combination of voice and rock in Echo who must wait for another to speak before being able to respond—and even then Echo can only repeat words already spoken. For Camões, then, speaking itself is a form of metamorphosis because the rocks of the cape become vocal and then revert, at the break of day, to their former muteness. Adamastor's self-initiated speech invests Africans with a subjectivity in epic narrative.

The simple, primordial verb of existence "Eu sou" also and more importantly marks Adamastor's speech as a deliberate act of self-constitution. Adamastor speaks to Gama as Gama speaks to the world. Gama wields the power and privilege of being. "I am" is a locution that defines an essence of self and acts as a performative in that it conjures and makes immanent an identity and a consciousness. One of the dangers Adamastor presents is that his melancholic lament might become the future lament of a nation if the imperial enterprise is not pursued in the face of, and despite, the certainty of occasional tragedy and defeat. If we allow, as some scholars maintain, that Camões mourns the loss of empire in *Os Lusíadas*, it is also possible to argue that the poem issues a call to arms (or at least to consciousness) for the rejuvenation of an epic past.[43] Adamastor, then, would stand as a negative exemplum, or, as Ronald de Sousa observes, "a counter-example to the effort upon which the Portuguese are embarked . . . The Portuguese effort will be a new Promethean act" (545). Adamastor is the failed "captain of the sea" whose unrequited desire and enduring grief leaves nothing but a ruins of the self, a spectral simulacrum of titanic greatness and strength.

Yet even if we do not subscribe to the antiepic hypothesis, Gama's response to Adamastor in the form of doubling the cape constitutes a moment of decision in that it overcomes the melancholic state of mind. It is Gama's choice not to submit to melancholy because it will stall the providential plan of imperialism. Gama's deliberate act of rounding Good Hope despite Adamastor's presence is the consequence of not giving in to fear and reaffirming his own *ousadia*. If Gama and his crew inhabit, albeit temporarily, a melancholic space that is both geographic (Africa)

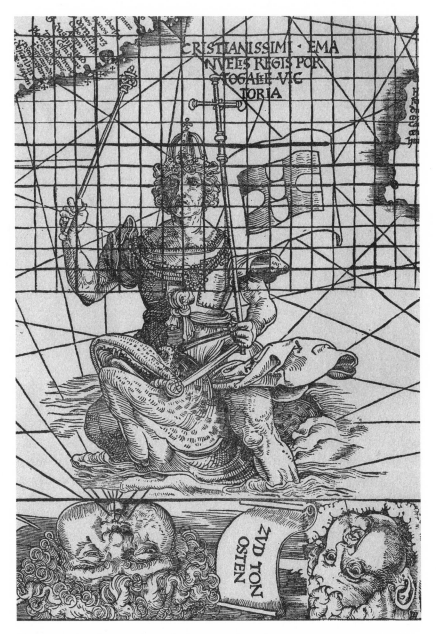

King Manuel I of Portugal rounds the Cape of Good Hope on a sea monster.
The rounding of Good Hope has here become part of navigational legend and lore.
From Martin Waldseemüller's *Carta Marina*, 1516. Courtesy of The James Ford Bell
Library, University of Minnesota, panel 11 of Bell facsimile 1959mWa.

and internal, this duality reflects the double nature of *ousadia* and the inevitability of deliberate acts of choice. In a discussion of scholars and the pursuit of truth in his *De vita libri tres*, Marsilio Ficino employs the metaphor of a traveler on land and sea (*terrimarique*) to denote the dilemma of ethical choice as a product of melancholy. Ficino writes:

> longissima via est quae ad veritatem sapientiamque perducit, gravibus terraeque marisque plena laboribus. Quicunque igitur hoc iter aggrediuntur, ut poeta quispiam diceret, saepe terra marique periclitantur. Sive enim mare navigent continue inter fluctus, id est humores duos, pituitam scilicet et noxiam illam melancholiam, quasi inter Scyllam Charybdimque iactantur.

> the road is very long which leads to truth and wisdom, full of heavy labors on land and sea. Hence people who undertake this journey are often at danger, as some poet might say, on land and sea. For if they sail on the sea, they are constantly tossed among the waves, that is, the two humors, namely phlegm and that noxious form of melancholy, as if between Scylla and Charybdis. (123)

Of significance also in this context is the long-standing connection between Saturn and melancholy. Saturn was thought to preside over long sea journeys (Klibansky, Panofsky, and Saxl 132) so that one of the typically Saturnine occupations is sailor or mariner.[44]

The internal or psychomachic conflict Gama confronts at Good Hope as the negotiation of fear and melancholy recalls passages in the medieval *Leal Conselheiro* of D. Duarte, the "philosopher king." Two of Duarte's chapters discuss melancholy as an impediment to the correct exercise of intellect, spirit, and will in Duarte's rigidly ethical universe. In chapters 19 and 20, Duarte presents an autobiographical account of his affliction with melancholy and his eventual recuperation from it. Duarte's bout with melancholy, he tells us, was a result of the onerous duties imposed on him as a young man of twenty-two to see to the bureaucratic matters of state while his father João I was occupied with the capture of Ceuta. Duarte's melancholy manifested itself in an abiding moroseness, an unshakable preoccupation with sadness, fear, and death. None of the remedies typically prescribed by physicians for curing melancholy alleviated his condition. In the end, Duarte recalls, he was restored to perfect health only by his faith and "good hope" (*boa esperança*), which suggests that ultimately the brand of melancholy Duarte describes is spiritual in nature, akin to *acedia* or religious melancholy, though Duarte himself is not a religious. The king contextualizes the discussion of melancholy in a discussion of *tristeza* (despair), the Portuguese rendering of *tristitia*.[45] Duarte conflates the humoral or somatic theory of melancholy (he refers to his malady as the "humor menencorico" [melancholic humor] and describes the symptoms of his "distempered" body as indicative of his unhealthy state) with the spiritual affliction of despair. So it is that in this Portuguese treatment of melancholy the somatic, melancholic self is inextricable from the ethical exercise of *viver bem* or "living well."

Duarte's melancholy, as he initially observes, originated in the circumstances attending the incipient African enterprise, and the *Leal Conselheiro* reveals the triumph over melancholy as a choice, a willed act. Duarte's vanquishing of melancholy adumbrates Gama's disavowal of fear in the face of Adamastor, a crucial moment in the voyage and expansionist ethos of *Os Lusíadas*. Gama's rounding of the cape is no accident—unlike his immediate historiographic sources, which describe the passage of Good Hope as an unremarkable, even felicitous event, Camões opts to shape this occurrence into an experience of danger and choice that marks the triumph of *ousadia*. The descent into a melancholic state of fear and apprehension, prompted by and mirrored in Adamastor's melancholy, parallels Duarte's melancholy as a direct result of the circumstances of expansion that is banished only by a concerted act of will and moral rectitude. The dissipation of the black cloud as Gama and crew steer past Good Hope—"Súbito de ante os olhos se apartou. / Desfez-se a nuvem negra . . ." (before us / In a twinkling he had vanished from our view. / The black cloud broke . . . V.60.i–iii)—might be read as symbolic of the victory over melancholy, as well as a reminder that Adamastor's own melancholic demeanor stands as an obverse to the spirit of *ousadia* embodied in Gama. Indeed, Adamastor's ire is tantamount to a faulty will and control of the sentiments. For Duarte, ire is born of a "fervor do coraçom" (upheaval in the heart, 56) that will seek to assuage itself with vengeance, a sentiment we find in Adamastor's threat to take vengeance on those who discovered him (V.44.i–ii).[46]

Crucial to the formulation of melancholy as part of the literary and cultural imaginary of medieval and Renaissance Portugal is *saudade*, a sentiment discussed by Duarte that shares some characteristics with melancholy as an expression of sadness, memory, and unfulfilled longing. *Saudade* means, roughly, "nostalgic yearning" or "bittersweet memory," an aching desire for someone or something lost or not present, and is discussed by Duarte in chapter 25, which is devoted to negative states of mind or affect. Duarte notes that *saudade*, unlike the other phenomena under analysis, originates in "senssualidade" or the sentimental affect as opposed to "rrazom" or reason. Duarte further isolates *saudade* from the other parts of his discussion with the claim that this sentiment cannot be found in "other books" and that "me parece este nome de ssuydade tam proprio, que o latym nem outro linguagem que eu saibha nom he pera tal sentido semelhante" (this word seems to me unique, since neither Latin nor any other language I know of has a similar sentiment, 95). This claim famously renders *saudade* as an untranslatable and therefore uniquely Portuguese sentiment—the "supreme icon of Portuguese culture," as Eduardo Lourenço puts it (107)—that is emblematic of the Portuguese temperament itself in cultural and literary history and which finds expression in a number of forms over the centuries.[47] Frequently, Duarte notes that *saudade* manifests itself through weeping (*chorar*) and sighing (*sospirar*). In Galician-Portuguese medieval lyric poetry (twelfth to fourteenth centuries), most notably in the *cantigas de amigo* (lover's songs) or poems in the voice of women who lament the absence of their lovers, we find melancholic aching prevalently incorporated into the sentimental universe of this poetry. The single young woman characteristically voices a plaint about her anguish and the uncertainty of the return of her *amigo*, who is frequently *além mar* (overseas). In Adamastor's voice we can hear an echo of these plaints, and it is perhaps with no little irony that Camões re-genders as masculine the voices of the *cantigas de amigo* whose beloved is not only "overseas" but is the very sea itself in the form of Thetis. Adamastor's sorrowful ire resonates as a transgeneric lament that conflates Duarte's and Camões's formulations of melancholy and *saudade* with the plangent medieval songs of abandoned lovers at water's edge.

We may, in this light, read Adamastor as a monstrous incarnation of *saudade*, a uniquely Portuguese version of melancholy, in addition to the more standard understandings of melancholy we have been discussing. What Freud and his interpreters such as Giorgio Agamben argue is that melancholy is a reaction to a lost object of love (in Adamastor's case, this would be Thetis), while Duarte identifies *saudade* as the sentiment, located in the heart, resulting from the affectionate "remembrance" of someone or from separation from that person.[48] Melancholy is inherently linked to the past and is "the first and most acute expression of temporality" (Lourenço 92), and *saudade* as well boasts this link with time (106). *Saudade* is a melancholically inflected form of memory and history, an affective relationship with the past. The suffering and anguish that *saudade* connotes and that is present in Adamastor's plaint also establishes a link to the world of Arabic thought. José Pedro Machado (*Dicionário* 165) derives *saudade* from Latin *solitate* (solitude), presumably implying that this emotional distress is a form of isolation or loneliness, or is caused by such isolation. Before Machado, Carolina Michaëlis de Vasconcellos likewise found the etymological origin in Latin in the feminine plural *solitates* (55), and considers *salutate* (health) as a possibility also. Against the perceived necessity of identifying a Latin root, Leo Pap turns to the Arabic *saudá*, which means "black bile," an etymon related to the adjective *aswad* (black) (99). Arabic *saudá* "literally refers to the 'blackened' or 'bruised' blood within the heart, and, figuratively, to a feeling of profound sadness. In (Arabic) medicine . . . *saudá* is a liver ailment which has as its symptom a bitter and melancholy sadness" (99).[49] So it is that *saudade*, if we accept the Arabic hypothesis, also boasts a link to humoral theory and melancholy and imputes an Arabic origin to this Portuguese form of suffering and anguish.

THE MASCULINE SHIP

The erotic connotations of lament suffusing Adamastor's autobiographical voice suggest that imperial pursuits can occasion loss and longing, and that therefore empire is a form of desire in the melancholic imagination. *Os Lusíadas* as such is Camões's greatest and most elaborate love poem, and Adamastor's loss constitutes part of its amatory universe. As a force of nature allegorized by the classical gods, desire pervades Camões's *oikoumene*. Adamastor's desire for Thetis is framed as both an erotic and (failed) imperial parable since the giant is unable to conquer the ocean and win the love of the Nereid. Adamastor's defeat in this respect is didactic, a warning against unmeasured and irrational desire. In this world of competing desires, the means by which Gama reaffirms his *ousadia* in the face of the Adamastorian menace participates in a gendered, sexualized metaphor of imperialism. Expansion is a masculine enterprise, an expression of male power and plenitude carried out under Venus's guidance. Juliana Schiesari argues that there is a "phallic essence of melancholia" (106), that it is an "empowering form of male eros" (110). It is possible to find a dramatization of this eros in the Adamastor episode because there is a confrontation between European and African desiring masculinities. Adamastor's exhortations and threats to the Portuguese explorers fail to deter them from braving the treacherous waters of the cape and tacking safely into the Indian Ocean. Camões fashions Adamastor's eros as a negative exemplum on the basis of his "choro" or weeping. Gama's masculine resolve trumps Adamastor's perpetually plaintive condition. If melancholy or melancholic suffering is a male prerogative, there is, according to Schiesari, a form of feminine grieving or suffering. Such grieving includes "inarticulate weeping, or other signs of ritualistic (but intellectually and artistically unaccredited) mourning" (12). Adamastor's grief, while not inarticulate, borders dangerously on a feminine or nonphallic expression of affect because it is an impotence.[50] Adamastor *melancholicus* threatens the exercise of imperial masculinity by degrading the prerogative of male melancholy into a feminized passivity. Camões, in line with many early-modern gendered formulations of the East, establishes a contrast between the masculine West and the feminine non-West, perhaps most clearly evidenced in canto VI as Gama's fleet comes within sight of Calicut. Here, "Easternness" mollifies Western masculine, bellicose passion, or, as David Quint observes, "the otherness of the Easterner becomes the otherness of the second sex" (28). As an African, Adamastor is subjected to an emasculating gaze that is realized in the symbolic interaction of ships and the natural elements as part of a gendered and sexualized worldscape.

Camões establishes the alliance between ships and the natural elements at the outset. In canto I, following several introductory stanzas, the action proper begins:

Já no largo Oceano navegavam,
As inquietas ondas apartando;

Os ventos brandamente respiravam,
Das naus as velas côncavas inchando;
Da branca escuma os mares se mostravam
Cobertos, onde as proas vão cortando
As marítimas águas consagradas,
Que do gado de Próteu são cortadas (I.19)

Already through the open sea they sailed,
Thrusting unquiet waves to either side.
And 'twas a gentle breath the winds exhaled,
That made the vessels' hollow sails spread wide.
White wakes all over the great seas they trailed,
Where through the deep the sharp cutwaters plied,
Cleaving the sacred wave where to and fro
The rushing cattle herds of Proteus go

Scholars generally identify here the epic convention of in medias res because the voyage to India is already under way when readers first enter the poem's linear sequence of events. The poet's choice of the ship at full sail on the high seas as the image that initiates the action freights the elements of this stanza with significations that will be repeated throughout the text. As we might expect from a poem so thoroughly saturated with the history and ideologies of maritime empire, Os Lusíadas favors ships, water, and travel as structuring devices of its various narratives. For Camões, ships (or boats) carry an important charge because they are the principal means through which worlds come into contact and through which knowledge of those worlds is acquired and exchanged. This primacy expresses itself in a metaphoric language of gender and eros. In the stanza above, the winds completely fill the sails and push the ship's prow through water in a manner that is both violent (the ship "cuts" the sea) and sexual. Helder Macedo argues that the winds that propel Camonian ships are symbolic of phallic power ("O braço e a mente" 66). In fact, the ship itself is a phallic icon as it cleaves the oceanic water and leaves a foamy residue ("branca escuma"). The sexualized energy symbolized by these winds, then, transforms the ships into agents of masculine imperialism and its phallic prerogative. The gods who represent the natural forces of the cosmos and who supervise the actions of the Portuguese implicate this sexual world force into the divine ordering of the universe. It is no accident that the patron goddess of the Portuguese enterprise is Venus, the goddess of erotic love who invests oceanic voyaging with decidedly erotic overtones.[51] The ship at full sail enters into a sexualized union with the sea and transports a fecundity of civilization to the world. Camonian water is feminine and the ships that move over it, navigate it, and inscribe it into an imperial *oikoumene* do so in a penetrative fashion. The natural elements in Camões's water-filled poem hence participate in a pervasive, restless eros where "woman drives the masculinist discourse of empire even in her absence" (Cohen, "The Discourse" 272). In this symbolic erotics of navigation, the ships and their occupants overcome the passive Adamastor and thus render him (and Africans generally) impotent.[52] Even so, the successful doubling of the cape leaves in its wake a testimony of the Portuguese/European preoccupation with the potent, African male body with its ability to block or impede imperial ambitions. This preoccupation is quasi-fetishistic because Camões expresses it initially as a heightened attention to, and awareness of, Adamastor's body parts, and then to the giant's potential (but unrealized) ability to hinder the voyage.

THE DEVIL'S MAP

In 1639, a two-volume commentary and translation into Castilian of *Os Lusíadas* was published in Madrid, a book that stands as a decisive moment in the history of Camonian criticism. The author of this edition, the *Lusíadas . . . comentadas,* is Manuel de Faria e Sousa (1590–1649), a prolific literary critic, historian, philologist, poet, and moralist whom the bibliographer Innocencio Francisco da Silva regarded as one of the most erudite men of his times.[53] By birth Portuguese, Faria e Sousa spent most of his life living and working in Madrid and writing in Castilian during the years of the dual monarchy (1580–1640) when Philip II of Spain also occupied the Portuguese throne as Philip I following the death of D. Sebastião in the battle of El-Ksar el-Kebir in 1578. Posterity has, to a great degree, ignored Faria e Sousa and his scholarly work, a fact no doubt due in part to his straddling of cultures that prompted his disavowal by critics in both Portugal and Spain.[54]

Faria e Sousa's edition of *Os Lusíadas* stands as a milestone in the criticism of Camões's poem in part because of its methodology and critical
apparatus. The scholar provides a line-by-line commentary in addition
to his translations of each stanza, and marshals a vast corpus of primary
and secondary sources into interpretive service. Frank Pierce concludes
that "Faria took the whole poem and presented a commentary which . . .
explained everything and drew together the rich variety of Camões' imagination into a satisfying rational statement" ("The Place of Mythology"
100).[55] Although the extent to which Faria e Sousa "explained everything"
may be debated, as well as the nature of the overall "rational statement"
Pierce claims is present in the commentator's work, Pierce is correct in
finding here the first systematic interpretation of the *Lusíadas* that seeks
to integrate the various episodes, historical and mythological actors, symbolic and metaphoric allusions, and the poet's own erudition. The critic
accomplishes this by positing an underlying allegorical structure to the
poem; for him, *Os Lusíadas* is a Christian allegory that trumpets the victory of the church militant in foreign lands. This interpretive gambit is in
itself reductionist and glosses over many of the poem's contradictions and
complexities. Yet although it is possible to disagree with Faria e Sousa's
assumption, it is much more difficult to assail his methodology, for he
"was not taken up only with gathering documentation, but with designing a method suitable for allegorizing the pagan elements in the poem"
(Glaser, "Manuel de Faria e Sousa" 137). Furthermore, Faria e Sousa's allegorizing readings are elaborated through an episode-based approach to
interpreting Camões's text, in itself a lasting contribution to Camonian
scholarship. The two volumes of dense commentary establish the study
of Camões as a discipline in and of itself in Iberian letters and launch
critical ideas that many scholars repeat, sometimes unknowingly, to the
present day.[56]

   One of the episodes Faria e Sousa examines closely is the Adamastor
episode, and indeed his comments on it constitute one of his lengthiest
disquisitions. Adamastor emerges as something of an icon of the process
of Camonian interpretation and as a bona fide topos in all subsequent
criticism of the poem. Arguably, no other writing has established the
domineering presence of Adamastor more than Faria e Sousa's interpretation. Faria e Sousa's reading finds in Adamastor a cartographic precept

that is part of the allegorical structure of the text. Early in his discussion, the critic provisionally designates Adamastor as the "frons Africae"
(the head of Africa) and claims that this is how readers generally understand the apparition's geographic symbolism, but the designation quickly
cedes to the postulation that lies at the core of Faria e Sousa's argument:
Adamastor is solely and unilaterally the representation of Muhammad
and Islam, and therefore the Devil, the antagonist of the Catholic church
represented by Vasco da Gama's fleet. Throughout the presentation of his
arguments Faria e Sousa takes recourse to the language of melancholy.

The critic recognizes the melancholic nature of Adamastor, though this
recognition does not explicitly connect the phantasm to the traditions of
melancholy we have been exploring in this chapter. The adjectives initially
used to describe Adamastor are "melancholic," "choleric," or "passionate,"
and there is a repeated insistence that "este Gigante representa al demo-
nio" (this Giant represents the Devil, for example, cols. 522 and 525) and
that he is the head of "la torpeza Mauritana" (Moorish turpitude, col. 541).
As Faria e Sousa inscribes Muhammad into the spiritual universe of *Os
Lusíadas* through Adamastor, he invests the apparition with a theoretical
importance as an expansionist negativity, a dark embodiment of the tenets
of imperialism. Adamastor issues forth from the pages of the *Lusíadas . . .
comentadas* as a body that impedes the smooth mapping of the world
according to a Christian cosmography which is the final epic achievement
of imperial Portugal. Adamastor's latent danger is that he threatens to un-
map the world into diabolical chaos. He looms ominously as a counter-
map to Christian imperialism, a devil's map. His phantasmal body bursts
into Camões's poem as the cartographic principle, demonically inflected,
underlying expansionist movement.

Faria e Sousa builds this reading of Adamastor by construing Africa
as solely and exclusively the seat of Islam, a gesture that wipes Africa clean
of its non-Islamic cultures with which Portuguese colonists had been familiar for more than two centuries by the time the *Lusíadas . . . comentadas*
appeared. The equation of African Moorishness with Islam in demonizing terms in part resuscitates a conception of the Saracen as foe to a militant Latin Christianity elaborated throughout the Middle Ages. With the
apocalyptic identification of Adamastor/Muhammad who was "el segundo
Lucifer, porque muchos dixeron, que Mahoma era el Antechristo" (the

second Lucifer, because many have said that Muhammad was the Anti-christ, col. 541), Faria e Sousa fuses a long-standing, Christian ideological practice with a more immediate anxiety—the threat of Islamic imperial-ism, especially in the form of the Ottoman Turks, to Portuguese expansion and conquest.[57]

The reading of Adamastor as an "estupenda fábula" (stupendous fiction, col. 539) overlays the giant's allegorical imperative with a melancholic nature: Adamastor is a "representación tristísima" (extremely sad figure, col. 516) who expresses himself in a "passión colérica" (choleric passion, col. 514). In commenting on the word *figura* in stanza 39 of canto V (recall that this stanza introduces Adamastor to the vision of the Portuguese onlookers), Faria e Sousa remarks on the sounds of the word itself, the "consonātes que eligiò el P. para descrivir un monstruo grāde de cuerpo, i cargado de semblante" (consonants that the Poet chose to describe a monster, huge of body and heavy of countenance, col. 515). The *ura* of *figura*, phonetically, "infunde malācolia . . . porque la *ur*, es triste diccion, que no en vano cupo en fuerte al nōbre de Saturno, patrō de los tristes" (inspires melancholy because *ur* is a sad sound, which not by accident appears in the name of Saturn, god of the sad, col. 515). In this analysis, onomatopoeia infixes melancholy into the structure of Camões's words. Faria e Sousa then announces that Adamastor is the rhetorical figure of *parascreve*, also known as *praeparatio*, the "dissimulated preparation of a thought which is to become known/revealed" (Lausberg 247). The giant is thus an interpretive key to something else, an enigma that will only be revealed through hermeneutic labor. The critic continues the rhetori-cal vein of his analysis by remarking on the correlation between Adamas-tor's gigantic, disproportionate stature, his "vozes agigantadas" (gigantic words, col. 517), and his monstrosity. Rhetorically, such a correlation is known as decorum, or the appropriate relation between form, purpose, and discourse.[58] Faria e Sousa ascribes to Camões a judicious use of poetic *mesura*, absent in Virgil, when the poet calls Adamastor the second Colos-sus of Rhodes:

El P . . . aborreció siempre las fabulas, por los hiperboles desmesurados . . . Descrive, pues, una cosa tan grande como aquel Promontorio, i dandole forma humana monstruosa, no solo por miembros, sino por grandeza se

> contenta con hazerle segundo al Colosso . . . al contrario de Virgilio, que
> descriviendo un Gigante . . . le haze . . . diziendo que llegava a las estrellas.
> (Cols. 518–19)

> the Poet . . . always abhorred fictions marred by unmeasured hyperbole . . .
> He describes . . . something as large as that promontory, and giving it a
> human, monstrous form, not only in its members but also in its greatness,
> is content with making it the second Colossus . . . [this is] contrary to
> Virgil, who in describing a giant . . . does so without restraint by saying that
> it reached the stars.

As the embodiment of Muhammad and "toda la Morisma" (all Moorishness, col. 573), this demonized, infernal, monstrous, and rhetorically deco-
rous body contravenes Portuguese *navegación,* a word in Faria e Sousa's pen
that means not only nautical science but Portuguese itinerancy through
the collective movement of ships as a coherent and sustained exercise
of Christian evangelism. Adamastor realizes his danger by mobilizing a
"Moorish navigation," the inimical, nautical practice that imbues Moors
with a cartographic capacity in that they are equally capable of traveling
across water and plotting and conquering parcels of space into which they
will write their infernal belief.

The cartographic power Adamastor darkly wields relies primarily on his
body that is partitioned and dispersed (but not disempowered) throughout the globe, a kind of anatomization that recalls the giant's physiological and melancholic body. This stretching of the partitioned body across
the space of the world mirrors the ancient Roman imperialist practice of
using the body as the organizing figure in designing cities, with the partitions or grid of the city corresponding to individual body parts.[59] The
key to the monster's exegesis, then, is his corporeality. The head of Africa
as a manifest danger to the pure and uncontaminated presence of the
verbum dei across the globe appears as a monstrously dispersed and con-
cealed body in the commentary on Adamastor's monstrous limbs:

> la gente Mahometana . . . possee . . . grandissimos miembros de todas las
> partes del mundo a la sazon descubiertas, no solo en toda la Africa, i en las
> dos Asias, sinò que en Europa posseyeron mucho . . . (Col. 541)

the Muhammadan people possess . . . extremely large members in all parts
of the world which may, in turn, each be discovered, not only in all of Africa
and in the two Asias, but also in Europe . . .

Faria e Sousa then explains Gama's use of the word *monster:*

> [L]e llama monstruo el Gama a este Gigāte. Esso cōviene mucho a Mahoma
> . . . de que tocava en mōstruosidad lo grande de su cabeça, como porque
> instituyô una seta mōstruosissima, tāto por su deformidad, como por cōs-
> tar de creencias contrarias, como tomada de Legisladores diferētes; i por
> esso mismo le llamā mōstruo todos los Autores Catolicos. (Col. 543)

> Gama calls this giant a monster. This is fitting for Muhammad . . . whose
> large head verged on monstrosity, as did his instituting a most monstrous
> sect, monstrous for its deformity, for its including contradictory beliefs, for
> being patched together from different authorities. That is why all Catholic
> writers call him a monster.

Adamastor's brand of monstrosity is a symbolic extension of a corporeality that Faria e Sousa likens to Jayán, a synonym for "giant."[60] Indeed,
Adamastor's very name contains within it a genealogy of monstrosity.[61]
Adamastor's limbs stretch to the four corners of the globe in a totalizing
attitude and touch all points of the *orbis terrarum.* Since, as Faria e Sousa
explains, a monster is "aquello que en la forma de su genero es despro-
porcionada, irregular, o sin medida" (that which, in its characteristic shape,
is disproportionate, irregular, or without measure, col. 535), Adamastor's
limbs enable him to act as a diabolical mapmaker because he insidiously
reaches the ends of the earth and emplots the coordinates of his sacrilege
across the globe. His body parts throw the spiritual cosmos out of order.
They are a deforming presence across the world's spaces and obstruct
the cosmic harmony that is negotiated by the gods and instantiated by
Portuguese imperialist action in every canto of the poem. Faria e Sousa's
Adamastor, therefore, suggests the mutability of the geographic body and
the imperative of imperial travelers and conquerors to delimit that body.
Camões, in ignoring the history of Portuguese colonization in the centur-
ies preceding his poem, returns Africa to a purely ideological existence,

a tabula rasa ripe for colonization. Faria e Sousa realizes this and con-
scripts this African blankness for the purposes of his allegorical reading.
As a body that takes on various shapes, Adamastor represents Africans
while also absenting them from the poem.

Adamastor, Muhammad, or Satan the imperialist rises up in Faria e
Sousa's analysis harboring an acquisitional avarice, an "ambicion de tierra,
i mas tierra" (ambition for land, and more land, col. 545), a desire that lies
at the heart of any imperialist enterprise. Adamastor is a monster of unenlightened earthiness, and his telluric metamorphosis is an appropriate
punishment for the false prophet blind to the sea of grace. In the explanation of Adamastor's transformation we hear something of a Dantesque
contrapasso:

> dize el Gigante que fue convertido en aquella tierra: i esto es, que por la
> providencia divina, tiene para los malos el castigo muy conforme a la culpa
> (de cuyo exemplo estan llenas las historias divinas, i profanas) no amando
> el Moro, sino tierra, i mas tierra, segun provamos arriba, fuè convertido en
> ella: i cūpliose la Filosofia de amor, que es transformar el amante en la cosa
> amada: i esso singularmente amo Mahoma: porque todas sus astucias no
> atēdieron màs de a hazerse poderoso terrenamente; i por esso fuè conver-
> tido en tierra hedionda. (Cols. 558–59)

> The Giant says that he was converted into that land, that is, that divine prov-
> idence reserves for the wicked a punishment in keeping with the crime
> (sacred and profane histories are full of such stories); in the Moor's loving
> only land and more land, as we demonstrated above, he was converted into
> it, and in this the philosophy of love is fulfilled which says that the lover is
> transformed into the beloved. This is what Muhammad singularly loved,
> because all of his skill was directed solely to making himself more power-
> ful in terrestrial terms, and for that reason was converted into this cursed
> land . . .[62]

This observation appears in the context of a larger argument in which
Muhammad's predilection for land accompanies the rejection of water as
sacred. Adamastor's desire for Thetis is sacrilegious because in her he does
not glimpse a power higher than himself. There is a warning here against

THE MONSTER OF MELANCHOLY

the dangers of improvident desire and misdirected spiritual questing. For Faria e Sousa, only Christianity allows for an understanding of water as sacred, and thus Portuguese *navegación* conflates sacramental water and imperial expansion.

For Faria e Sousa, Adamastor and monsters relate to his own exegetical enterprise. At the outset of his comments on the episode he writes:

> Pondrème aqui a componer una monstruosa nota de monstruos, para que me tēgan por monstro de erudicion? Hagalo quien tuviere essa codicia, que yo con actos vio[l]entos no quiero mostrarme ciente . . . (Col. 535)

> Shall I set myself to composing a monstrous note on monsters here, so that my readers will take me for a monster of erudition? Let whoever might wish to understand it in this way do so, because I do not wish to show myself knowledgeable by violent acts . . .

The monster and the monstrous may turn the critic into a monster, as Faria e Sousa humorously suggests but in doing so acknowledges an inbuilt reciprocity between monsters and exegesis. Perhaps not a little disingenuously does Faria e Sousa disavow an overly ambitious erudition as a "violent act," only then to posit an apologia of monsters, backed by numerous *auctoritates,* that embraces the four corners of Camões's poem in metonymic efficiency. Faria e Sousa stands as one of Camões's most influential mythographers because he establishes *Os Lusíadas* itself as a mythos, a decisive, foundational moment in the Iberian cultural archive. Within the critic's "alegoría líquida" (liquid allegory), Adamastor functions as an appeal to the pleasure of reading: "Con aver pintado un monstruo fiero, fabrica en el un caso apetecible al gusto del leer" (having depicted a fearsome monster, [Camões] creates with him an appealing case for the pleasure of reading, col. 580).[63] The complex hermeneutic dimension of Adamastor is perhaps one of the greatest discoveries recorded by the critic.

❧ ❧

Melancholy in the maritime world, as Ulrich Kinzel suggests, is an oceanic dislocation of the self (37). It is also an experience of alienation, and perhaps that is why Adamastor is so unsettling, so disturbing to Camões's travelers as they make their way east. The startling appearance of Adamastor in the middle of this journey marks a moment of mythmaking that remains vital to this day. In the literatures and intellectual culture of South Africa, Adamastor lives on in critical debates and in the memories of a society once divided by apartheid; he has surfaced in André Brink's novel *The First Life of Adamastor,* and in the painting by Cyril Coetzee based on Brink's novel that now hangs in the Cullen Library of the University of the Witwatersrand.[64] However we choose to interpret Adamaster, within whatever cultural or historical moment, Camões's giant remains one of the poet's most strident calls to the interpretive endeavor, to an awareness of human connectivity through time that any myth promotes. By reading Adamastor as a melancholic and as a dark reflection of the expansionist subject that travels the seas of the world, we are able to appreciate the specter's link to the classical world at the same time as we are able to glimpse something new, something different that exceeds the Renaissance practice of *imitatio.* Like the turbulent currents of water that meet and clash at the Cape of Good Hope, Adamastor's fearful voice disturbs his hearers because it brings together, dissonantly, strands of time. His voice is at once alive and dead, a ghost of the past that speaks in the present of the future. Adamastor, it seems, will never rest, will never find calm. He will always provoke. Perhaps that is why he laments so fiercely, locked in his storm-tossed prison at the end of the world.

Notes

INTRODUCTION

1. For a study of the capture of Ceuta and its early years of Portuguese occupation and rule, see Livermore, "On the Conquest of Ceuta," and Russell, *Prince Henry,* chapters 2 and 3.

2. On the possible chivalric motives for the capture of Ceuta, see Goodman, chapter 5. Goodman argues for the central role of João I's queen, Filipa of Lancaster, in the formulation of such motives.

3. Beginning in the eleventh century, Spain's incursions into North Africa for political and mercantile gain also prolonged the impulses of *reconquista,* according to García-Arenal and Bunes (22–24).

4. Emily C. Bartels, also writing on the culture of Renaissance England, notes that "Renaissance representations of the Moor were vague, varied, inconsistent, and contradictory" ("Making More of the Moor" 434). The Moor is a boundary marker of shifting signification.

5. Of Zurara's chronicles, only the *Crónica de Guiné* has been translated in its entirety into English; see Beazley and Prestage. Extracts in English from Zurara's other texts can be found in the anthologies by Prestage and Miall, though Miall's collection must be treated with caution because the English translations are based not on the original Portuguese texts but on a French translation. Lomax and Oakley provide English translations of selected parts of the chronicles of Fernão Lopes. Pedro de Meneses was the first captain-governor of Ceuta (see Russell, *Prince Henry* 59–60), and Zurara's chronicle of him details the period between the capture of Ceuta in 1415 to Pedro's death in 1437. Pedro's son was Duarte de Meneses and a governor of Alácer-Ceguer; Zurara's chronicle of his rule extends the history of Portuguese presence in Africa to 1464. The chronicles of the Meneses are only of secondary interest to this study because they deal primarily with the histories of the two colonies in northern Africa, especially their military

histories, and less with the initial Portuguese encounters with Africa. For the printing history of Zurara's chronicles, see Dinis 171–254. A decade after Zurara completed *Ceuta,* the Italian scholar Mateus de Pisano, tutor to Afonso V, produced a condensation in Latin of Zurara's chronicle titled *De Bello Septensi* in order for knowledge of the expedition to be more widely disseminated abroad (Rogers, *The Travels* 69). This Latin text, also given the Portuguese title *Livro da guerra de Ceuta* (Book of the Ceuta War) in the eighteenth-century collection in which it is printed, appears to be the only surviving work of Pisano (for a Portuguese translation of Pisano's text, see Pinto). Serra, the editor of this collection, speculates that Pisano was the son of Christine de Pisan (3–4).

6. Hess studies the Ottoman imperial enterprises that were contemporaneous with Portugal's in the fifteenth and sixteenth centuries. Hess notes that "[t]he historical importance . . . of this simultaneity is not that Ottoman imperialism caused Portuguese expansion but that the Indian Ocean contact brought together the most militant representatives of the two cultures" ("The Evolution of the Ottoman Seaborne Empire" 1915).

7. For English translations of some of these narratives, see Boxer, *Tragic History;* also see Blackmore, *Manifest Perdition.*

8. For some case studies that seek to "unsettle old simplifications about the political, social, and economic character" of Portuguese empire, see Curto, "Portuguese Imperial and Colonial Culture."

9. Of note here is the Portuguese/Castilian rivalry during the early years of expansion: "The nationalistic element was a crucial addition to the religious identity because since the late Middle Ages the Portuguese did not simply define themselves as Christians against Moors or, secondarily, as missionaries amongst the blacks whom they enslaved; they were also, within Christianity, Portuguese as opposed to Castilians. In fact the explorations of the fifteenth century gave expression to the idea of a separate providential history against the Castilian threat of a Spanish Christian empire that would include the whole of the Iberian Peninsula once lost to the Moors" (Rubiés, *Travel and Ethnology* 177n29).

10. Washburn also studies other terms related to discovery, such as "continent," "terra firma," and "Indies."

11. "A concrete example which shows there was already some knowledge [of Africa] is the melancholy matter of da Gama's contacts with Muslims in east Africa. Pero da Covilham found that the east African coast as far south as Sofala was Islamic, and that Muslim traders linked these areas with the Muslim heartland further north, and indeed with other areas all over the Indian Ocean. The first Muslim ruler da Gama met was the sultan of Mozambique Island. Immediately age-old prejudice appeared on both sides, fuelled by remembrances of the Crusades, endemic warfare for decades in north Africa, and the Portuguese reconquest of their homeland from Muslims. When they met Muslims, the Portuguese

knew exactly what they thought: they hated them and were hated in return. This certainly was not a new and unfamiliar world" (Pearson 147).

12. In terms of scholarly work on Africa during the Renaissance, Bartels questions the model that postcolonial studies assumes as underlying its own practice by arguing that "[postcolonial critiques] continue . . . to recreate the history of silenced voices through only one model of cultural exchange: one in which European domination is both the motivating force and the inevitable outcome" ("*Othello* and Africa" 46).

13. Mills, it should be noted, argues that it is possible to conceive of the kind of discourse produced by empire as "colonial" even if there is no explicit presence of colonies as part of that discourse: "[c]olonial discourse does not . . . simply refer to a body of texts with similar subject-matter, but rather refers to a set of practices and rules which produced those texts and the methodological organisation of the thinking underlying those texts" (107).

1. ENCOUNTERING THE AFRICAN

1. For historical summaries of Portugal in Africa during this time, see Boxer, *Portuguese Seaborne Empire* (chapter 1), Brooks (chapters 7–9), the relevant chapters of Diffie and Winius, Duffy (chapter 1), Newitt, *Portuguese Overseas Expansion* (chapters 1 and 2), Parry (chapter 8), Penrose (chapter 3), Russell-Wood (chapter 1), Santos, *Viagens de exploração*, Thornton, "The Portuguese in Africa," or van Wyk Smith, "Introduction." For Portuguese presidios in North Africa, see Coates 56–64. For a recent overview that includes the Americas, see Hart, chapter 2. Valladares considers Portuguese expansion in the modern historiography of Atlantic studies. For early cartography on Africa, see La Roncière and Relaño.

2. See Snowden's chapter 1 for a discussion of the several terms used by Greco-Roman writers to describe Ethiopians and Africans in general and the physical attributes indexed by this vocabulary. Throughout the Middle Ages and into the early-modern period "Ethiopia" referred to a much larger and imprecise geographic space than its modern counterpart, much like "India." Ethiopia could designate vast stretches of East African land, the Indian Ocean, Asia, or the southern regions of the world. Relaño notes that Ethiopia was "conceived of in the late Middle Ages as a sort of sociological space signifying all territories beyond the Islamic world. It was the land south of the Sahara and Egypt. . . . More than a real space, it was a symbolical one where legends like that of Prester John were the only means at hand to organize and attain geographical knowledge" (58).

3. Throughout the Middle Ages and even into the early decades of the fifteenth century following the Portuguese capture of Ceuta, Isidoro remained an authority on Africa. A good example of this authority appears in the Portuguese/Castilian dispute regarding rights to the Canary Islands in the 1430s. Alfonso de

Cartagena, bishop of Burgos, drafted a series of *Allegationes* (Allegations) in 1435 in defense of Castile's right to the islands. The document registers prevalent ideas about Africa and Isidoro's "indisputable authority" on the topic. Among these ideas is the division of Mauritania into two provinces (pace classical geographers), Caesariense and Tingitania; the Canaries are part of this latter province, which, according to the bishop, belongs to Spain. For the Latin text of the *Allegationes* and a translation into Portuguese, see documents 281 and 282 in Marques, *Descobrimentos portugueses.*

4. In another book, Harvey discusses the "insidious ideological bias inherent in this use of [*morisco*]" (*Muslims in Spain* 4). For a summary of the *mouro* as *muçulmano* from the early Middle Ages through the initial centuries of overseas expansion from a Portuguese perspective, see Thomaz, "Muçulmanos." Barletta, in a study of the literature of the *moriscos* in Spain, notes that *morisco* was the common early-modern term for the Muslims of Spain before their expulsion in 1492 (ix).

5. I cite Scott's translation of the *Partidas*. "Moor" and "Saracen" in Alfonso's laws are synonymous: "*Sarracenus* en latín tanto quiere decir en romance como moro: et tomaron este nombre de Sarra que fue muger libre de Abraham" (*Sarracenus*, in Latin, means Moor in the vernacular, and this name is derived from Sarah, the free wife of Abraham, 5:1438). One glimpses here the conflation of Moor and Saracen that reappears two centuries later in the papal bulls authorizing Portuguese appropriation of African lands and resources, including its inhabitants.

6. *Partida* 6, title 7, law 7, for example, stipulates that a son can be disinherited if he becomes a Moor.

7. "And the Lord said . . . 'And now you are cursed from the ground . . . If any one slays Cain, vengeance shall be taken on him sevenfold.' And the Lord put a mark on Cain, lest any who came upon him should kill him" (Genesis 4:10–11, 15).

8. See the seventh *Partida* for these regulations, and Liu's analysis of them in the context of religious mixing and poetry in chapter 5 of his *Medieval Joke Poetry.*

9. I use Mettmann's numbering of the CSM.

10. For the CEM that incorporate same-sex imagery and innuendo, see Blackmore, "Poets of Sodom." Gregory S. Hutcheson's analysis of the sodomitic Moor as a product of historiographic discourse in medieval Spain provides an interesting case study in the politics of sodomy as impinging on Moorishness.

11. The numbers of the *cantigas* follow Lapa's edition.

12. See Pedro's *Livro de linhagens* 204–11.

13. The traditional view of Reconquest presumes a clear distinction between Christian (re)conquerors and Moorish infidels. The realities of medieval Iberia, however, were quite different and not as clean as this mainstay of historiographic

thought would suppose, because the separation of Christian and Moorish elements in the cultures of Iberia was difficult. For further analysis of this topic in a slightly later time period, see the relevant portions of Fuchs, *Mimesis and Empire*.

14. See documents 286, 287, and 288 in Marques, *Descobrimentos portugueses* 352–65. In an opinion written ca. 1433, Prince João states: "Ajnda guerra dos mouros nõ somos çertos se he serujço de deus; por que eu nõ vy nem ouuy que noso senhor nem algum dos seus apostolos nem doctores da Jgreja mandassem que guerreasem jnfieis mas antes per pregação e mjlagres os mandou conuerter" (We are yet unsure if the war on the Moors is in God's service, for I have not heard or read that Our Lord, or any of his apostles or doctors of the holy church, mandate that we should enter into battle with the infidels. Rather, preaching and miracles should be the manner of their conversion, Marques, *Descobrimentos portugueses* 354). This document is also reproduced in *Livro dos conselhos de El-Rei D. Duarte* 43–49. Prince Henry's response to this question is definitive: "E da guerra dos mouros ser serujço de deus nõ ha que duujdar" (And the war on the Moors as a service to God is beyond doubt, Marques 361).

15. On the various understandings and metaphors of "India" and the "East" in early modern colonialism, see Raman, who dedicates a chapter of his book to Camões and *Os Lusíadas*.

16. See Cass for a summary of criticism on Saidian Orientalism.

17. Irwin reconfirms this gap by leaving Portugal out altogether in his rebuttal of Said, which he considers to be a work of "malignant charlatanry" (4), a charge based in part on Said's narrow selection of sources.

18. Strandes notes that "India" embraced southern Arabia, Ethiopia, East Africa, and the East Indies, but that it would be more accurate to say that "India" meant the lands that produced spices, aromatics, and precious stones (3).

19. In the sixteenth century, João de Barros follows Zurara's partitioning of Africa by identifying the Senegal River (and the Sahara generally) as the dividing line between the lighter-skinned Arabic Moors and the first "negros da Guiné" (blacks of Guinea) or the *jalofos* (Wolofs). In writing of this region, Barros refers to the Torrid Zone: "Ora onde o Infante manda descobrir, é já dentro no fervor do sol, que de brancos que os homens são, se lá fôr algum de nós, ficará (se escapar) tam negro como são os guinéus, vezinhos a esta quentura" (Now where the Prince [Henry] has ordered expeditions of discovery is so subjected to the intensity of the sun, that however white a man might be, if any of us were to go there, he would become [if he indeed is able to escape] as black as Guineans, who are neighbors to this heat, *Ásia* 24–25). The comment echoes commonly held beliefs about geohumoralism or the climatologically influenced body, and proposes that the body may be changed in the course of one lifetime, a slight recasting of the geohumoral tenet that physical traits were shaped by environmental factors over time and through the generations.

20. For Zurara's use of the historiography of Alfonso X, also see Carvalho, *Estudos* 166–67, 227–39, and Fonseca, "A Crónica de Guiné" 155.

21. For a transcription of this Latin document and further comments on the Portuguese understanding of India, see Randles, "Notes."

22. See Bourdon 47n1 for a summary of this hypothesis.

23. Although "Europe" is a standard term in debates on Orientalism, it should be noted that it is uncommonly used as a Western qualifier for "us" in the Portuguese writings studied here. Zurara, for instance, does not use the term; when the chronicler refers to a collectivity against which the inhabitants of Africa are compared, it is usually *cristãos* (Christians) or, less frequently, Portugal.

24. Curto makes his observations in the context of the work of Charles Boxer on sixteenth- and seventeenth-century Portuguese historiography. In an essay published in 1948 ("Three Historians"), thirty years before the appearance of *Orientalism*, Boxer makes the case for João de Barros as a "pioneer Orientalist" (18).

25. Américo Castro proposed a peaceful model of *convivencia* in *España en su historia*, one that has been revised by historians such as David Nirenberg in *Communities of Violence*, who advocates for a conflictual, violent tenor of "living together" in the Spanish Middle Ages.

26. See chapter 6 of *Medieval Identity Machines*.

27. Moors as one kind of African would thus be "agents of empire," in McClintock's expression (5).

28. Werner Sollors (446–47n50) offers further etymological documentation and finds earlier uses of the word that adumbrate modern use predating those cited by Hannaford.

29. Sollors notes the "importance of 'conversos' for the rise of the concept of 'race'" (447n55).

30. See chapters 16, 17, and 30.

31. In a comment on Castilian *negro* (black), Casares lists several groups of people who might fall under this designation in early-modern Spain and notes that there were internal differences in "black" Africa as well as in "white" Europe (248).

32. For a study of sexual/nuptial unions between Portuguese and Africans, see Elbl.

33. Horta's study documents the many kinds of Africans reported in Zurara's chronicle and in subsequent, mostly Portuguese texts, and provides a chart of the descriptions of the physical attributes of Africans that are culled from numerous sources.

34. Unlike Spanish *guineo*, which denotes any person of black skin, including Ethiopians (Grubb 72), Portuguese *guinéu* is generally restricted to western Africa as opposed to the *etíope* (Ethiopian). Zurara's irregular use of *mouro* as a label applicable to Africans outside of Mauritania contrasts with later, early-modern

Spanish historiography in which Moors are defined by where they reside (Bunes Ibarra 111).

35. I cite Kimble's translation.

36. For other comments on *lançados,* see Haydara 34–36 and Voigt.

37. In the sixteenth century, al-Hasan ibn Muhammad al-Wazzan, the Granadan Moor who converted to Christianity and became known as Leo Africanus, published his *Della descrittione dell'Africa* (Description of Africa) in volume 1 of Ramusio's collection of travel narratives which appeared in 1550. Here, too, Africa is divided into regions that are defined, in part, by the skin color of inhabitants. Two decades after Leo's book, Luis del Mármol Carvajal published the *Descripción General de África* (General Description of Africa) in 1573, one year after *Os Lusíadas*. Mármol Carvajal's book was the only global study of the practitioners of Islam (Bunes Ibarra 3); its mapping of Islam onto Africa predates the kinds of arguments to be made by Faria e Sousa (see chapter 3, below). For the influence of Leo Africanus and the Portuguese chronicler Damião de Góis on Mármol Carvajal, see Bunes Ibarra 9–10. On Leo Africanus, see Davis, *Trickster Travels*.

38. The idea of uninhabitable regions of the globe such as the Torrid Zone is formulated in Macrobius's climatic map, where the sphere is divided into climatic zones "whose placements determine the habitable and uninhabitable regions" (Jacob 296). Fonseca's correlation between bodies and space that we noted above would, in the case of the Torrid Zone, mean that since no bodies inhabited it, it was a non-space or an aspatial swath across Africa. The expeditions recorded by Zurara quickly disproved the legend of an uninhabitable Torrid Zone.

2. Expansion and the Contours of Africa

1. Perhaps the most extensive bibliography of mainly Portuguese primary sources on early-modern Africa (fifteenth to seventeenth centuries) is the one compiled by Horta ("O Africano"). This list is arranged according to geographic region. Also see Winius, "Bibliographical Essay." Newitt (*East Africa*) presents a selection of translations into English of documents relating to the Portuguese presence on the eastern littoral.

2. There are also collections of bureaucratic documents from this time relating to the details of imperial administration, such as trading rights, duties levied on imported goods, or royal grants and privileges. For these, consult the volumes compiled by Brásio, and Marques, *Descobrimentos portugueses*.

3. "Espanha" (Spain) in the fifteenth and sixteenth centuries was often synonymous with "Iberia," which is the sense of the word here.

4. Arguim was the first European slave station in Africa.

5. For an analysis of two treatises on Guinea from the late-sixteenth and early-seventeenth centuries, see Saive.

6. See Branche 32–48.

7. Barreto similarly finds in Zurara the first historiographic foundations for an official imperialist ideology that construes the discoveries as a civilizing mission (108–9).

8. Of note here is an observation made by António Martins, secretary to D. João I and representative at the Council of Constanza (1415): "O nome do infiel Maomé foi apagado e retirado e Cristo é hoje aí [em Ceuta] honrado e adorado . . . pela tomada da cidade, poderosa por terra e mar, porto e chave de toda a África, o Altíssimo abriu o caminho ao povo cristão para que a partir daí prossigam na salvação das suas almas realizando venturosas operações contra os sarracenos" (The name of the infidel Muhammad was extinguished and removed and Christ today is revered and worshipped [in Ceuta] . . . with the seizure of this city that wields power both on land and sea and is the port and key to all of Africa, the One Most High opened the way to Christians so that, following in Ceuta's wake, they may continue the fortuitous work of saving their souls by fighting the Saracens; quoted in Horta, "A imagem do Africano" 50).

9. See, for example, chapter 138 of Pina's chronicle. Afonso V (1438–81), because of his interest in maintaining Portugal's interest in Africa, came to be known as "o Africano" (the African).

10. João II was the first to add "Senhor de Guiné" to the crown's title. Manuel I, under whose orders Vasco da Gama made his voyages to India, expands the title to "Senhor da Navegação, Conquista, e Comércio da Etiópia, Arábia, Pérsia, e Índia" (Lord of the Navigation, Conquest, and Commerce of Ethiopia, Arabia, Persia, and India).

11. For a summary of these conflicts, see Davenport 9–12.

12. Boxer notes that "Indies" was a shifting term that often included Ethiopia and East Africa, as well as the known parts of Asia (*Portuguese Seaborne Empire* 19).

13. I cite Davenport's Latin text and translation.

14. Lahon states that Zurara's *Crónica dos feitos de Guiné* was sent to Rome as a Portuguese strategy in obtaining the *Romanus Pontifex* (*Os negros* 98n15).

15. See Machado's etymological study (227–37) for further comments and textual attestations; also see Domingues (215–16).

16. The conquest of Lisbon in 1147 by Alfonso Henriques, first king of Portugal, traditionally marks the final, decisive action of Reconquest in Portugal, much as the fall of Granada in 1492 does for Spain. Thus Reconquest and the formation of the nation of Portugal are intertwined. See Marques, *History of Portugal* 41–45, 76–77, and Read 152–62.

17. Cadamosto's account first appeared in print in 1507 in Montalboddo's *Paesi nouamente retrovati & Novo mondo da Alberico Vesputio Florentino intitulato,* and then again in Giovanni Battista Ramusio's famous collection of travel narratives, *Navigationi et viaggi* (1550).

18. Quotations of Cadamosto's Italian are from the Italian-Portuguese edition of his text, *Viagens*.

19. The other ships and their captains were the *São Gabriel* (Vasco da Gama), the *Bérrio* (Nicolau Coelho), and a supply vessel (Gonçalo Nunes) that did not reach India. On the doubts surrounding the authorship of the *Relação*, see Subrahmanyam 80–83.

20. Such practical texts do exist in the world of nautical writing—they are known as *regimentos* or sailing instructions. *Regimentos* do not exhibit the same engagement with narrative episodes as the texts being studied here. For an example of *regimentos* (with English translations) and other documents on the materialities of expansionist voyages, see *Documentos sobre os portugueses em Moçambique*. Other information about life on board expansionist ships may be found in Boxer, *Tragic History of the Sea*, Pérez-Mallaína, and Smith.

21. Also see Madureira's discussion for reading the nautical charts of Arab pilot Ahmad Ibn-Mādjid against the Portuguese *roteiros*.

22. Translations of Velho's text are mine. A full English translation by E. G. Ravenstein was published by the Hakluyt Society in 1898; part of that translation is reprinted in Ley 3–38.

23. The *padrões* or pillars were carried on board ships and were implanted on foreign soil both as a marker of Portuguese passage and as a symbolic possession of lands.

24. The fourth and fifth *Décadas* were published posthumously. Barros's successor, Diogo do Couto (1542–1616) endeavored to continue the *Décadas,* but only his fourth, fifth, and seventh *Décadas* were published.

25. According to the time line Barros sets out for his history in chapter 1 of the first *Década da Ásia, África* begins with the capture of Ceuta (13).

26. In the obedience oration delivered to Pope Innocent VIII in 1485 by Vasco Fernandes on behalf of João II of Portugal (reigned 1481–95 and oversaw the consolidation of the Guinea trade), "[the kings of Lusitania] never considered as foreign anything that pertains either to the defense or to the propagation of the Christian religion" (Rogers, *The Obedience of a King of Portugal* 42).

27. The panegyric (*panegírico*) was a favored genre among Renaissance humanists (Boxer, *João de Barros* 63) and allowed the writer to display classical learning.

28. "vieram a estes Regnos muitos homẽs letrados, & curiosos . . . cõ tenção de ir ver estas terras . . . ou pera tambẽ ajudarẽ a descobrir outras, cõ sperança do proueito que se lhes disso podia seguir" (many curious and learned men came to these realms, with the intention of traveling to see these lands . . . or also, to help in their discovery, with hopes of the benefits to be derived from these trips . . . , 11).

29. "'Africa' has no native source and so did not exist before its definition as an other in relation to Europe and Asia" (Miller 13).

30. Miller also posits an acephalic vision of Africa: "Africanist discourse in the West is one in which the head, the voice—the logos, if you will—is missing" (27). Camões imaginatively gives the continent a head and a voice in the figure of Adamastor by construing him as the speaking culmination of the African landmass, an idea explored in chapter 3.

31. All English translations of *Os Lusíadas* are from Bacon. Portuguese citations are from Ramos.

32. Islam is the presence that makes Gama's voyage not one of discovery of a new world but of a preexisting competitor empire, according to Jacqueline Kaye's argument: "What we see in *The Lusiads* is da Gama's discovery not of a new world of unknown territories but of the precedence of Islam everywhere" (67). On the coexistence of the Portuguese and Ottoman maritime empires in the Indian Ocean, see Hess, "The Evolution."

33. The bibliography on this topic is considerable. For explanations of the interior wits and the workings of faculty psychology, begin with Babb (chapter 1), Burke (chapter 1), Carruthers (47–60), Folger (27–33), and Harvey (*Inward Wits*).

34. Juan Luis Vives (1492–1540) also summarizes this process in his *Tratado del alma* (1170–72) in the *Obras completas*. For further explanation of the workings of the *imaginatio*, see Carruthers 51–54.

35. Alfonso's discussion of the interior wits is in the second *Partida*, title 13, laws 6–11. For Alfonso, imagination has greater power than phantasy because the imagination causes the mind to portray matters relating to past, present, and future.

36. Vaughan and Vaughan note that the climatic explanation of the African's— and here, Ethiopian's—pigmentation was commonplace in Europe in the fifteenth and sixteenth centuries (23).

37. Geohumoral descriptions of non-European natives will survive into the sixteenth century and the conquest of the Americas. In 1574 Juan López de Velasco describes the physical traits of American indigenes according to the heat and characteristics of the land. But unlike Alfonso's and Zurara's sun-scorched Ethiopians, López de Velasco's natives of the Equator and highlands of Quito exhibit varying hues of whiteness, distinct from the "negro atezados" (sunburned blacks) of the Cape of Good Hope (14; also see 20). This challenges the idea that proximity to the sun causes black skin. For further comments, see Floyd-Wilson 78–86.

38. In a discussion of the spirits as adversely affected by the body's humors, Burke notes that "[w]ithin the body once the vital spirit is corrupted the correct functioning of the faculties of the sensitive soul in concert with those of the higher powers is no longer possible" (60–61). The physician Galen, one of the main proponents of humoral physiology, also proposed "bodily sources of cognitive error" (Clark 48), which may include the vital spirits.

3. THE MONSTER OF MELANCHOLY

1. For José Benoliel, the episode runs to stanza 70; Benoliel gives no reason for extending the limits of the episode beyond stanza 60. To my knowledge, Benoliel is the only scholar to argue for a possible Arabic source of the Adamastor episode, which he finds in the "Conto do Pescador" (Fisherman's story) of the *Thousand and One Nights* (the Bible and Greek mythology are the other sources identified by Benoliel). Castro rejects this hypothesis (*O episódio do Adamastor* 6n6); Ramalho classifies Benoliel's suggestion as "fantastic" (11n1) and that one possible source of Adamastor's name is the Hebrew word *Adamah*, "earth" ("Sobre o nome de Adamastor" 29). We should be cautious, however, to dismiss too quickly the possibility of cross-fertilization of Hebrew and Arabic literature into Portuguese texts of the Renaissance (and earlier), given the presence of Hebrew and Arabic scholars and learning in the Portuguese court and in the science of navigation.

2. Voltaire's pronouncement was influential because he was the sole authority on Camões in England for most of the eighteenth century, until the appearance of William Julius Mickle's translation with accompanying introductory essay in 1776 (Williams, "Introduction" 250). Mickle vigorously criticized Voltaire's comments on Camões's poem. For this polemic, see Williams, "Introduction" 251–54, and Pierce, "The Place of Mythology" 100–105; for a general study of the neoclassical criticsm of *Os Lusíadas*, see Willis. Voltaire also criticized Spanish epic; Elizabeth R. Davis argues that Voltaire's judgments "were influential in swerving the European epic canon away from Spanish epic" (8). The same would hold true for Portuguese epic.

3. In Adamastor's fearful form as the protector of secrets we might glimpse a possibility of the epic uncanny as Elizabeth J. Bellamy argues for it: "Freud, quoting Schelling, offers the *Unheimliche* as '*the name for everything that ought to have remained . . . secret and hidden but has come to light*' . . . The supernatural spirit of Virgil's Polydorus, staining the ground with his own gore, *ought* to have remained buried in its obscure Thracian mound. But his ululating moans and mangled roots persist in making their ghostly returns to constitute epic history's privileged mise-en-scène of dread and ontological uncertainty" (208–9, emphasis in original). Adamastor is a terrifying return of the fabled dread surrounding the southern threshold and the secrets of nature he guards, dramatically presented by his outrage at being surpassed. Gama and his mariners may well experience a frisson of ontological uncertainty when faced with such a strange yet familiar apparition.

4. This dual nature of Adamastor's voice prompts Vieira to interpret Adamastor as two separate monsters (30). However, as I argue here, the two registers of Adamastor's discourse can be reconciled into one speaking subject through melancholy.

5. See Quint, chapter 3.

6. Jared Banks, in comments relating to historiography, notes that the Portuguese chronicles of discovery "act as master narratives which subsume all resistance within an imperialist *telos*" (3).

7. Brink continues: "That this is no fanciful postcolonial reading of the text is borne out by the way in which Camões describes the continuation of Da Gama's voyage after the unsettling encounter at the Cape: when next the Portuguese venture ashore . . . the Africans they meet on the beach are described as 'the people who owned the country here'. There is no hint of the would-be coloniser's greedy gaze in this passage (stanza 62), which confirms the impression of Adamastor as the legitimate protector of the subcontinent who has every reason to hold his territory against any threat of foreign invasion and appropriation" (45).

8. Saraiva points out that Adamastor does not belong to the circle of Olympian gods but to the giants of earth who were defeated by the gods ("Função e significado" 49). Other precedents to Adamastor include Claudiano's *Gigantomachia*, the *Officina* of Joannes Ravisius Textor, *Orlando Furioso*, and *Pantagruel*. For an inventory and discussion of these precursors, see the studies by Ramalho ("Aspectos clássicos") and Santos ("A denominação").

9. In referring to Ceuta as a place of beauty, Zurara may be thinking of the precepts set out by Cicero in the *De Officiis*, translated into Portuguese as the *Livro dos ofícios* by D. Pedro, duke of Coimbra, sometime before 1438. In this text, a chapter on the destruction of cities (chapter 23, "Que cousas se devem guardar na destroyçom das cidades" [What matters should be observed in the destruction of cities]) notes that this feat is reserved for great men (*grandes barõoes*, 49). Some pages later, a pair of chapters considers honesty and the beauty of deeds (*fremosura das obras*) or decorum, and defines decorum as that which distinguishes humans from other creatures and that which is in accordance with nature (57–59). Zurara fashions the capture of Ceuta as "natural" in an early chapter of his chronicle since it is an action allowed by the order of nature and the turning of the celestial wheels; by referring to Ceuta as the commencement of beauty, the chronicler may be fashioning the destruction of Ceuta according to Ciceronian precepts.

10. Recall that Bartolomeu Dias had successfully doubled the cape nine years before Gama's trip, in 1488.

11. The location of the Pillars of Hercules would move south as exploration progressed. In the *Códice Valentim Fernandes*, we find a reference to the legend of Hercules at Cape Non: "quando chegou a este cabo achou as correntes muy fortes que nom podia passar E pos neste cabo hũa columna em que estaua esprito em letras gregas que quem pasasse este cabo tornaria ou nom" (when [Hercules] arrived at this cape he found the currents so strong that he could not pass; and he placed a column on this cape with Greek letters on it that said whoever passed this cape would return, or not, 14).

12. See Cochran, chapters 4 and 5. Cochran builds his argument on the nineteenth-century polemic on Adamastor in José Agostinho de Macedo's attack on Camões (*Reflexões críticas*, portions of which also appear in Macedo's *Censura dos Lusíadas*). In addition to Cochran's analysis of *figura* as a confluence of figuration, discourse, and history, it should be noted that *figura* might also be understood as "map," as Ricardo Padrón notes (93) in his discussion of Hernán Cortés. A spirited response to Macedo was published by Francisco de S. Luiz in 1819, who takes Macedo to task on many of his "factual" accusations by presenting what is essentially an antipositivistic reading of Camões's text and a defense of Camões's use of sources.

13. I depart from Bacon and provide a different translation here of "esse estupendo / Corpo, certo, me tem maravilhado!" in order to remain closer to Camões's Portuguese and to emphasize the sense of wonder that Adamastor's physicality clearly occasions.

14. In my view, Cohen's essay is one of the best theoretical treatments to date of monsters and monster culture, since it accounts for monsters across the chronological spectrum of Western culture without abandoning historical specifics, and provides a number of monstrous *modi legendi*.

15. Some studies that advance these ideas are Cidade (126–29), Santos ("A denominação" 627), Pierce ("Camões' Adamastor"; "The Place of Mythology"), or Bowra (123–26). For a discussion of Adamastor and prosopopeia, see Cochran, chapter 5. António José Saraiva ("Função e significado"; "Lugar do Adamastor") argues that Adamastor is not a figure of allegory (allegory is reserved only for the Olympian gods) but of human subjectivity in the form of a "hallucination," an idea that borders on the place of Adamastor in the imagination, as I argue below. Neves concurs with Saraiva's argument and postulates that Adamastor's sphere of existence is the human, not the supernatural. Hardie (chapters 3 and 4) studies gigantomachic allegory in Virgil and the association of giants and monsters with elemental forces of nature, including storms.

16. Some of these monsters appear in other Iberian texts, such as the *Libro del infante D. Pedro*, written in Castilian by Gómez de Santisteban about the real and imagined travels of D. Pedro, brother of Prince Henry, the Navigator; see Rogers, *The Travels*. The *Book of Marco Polo* was translated into Portuguese as the *Livro de Marco Paulo* and printed by Valentim Fernandes in 1502. Mandeville was translated into Castilian as the *Libro de las maravillas del mundo*. Camões's knowledge of Pliny was probably based on the *Commentum in Plinii Naturalis Historiae* by the humanist Martinho de Figueiredo. According to Artur Anselmo, Figueiredo's commentary was "one of the most important books at the dawn of humanism in Portugal" (20). For a catalog of this kind of monster in *Os Lusíadas*, see Lima. Also see the studies by Friedman, Gil (*Monstros*), and Río Parra.

17. "[W]ell-settled myths had a life of their own, and this was difficult to

eradicate even with perceptual knowledge" (Relaño 37). Since the Portuguese exploration of Africa was almost entirely a coastal enterprise, the old legends of monsters could be maintained by pushing the monster's dwelling place inland.

18. See Burke 13–14, 65.

19. Perhaps the most famous representation of the intersections between melancholy and the sciences is Albrecht Dürer's engraving *Melencolia I*. For comments, see Klibansky, Panofsky, and Saxl 284–402, and Yates, chapter 6.

20. Overviews of the details of humoralism as it relates to melancholy may be found in Babb (chapters 1–3), Klibansky, Panofsky, and Saxl (passim), and Lyons (chapter 1). Radden provides a selection of primary texts documenting the development of the concept of melancholy over the centuries. For a brief recapitulation of theories of melancholy in the context of Camões's lyric, see Silva, *Camões* 209–28 and "The Songs of Melancholy." Earle also addresses the question of melancholy in Camões's Petrarchan lyrics.

21. The yellow of Adamastor's teeth is significant in this humoral explanation of melancholy. It is therefore not an arbitrary color choice. Letzring notes some of the changes made by English translators of Camões in the eighteenth century, among them the color of Adamastor's teeth. Some translators avoid mention of the teeth altogether, while William Julius Mickle made the teeth blue (Letzring 423). Letzring posits that "[a] possible explanation for the changes is that 'yellow teeth' is too 'low' an image for the dignity required for the epic genre . . . Yellow teeth may be repulsive, even disgusting, but they are not particularly terrifying" (ibid.). Henry Hallam, a nineteenth-century scholar, believes that "[t]he formidable Adamastor is rendered mean by particularity of description, descending even to yellow teeth" (quoted in Letzring 424). Adamstor's choleric temperament may best explain Camões's choice of yellow.

22. Camões did, however, have a direct connection with melancholy "exposition books" (to use Lyons's term) through his involvement in Garcia de Orta's *Colóquio dos simples e drogas da Índia* (1563). Camões composed an introductory poem for this book which, in its scientific treatment of simples, drugs, diseases, and cures, mentions both melancholy and choler. Boxer notes that Garcia de Orta's book brings Asiatic cholera (*cholera morbus*) to the attention of the Western world (*Two Pioneers* 17).

23. Horta ("A representação do Africano" 221–32) culls numerous descriptions of the physical attributes of Africans in texts to 1508, among which is the regular occurrence of "crespos cabelos." Other texts closer to Camões's time attest to the same link between "crespos cabelos" (or "revoltos") and blackness: João de Barros refers to the inhabitants of Good Hope (which he terms "outra fábula de perigos" [another legend of dangers, *Década da Ásia* 130]) as being "negros de cabelo revolto" (blacks with curly hair, 138); Damião de Góis describes the same inhabitants as "gente de cabelo revolto" (people with curly hair, *Crónica do felicíssimo*

rei D. Manuel 78) and as "homens pretos" (black men, 74); and Lopes de Castanheda describes Good Hope inhabitants as "gente baça" (dark people, 12). In 1563,
António Galvão writes that Good Hope is a storied locale of sorcerers and
enchanters who are "negros" (black, 63).

24. Both Portuguese and Latin versions of Aristotle's works were in circulation
in sixteenth-century Portugal. See, for example, the entries for *Os Problemas de
Aristóteles* and *Aristoteles de animalibus* in Carvalho, "A livraria" 165, 171.

25. Schiesari notes that Ficino was responsible for melancholy's "reevaluation as
a cultural value" (110). Floyd-Wilson observes that "it was the legacy of Aristotle's
Problem XXX . . . together with Marsilio Ficino's reorientation of melancholic
genius within both the pragmatics of humoral medicine and the transcendent
framework of Neoplatonism that succeeded in imbuing melancholia with a power
and agency that outstripped the other humors" (67), so that "Ficino's work may
be more important for initiating the concept that melancholy is a humor to be
cultivated" (70). Klibansky, Panofsky, and Saxl explain that "[r]eally 'outstanding'
talent, as shown in objective achievement, presupposes a double limitation of the
effects emanating from black bile . . . the amount of melancholy humour must
be great enough to raise the character above the average, but not so great as to
generate a melancholy 'all too deep', and that it must maintain an average tem-
perature, between 'too hot' and 'too cold'. Then and only then is the melancholic
not a freak but a genius" (32).

26. The idea of the melancholic genius as a spirit will reappear in Robert Burton's widely influential *The Anatomy of Melancholy*, published in 1621 just decades
after Camões's poem. Burton speaks of "those Genii, Spirits, Angels, which rule
and domineer in several places; they cause storms, thunder, lightning, earthquakes,
ruins, tempests, great winds, floods" (418), some elements of which are present in
Adamastor's meteorological turbulence and his threat to cause shipwrecks and
ruination of all kinds.

27. Although not specifically referring to lovesickness, Silva argues that the
melancholic man, "in his anxiety and agitation, often exhibits an almost pathological verbosity" ("Songs of Melancholy" 47), a fact reflected in Adamastor's
loquaciousness.

28. In a study of Luis de Góngora's *Polifemo y Galatea* (Polyphemus and Galatea,
1612), Parker remarks on the use of *pálido* to describe the Cyclops Polifemo's cave.
Polifemo is one of the Iberian heirs of Adamastor. Parker notes that the word
carried associations with death and that it is part of the first image-complex of
Góngora's poem in which darkness, night, blackness, and death are linked (61, 63).
The same associations could be posited for Adamastor with his nocturnal and
deathly abode at the cape as a netherworld of the spirit.

29. The Iberian Peninsula, and in particular Spain, functioned as one of the
ports of entry of Arabic notions of passionate love (Wack 38).

30. Braga (*História da Universidade de Coimbra* 211) lists a manuscript copy of the *Viatico* as part of the library of D. Duarte (reigned 1433–38). Braga remarks: "This book is also titled '*Breviarium Constantini, dictum Viaticum*' . . . The preference for the *Viatico* in Portugal can be explained because of the presence of Arabic learning, which also bears on philosophical inquiries; medicine was practiced by the *Mudjares* [*sic*], and their books, though written in Portuguese, were *aljamiados*, that is, written in the Arabic alphabet" (211–12). Avicenna also shows up in the libraries that Braga inventories, though it is not clear if the *Canon* is part of these holdings (there is a copy of the *Dialectica* in Duarte's library, and the Constable Pedro's library contains a simple entry "Evicenna" [232]).

31. Constantine notes: "Sometimes the cause of eros is also the contemplation of beauty. For if the soul observes a form similar to itself it goes mad, as it were, over it in order to achieve the fulfillment of its pleasure" (trans. in Wack 189).

32. Freud famously reflects on the lost or absent object as a cause of melancholy in "Mourning and Melancholia." For discussions of the Freudian formulation of melancholy and erotic love situated within the context of medieval literature and culture, see Agamben and Wells. For comments relating this loss to the lyric poetry of Camões, see Silva, "Songs of Melancholy" 40–52.

33. In a symbolic linking of earthiness, landscape, and melancholy, Lyons argues that "[t]he heart that was oppressed by gross and heavy melancholy humours was imprisoned . . . [t]here was no clear line of distinction . . . between the state of the melancholic's mind and the landscape that he inhabited or projected" (14–15). Similarly, Susan Stewart's remarks on giants as telluric and disproportionate in *The Faerie Queene* recall Adamastor's ancestral claim that "Fui dos filhos aspérrimos da Terra" (I was Earth's child, like those of ruthless might; V.51.i) as they do his corporeality: "the giant is linked to the earth in its most primitive, or natural, state . . . the gigantic presents a physical world of disorder and disproportion" (74).

34. The Italian text and translation are from Durling.

35. Klibansky, Panofsky, and Saxl, in a discussion of Aristotle's *Problemata* XXX, note that "effects of the sinister substance [black bile] . . . conjured up the idea of all that was evil and nocturnal" (15–16) and that for some classical heroes melancholy imbued them with a "nimbus of sinister sublimity" (16). As an incarnation of that which is "evil and nocturnal," Adamastor's darkness is both a sign of imminent danger at the end of the day and a symbolic darkness of Africa and its natives—a land and people blind to the true faith.

36. According to Avicenna, other afflictions caused by melancholy (in addition to insomnia) are sleepiness, amnesia, and hydrophobia (David-Peyre 194).

37. Klibansky, Panofsky, and Saxl note that an afflicted imagination can result in seeing black men (93). In stanza 36 of canto V, the stanza immediately preceding the beginning of the Adamastor episode, the episode of Fernão Veloso ends.

Veloso went ashore and was chased by a group of black men (to the bemusement of his shipmates) who shot at him with bows: "Por que, saindo nós pera tomá-lo, / Nos pudessem mandar ao reino oscuro" (As he returned, their ambush they prepare, / In hope to send us all to darkest Hell, V.36.vi–vii). There is a dramatic, transitional swing from the comic to the menacing in the expression "reino oscuro" (literally, "dark realm"). Camões clearly plays on understanding sub-Saharan Africa as a "reino oscuro"; these lines also announce the dark realm of Adamastor and the terrifying recesses of the mind.

38. The ambivalent nature of *ousadia* is apparent in canto II when, as Gama's fleet endeavors to make port in East Africa, Bacchus disguises himself as a priest and delivers false information to two Portuguese envoys in an attempt to ambush the Portuguese: "Neles *ousadamente* se subissem; / E nesta treïção determinavam / Que os de Luso de todo destruíssem" (In fury they [the Moors] might fall on them straightway. / And by this treachery they were well assured / The Portuguese to the last man to slay, II.17.iv–vi, emphasis mine).

39. See Fisher's discussion, 4–16.

40. The obstacle to expansionist daring incarnated by Adamastor may also be a symbolic representation of the Khoikhoi herders of southern Africa, according to Madureira, who are hostile and "the very negation of discovery" (54).

41. Fisher argues that "the . . . passion that has closest links in all analysis to either anger or fear [is] the passion of grief or mourning" (14). Fisher proposes melancholy as a kind of lack or negativity, the absence of high-spiritedness typical of the passions (229–30) and links this understanding to Greek medicine: "the details of the state of melancholia were closely modeled on the symptoms of malaria—low energy, indifference, dispiritedness" (229). Fisher's notion of melancholy contrasts with Adamastor's more choleric and confrontational demeanor.

42. André Brink observes: "Most significantly, in narrative terms, by allowing Adamastor to speak for himself, to tell his own story, his presence demands from the reader an effort to *understand*" ("A Myth of Origin" 45, emphasis in original).

43. Dorothy Figueira, for example, argues that "*The Lusiads* is really an anti-epic, concluding with a prophetic vision suggesting the demise of the Portuguese Indian empire. Although the Portuguese achievement is presented as part of providential design to win the world for the faith and Camoens presents it as part of God's purpose for the universe as a whole, the tenth canto clearly shows how the Portuguese fight for the faith is determined by the spiritual values of Europe. Camoens' need for a new myth suggests that these values are bankrupt and that the forces of error and darkness will, in fact, prevail" (396).

44. Walter Benjamin also notes the "melancholic's inclination for long journeys" (149).

45. Although *acedia* and *tristitia* are technically different states of spirit and mind, they were often conflated in the Middle Ages (Soufas 39). Duarte dedicates

a separate chapter to the discussion of the sin of *occiosidade* or sloth, but there are elements of this sin in his discussion of *tristeza* as well.

46. In his *Panegíricos,* João de Barros opines that nothing is more contrary to knowledge of the truth than ire, and notes that frequently "menencoria . . . vence os sabedores, e os olhos d'alma" (melancholy triumphs over wise men, and the eyes of the soul, 150).

47. Lourenço does not find in Duarte's book the origin of the "mythification" of *saudade* as a mainstay of Portuguese culture and argues against identifying the *Leal Conselheiro* as its origin (*Mitologia* 103); for Lourenço, the birth of *saudade* as a (national) "mythology" is Camões's "Christianized Neoplatonic vision" (110). Although the plausibility of identifying only a single origin of the mythification of *saudade* is open to question, it cannot be denied that, though Duarte's objective may have been more "modest" (Lourenço 103), the subsequent effect of his proclamation about the untranslatability of *saudade,* in conjunction with the work of Camões, was substantial.

48. See especially Agamben, chapter 4. According to Aristotle, the passions are part of the sensitive soul and are located in the heart (Babb 3–4). But "passion" also carries a physiological meaning as "a muscular expansion or contraction of the heart" (Babb 12). This physiological phenomenon may be what Duarte is referring to at the outset of his chapter on *saudade* when he observes that "a tristeza, per qual quer parte que venha, assy embarga sempre contynuadamente o coraçom" (sadness, wherever it comes from, always and continuously constricts the heart, 93).

49. Klibansky, Panofsky, and Saxl also note the Arabic expression *saudāwī al-mizāğ,* "black by admixture, melancholy" (36n81); "the Arabic expression for 'black' or 'melancholic' became synonymous with 'passion'" (36).

50. Moira Richards reads Adamastor as the would-be rapist of Thetis, arguing that the *Lusíadas* in this episode contains a "delightful feminist revenge parable" (73). I agree with Richards's underlying assumption that the dynamics of colonial/sexual aggression are often frequently intertwined throughout the poem, but stop short of applying "feminism" in its contemporary understandings to Camões and his poetic constructions of women and female sexuality.

51. René P. Garay, in fact, finds the eros of the poem to be supervised by a woman and argues that "the Portuguese venture in *Os Lusíadas,* for all the chauvinistic bravado that the enterprise entails, still falls clearly within the controlled domain of a well-defined feminine principle. It is the archetypal woman (i.e., Venus), after all, who not only inspires, but at times commandeers the epic enterprise" (87).

52. Bethlehem studies the possible associations between Adamastor's stoniness and his phallic nature, and suggests that he calls up the threat of castration (53).

53. For a catalog of Faria e Sousa's works, see Silva, *Diccionario bibliographico* 414–18.

54. "[B]y choosing to write most of his works in Spanish, Faria e Sousa placed himself in a no-man's land of literary history. Students of Portuguese culture tend to leave aside an author who willfully neglected to cultivate the national language at a moment when its very existence as a tool of artistic expression was at stake. Students of Spanish civilization are not particularly attracted to a writer who betrays in his work a marked Portuguese bias, even when he does not openly glorify his countrymen" (Glaser, *The "Fortuna"* 5). For a summary of some of the conflicting critical views on Faria e Sousa, see Silva, "Exile under Fire" 61–63. Sena traces Faria e Sousa's genealogy and provides notes on the historical/political contexts of his work.

55. For Pierce, Camões is a humanist poet working within a rhetorical tradition; for a rebuttal of this view, see Glaser, "Manuel de Faria e Sousa" 135–36.

56. Faria e Sousa took cognizance of the fact that the vicissitudes of the physical book necessarily impinge on the acts of reading and interpretation, and so it was that he presented the first formal treatment of the two putative "first editions" of *Os Lusíadas*. For a comprehensive study of the problems surrounding the *editio princeps* along with a reproduction of twenty-nine of its exemplars on CD-ROM, see Jackson, *Camões and the First Edition*.

57. Shankar Raman notes, "The Portuguese colonial empire began and ended . . . with its military struggles against the Islamic powers of the Mediterranean . . . It is at the hands of the deliberately erased colonial power that preceded and shaped Portugal's own outward expansion that King Sebastian meets his death" (155–56).

58. Part of Adamastor's decorum is that his words reflect his monstrous body and his temperament: "Rōpe el Gigāte su furor en razones, i palabras con gran estudio, proporcionadas a su estatura, colera, pasion, i bravosidad, i vengança" (the Giant's furor comes out in speech and proper words, proportionate to his stature, choler, passion, arrogance, and vengefulness, col. 520).

59. See Sennett 106–8.

60. Covarrubias, in his renowned dictionary of 1611 and one of the many textual authorities Faria e Sousa cites, defines "Jayán" as a "hombre de estatura grande, que por otro término decimos gigante" (a man of large stature, whom by another word we call giant, 680).

61. Faria e Sousa is the first critic to posit the etymological origins of "Adamastor": "Adamastor: nōbre que tiene mucho del de Duma, ascendiente de Mahoma, como hijo de Ismael . . . Pudo tambien cōponerlo el P. de adamas, por la consideraciō que veremos luego . . . el P. formò este nōbre de *Adamastos*, que segū los Gramaticos, vale indomito, qual fue Mahoma, i es ingente en sus errores, i ambiciō: i tābien del verbo *adamo*, que vale enamorar, pues el P. le finge luego

muy perdido de amores por Tetis: i Mahoma fue primero enamorado de muger agena ... I es de creer, que el P. con este nombre quiso de alguna manera alumbrarnos, para que viessemos a Mahoma en lo recondito desta fabula, pues teniendo en los Poetas anteriores el nõbre de Damastor, dado a uno de los Gigantes, no avia para que alterar en el quando pintava un Gigante, si no quisiera con el pintar a Mahoma en essa parte. Dize màs aì, que de la guerra de los Gigantes le tocò la parte de conquistar el Oceano, siendo Capitan de aquella armada: esso puntualmente toca a los Mahometanos, que fueron Capitanes desta navegacion, i la conquistarõ primero, i en virtud della estavan muy poderosos agora en aquellos mares" (Adamastor [is a] name that has Duma in it, related to Muhammad as the son of Ishmael ... The poet could also have composed the name from adamas, which we will presently consider ... the poet created this name from *Adamastos*, meaning indomitable according to the Grammarians, which Muhammad was in the magnitude of his erroneous ways and ambition; the name also comes from *adamo*, meaning to fall in love, evident when the poet makes him hopelessly in love with Thetis as Muhammad also was in love with a foreign woman ... And it is to be believed that, with this name, the poet wished in some manner to enlighten us so that we could see Muhammad lying hidden in this fiction. For since the name Damastor appears in earlier poets as one of the giants, no change was necessary here in order to create and describe a giant, even if, in using the name, Muhammad was not described in this passage. Furthermore, in the war of the giants, it fell to him [Adamastor] to conquer the ocean since he was the captain of the fleet. This immediately points to the Muhammadans, who were captains of navigation and conquered the ocean first, and because of that they were very powerful in those waters, col. 545). For a recent study of possible classical sources of Adamastor's name, see Hilton "'Chamei-me Adamastor.'"

62. The locution "transformar el amante en la cosa amada" is a reference to the first verse of Camões's sonnet "Transforma-se o amador na cousa amada." The Platonic-Aristotelian undertones of this emblematically Camonian "philosophy of love" are redirected here to indict Muhammad as intrinsically unable to rise above an earthly desire to behold the one, true Beauty.

63. See Figueiredo, *A autocomplacência da mimese*, chapter 4, for an analysis of how the Adamastor episode relates to Camões's mimetic art and how it may be read as a "lesson" in literary criticism and the practice of narrative.

64. For studies of Adamastor in South African literature, see Gray, Bethlehem, Graham, and Hanzimanolis. Also see van Wyk Smith, *Shades of Adamastor*. Monteiro (chapter 9) comments on the Adamastor legacy in English-language literature. Coetzee's painting *T'Kama-Adamastor* is the focal point of a collection of essays by South African scholars, edited by Vladislavić.

Works Cited

El Abencerraja (novela y romancero). Ed. Francisco López Estrada. Madrid: Cátedra, 2000.

Alfonso el Sabio. *Cantigas de Santa Maria*. Ed. Walter Mettmann. 4 vols. Coimbra: [Universidade de Coimbra], 1959–72.

———. *General estoria*. Primera parte. Vol. 1. Madrid: Funación José Antonio de Castro, 2001.

———. *General estoria*. Segunda parte. Vol. 1. Ed. Antonio G. Solalinde, Lloyd A. Kasten, and Víctor R. B. Oelschläger. Madrid: Consejo Superior de Investigaciones Científicas/Instituto "Miguel de Cervantes," 1957.

———. *Libro de las cruzes*. Ed. Lloyd A. Kasten and Lawrence B. Kiddle. Madrid: Consejo Superior de Investigaciones Científicas, 1961.

———. *Primera crónica general de España que mandó componer Alfonso el Sabio y se continuaba bajo Sancho IV en 1289*. Vol. 1. Ed. Ramón Menéndez Pidal. Madrid: Gredos, 1955.

———. *Las Siete Partidas*. Trans. Samuel Parsons Scott. Ed. Robert I. Burns. 5 vols. Philadelphia: University of Pennsylvania Press, 2001.

———. *Las siete partidas del rey Don Alfonso el Sabio: cotejados con varios códices antiguos por la Real Academia de la Historia*. 3 vols. Madrid: Atlas, 1972.

Alighieri, Dante. *The Divine Comedy: Inferno*. Vol. 1, part 1. Trans. Charles S. Singleton. Princeton, N.J.: Princeton University Press, 1970.

Aristotle. *Problems, Books XXII–XXXVIII*. Trans. W. S. Hett. Cambridge: Harvard University Press, 1957.

Azurara. See Zurara.

Barros, João de. *Ásia de João de Barros: Dos feitos que os portugueses fizeram no descobrimento e conquista dos mares e terras do Oriente*. Ed. Hernani Cidade. Vol. 1. Lisbon: Agência Geral das Colónias, 1945.

————. *Crónica do imperador Clarimundo*. Ed. Marques Braga. 3 vols. Lisbon: Sá da Costa, 1953.

————. *Panegíricos (Panegírico de D. João III e da infanta D. Maria)*. Ed. M. Rodrigues Lapa. Lisbon: Sá da Costa, 1943.

Brásio, António, ed. *Monumenta missionaria africana. África ocidental*. 15 vols. Lisbon: Agência Geral do Ultramar, 1952–88.

Brink, André. *The First Life of Adamastor*. London: Secker and Warburg, 1993.

Burton, Robert. *The Anatomy of Melancholy*. Ed. Floyd Dell and Paul Jordan-Smith. New York: Tudor Publishing, 1941.

[Cadamosto, Alvise.] *Viagens de Luís de Cadamosto e de Pedro de Sintra*. Lisbon: Academia Portuguesa da História, 1988.

Camões, Luís de. *The Lusiad, or, The Discovery of India: An Epic Poem*. Trans. William Julius Mickle. Oxford: Jackson and Lister, 1776.

————. *Os Lvsiadas do grande Lvis de Camoens. Principe da poesia heroica . . .* Ed. Manoel Correa. Lisbon: Pedro Crasbeeck, 1613.

————. *Lvsiadas de Lvis de Camoens, principe de los poetas de España . . . Comentadas por Manvel de Faria i Sousa, Cavallero de la Orden de Christo, i de la Casa Real*. Vol. 1. Madrid: Ivan Sanchez, 1639.

————. *Os Lusíadas*. Ed. Francisco Gomes de Amorim. 2 vols. Lisbon: Imprensa Nacional, 1889.

————. *Os Lusíadas*. Ed. Emanuel Paulo Ramos. Porto: Porto Editora, 1990.

————. *The Lusiads*. Trans. Leonard Bacon. New York: Hispanic Society of America, 1950.

Castanheda, Fernão Lopes de. *História do descobrimento e conquista da Índia pelos portugueses*. Ed. Pedro de Azevedo. Books 1 and 2. Coimbra: Imprensa da Universidade, 1924.

Correia, Gaspar. *Lendas da Índia*. Ed. M. Lopes de Almeida. Vol. 1. Porto: Lello e Irmão, 1975.

Couto, Diogo do. *Da Ásia. Década 7*. Lisbon: Regia Officina Typografica, 1783.

Covarrubias Orozco, Sebastián de. *Tesoro de la lengua castellana o española*. Madrid: Castalia, 1994.

Davenport, Francis Gardiner, ed. *European Treatises Bearing on the History of the United States and Its Dependencies to 1648*. Gloucester, Mass.: Peter Smith, 1967.

Documentos sobre os portugueses em Moçambique e na África central, 1497–1840/ Documents on the Portuguese in Mozambique and Central Africa, 1497–1840. Vol. 1. Lisbon: National Archives of Rhodesia and Nyasaland; Centro de Estudos Históricos Ultramarinos, 1962.

Eduarte [i.e., Duarte], D. *Leal Conselheiro*. Ed. Joseph M. Piel. Lisbon: Bertrand, 1942.

Fernandes, Valentim. *Códice Valentim Fernandes*. Ed. José Pereira da Costa. Lisbon: Academia Portuguesa da História, 1997.

Ficino, Marsilio. *Three Books on Life*. Ed. and trans. Carol V. Kaske and John R. Clark. Binghamton, N.Y.: Medieval and Renaissance Texts and Studies, 1989.

Figueiredo, Martinho de. *Commentum in Plinij naturalis historiae . . .* [Lisbon: 1529].

Galvão, António. *Tratado dos descobrimentos*. 4th ed. [Porto]: Civilização, 1987.

Góis, Damião de. *Chronica do prínçipe Dom Ioam, rei que foi destes regnos segundo do nome, em que summariamente se trattam has cousas sustançiaes que nelles aconteçerão do dia de seu nasçimento atte ho em que elRei Dom Afonso seu pai faleçeo*. New ed. Ed. A. J. Gonçálvez Guimarãis. Coimbra: Imprensa da Universidade, 1905.

———. *Crónica do felicíssimo rei D. Manuel*. Part 1. Coimbra: [Universidade de Coimbra], 1949.

The Holy Bible. Revised Standard Version Containing the Old and New Testaments. Ed. Herbert G. May and Bruce M. Metzger. New York: Oxford University Press, 1973.

Homer. *The Odyssey*. Trans. Robert Fagles. New York: Viking, 1996.

Huarte de San Juan, Juan. *Examen de ingenios para las ciencias*. Ed. Guillermo Serés. Madrid: Cátedra, 1989.

Isidoro de Sevilla. *Etimologías*. 2 vols. Edición bilingüe. Ed. and trans. José Oroz Reta and Manuel-A. Marcos Casquero. Madrid: Biblioteca de Autores Cristianos, 1982–83.

Lapa, M. Rodrigues, ed. *Cantigas d'escarnho e de mal dizer dos cancioneiros medievais galego-portugueses*. Lisbon: João Sá da Costa, 1995.

Leo Africanus. See Ramusio.

Ley, Charles David, ed. *Portuguese Voyages, 1498–1663*. London: Phoenix Press, 2000.

Libro d'las marauillas del mūdo y d'l viaje de la terra sancta de jerl'm. y de todas las provincias y cibdades de las Indias y d'todos õbres monstruos q. ay por el mūdo. Valencia: Costilla, 1521.

Livro dos conselhos de El-Rei D. Duarte (Livro da cartuxa). Ed. João José Alves Dias. Rev. A. H. de Oliveira Marques and Teresa F. Rodrigues. Lisbon: Estampa, 1982.

Livro dos ofícios de Marco Tullio Ciceram, o qual tornou em linguagem o Ifante D. Pedro, duque de Coimbra. Ed. Joseph M. Piel. Coimbra: [Universidade de Coimbra], 1948.

Lopes, Fernão. *Crónica del Rei Dom Joham I de boa memória e dos reis de Portugal o décimo*. Parts 1 and 2. Pref. Luís F. Lindley Cintra. Lisbon: Imprensa Nacional-Casa da Moeda, 1977.

———. *The English in Portugal, 1367–87*. Trans. and ed. Derek W. Lomax and R. J. Oakley. Warminster, UK: Aris and Phillips, 1988.

López de Velasco, Juan. *Geografía y descripción universal de las Indias*. Ed. Marcos Jiménez de la Espada. Madrid: Atlas, 1971.

Mármol Carvajal, Luis del. *Descripción general de África*. Vol. 1. Madrid: Instituto de Estudios Africanos/Consejo Superior de Investigaciones Científicas, 1953.

Marques, João Martins da Silva. *Descobrimentos portugueses: documentos para a sua história*. Vol. 1 (1147–1460). Lisbon: Instituto para a Alta Cultura, 1944.

Mela, Pomponius. *Pomponius Mela's Description of the World*. Trans. F. E. Romer. Ann Arbor: University of Michigan Press, 1998.

Melville, Herman. *Billy Budd, Sailor, and Selected Tales*. Oxford: Oxford University Press, 1997.

Mexía, Pedro. *Silva de varia lección*. Vol. 1. Ed. Antonio Castro. Madrid: Cátedra, 1989.

Montalboddo, Fracanzano da, comp. 1508. *Paesi nouamente retrovati & Novo mondo da Alberico Vesputio Florentino intitulato*. Princeton, N.J.: Princeton University Press, 1916.

Orta, Garcia de. 1563. *Colóquios dos simples e drogas e cousas medicinais da Índia*. Lisbon: Academia das Ciências de Lisboa, 1963.

Ovid. *Metamorphoses*. 3d ed. Trans. Frank Justus Miller. Vol. 1. Cambridge: Harvard University Press, 1984.

Paré, Ambroise. *Des monstres et prodiges*. Ed. Jean Céard. Geneva: Droz, 1971.

Pedro, D. *Livro de Linhagens do conde D. Pedro*. Portugaliae Monumenta Historica. New ser., vol. 2, part 1. Ed. José Mattoso. Lisbon: Publicações do II Centenário da Academia das Ciências, 1980.

Pereira, Duarte Pacheco. *Esmeraldo de situ orbis*. 3d ed. Ed. Damião Peres. Lisbon: Academia Portuguesa da História, 1954.

———. *Esmeraldo de situ orbis*. Trans. and ed. George H. T. Kimble. London: Hakluyt Society, 1937.

[Petrarca, Francesco.] *Petrarch's Lyric Poems: the Rime sparse and Other Lyrics*. Trans. and ed. Robert M. Durling. Cambridge: Harvard University Press, 1976.

Pina, Rui de. *Crónicas*. Ed. M. Lopes de Almeida. Porto: Lello e Irmão, 1977.

Pinto, Roberto Corrêa, trans. *Livro da guerra de Ceuta*. Lisbon: Academia das Sciências de Lisboa, 1915.

Pisano, Mateus de. *De Bello Septensi*. *Collecçaõ de livros ineditos de historia portugueza, dos reinados de D. Joaõ I, D. Duarte, D. Affonso V., e D. Joaõ II*. Ed. José Correia da Serra. Vol. 1. Lisbon: Academia Real das Sciencias, 1790. 7–57.

Pliny the Elder. *Natural History*. Trans. H. Rackham. Vol. 2. Cambridge: Harvard University Press; London: William Heinemann, 1942.

Polo, Marco. *The Book of Ser Marco Polo*. Trans. Henry Yule. New York: AMS Press, 1986.

———. *O Livro de Marco Paulo—O livro de Nicolao Veneto—Carta de Jeronimo de Santa Estevam, conforme a impressão de Valentim Fernandes, feita em Lisboa em 1502; com tres fac-símiles*. Ed. Francisco Maria Esteves Pereira. Lisbon: Biblioteca Nacional, 1922.

Prestage, Edgar. *The Chronicles of Fernão Lopes and Gomes Eannes de Zurara, with translated extracts and seven illustrations*. [N.p.]: Watford, 1928.

Ramusio, Giovanni Battista. *Navigationi et viaggi*. Vol. 1. Amsterdam: Theatrvm Orbis Terrarvm, 1970.

Resende, Garcia de. *Crónica de D. João II e miscelânea*. Lisbon: Imprensa Nacional-Casa da Moeda, 1991.

Schwarzafrika. Graz: Akademische Druck- u. Verlagsanstalt, 1962.

Sintra, Diogo Gomes de. *Descobrimento primeiro da Guiné*. Ed. Aires A. Nascimento. Lisbon: Colibri, 2002.

Sousa, Manuel de Faria e. See Camões.

Strabo. *The Geography of Strabo*. Trans. Horace Leonard Jones. Vol. 8. London: William Heinemann, 1932.

Torquemada, Antonio de. *Obras completas*. Vol. 1. Madrid: Turner, 1994.

van Wyk Smith, M., ed. *Shades of Adamastor: Africa and the Portuguese Connection: An Anthology of Poetry*. Grahamstown, South Africa: Institute for the Study of English in Africa, Rhodes University; National Literary Museum, 1988.

Velho, Álvaro. *A Journal of the First Voyage of Vasco da Gama, 1497–1499*. Trans. and ed. E. G. Ravenstein. London: Hakluyt Society, 1898.

———. *Relação da viagem de Vasco da Gama*. Ed. Luís de Albuquerque. Lisbon: Comissão Nacional para as Comemorações dos Descobrimentos Portugueses/Ministério da Educação, 1989.

Virgil. *Eclogues. Georgics. Aeneid 1–6*. Trans. H. Rushton Fairclough. Cambridge: Harvard University Press, 1935.

Vives, Juan Luis. *Obras completas*. Vol. 2. Madrid: Aguilar, 1948.

Voltaire. "An Essay on Epic Poetry/Essai sur la poésie épique." Ed. David Williams. In *The Complete Works of Voltaire*. 3B. Oxford: Voltaire Foundation, 1996. 303–497.

Zurara, Gomes Eanes de. *The Chronicle of the Discovery and Conquest of Guinea*. 1896. Trans. Charles Raymond Beazley and Edgar Prestage. Vol. 1. New York: Burt Franklin, n.d.

———. *The Chronicle of the Discovery and Conquest of Guinea*. Trans. Charles Raymond Beazley and Edgar Prestage. Vol. 2. London: Hakluyt Society, 1899.

———. *Chronique de Guinée*. Mémoires de l'Institut Français d'Afrique Noire 60. Ed. and trans. Léon Bourdon and Robert Ricard. Notes by L. Bourdon, E. Serra Rafols, Th. Monod, R. Ricard, and R. Mauny. Dakar: IFAN, 1960.

———. *Conquests and Discoveries of Henry the Navigator, being the chronicles of Azurara: Portuguese Navigators and Colonizers of the Fifteenth and Sixteenth Centuries*. Trans. Bernard Miall. Ed. Virgínia de Castro e Almeida. London: George Allen and Unwin, 1936.

———. *Crónica da Tomada de Ceuta por El Rei D. João I*. Ed. Francisco Maria Esteves Pereira. Lisbon: Academia das Sciências de Lisboa; Coimbra: Imprensa da Universidade, 1915.

————. *Crónica de D. Duarte de Meneses*. Ed. Larry King. Lisbon: Universidade Nova de Lisboa, 1978.

————. *Crónica de Guiné*. Ed. José de Bragança. [Porto]: Livraria Civilização, 1973.

————. *Crónica do conde D. Pedro de Meneses*. Ed. Maria Teresa Brocardo. Lisbon: Fundação Calouste Gulbenkian/Junta Nacional de Investigação Científica e Tecnológica, 1997.

————. *Crónica dos feitos notáveis que se passaram na conquista da Guiné por mandado do infante D. Henrique*. Vol. 1. Ed. Torquato de Sousa Soares. Lisbon: Academia Portuguesa da História, 1978.

SECONDARY SOURCES

Agamben, Giorgio. *Stanzas: Word and Phantasm in Western Culture*. Trans. Ronald L. Martinez. Minneapolis: University of Minnesota Press, 1993.

Akbari, Suzanne Conklin. "From Due East to True North: Orientalism and Orientation." In *The Postcolonial Middle Ages*, ed. Jeffrey Jerome Cohen. New York: St. Martin's Press, 2000. 19–34.

Anselmo, Artur. *Camões e a cultura portuguesa do século XVI*. Viana do Castelo: n.p., 1980.

Babb, Lawrence. *The Elizabethan Malady: A Study of Melancholia in English Literature from 1580 to 1642*. East Lansing: Michigan State College Press, 1951.

Bagby, Albert I., Jr. "Some Characterizations of the Moor in Alfonso X's 'Cántigas.'" *South Central Bulletin* 30 (1970): 164–67.

Banks, Jared. "Adamastorying Mozambique: *Ualalapi* and *Os Lusíadas*." *Luso-Brazilian Review* 37.1 (2000): 1–16.

Barbour, Nevill. "The Significance of the Word *Maurus*, with its Derivatives *Moro* and *Moor*, and of Other Terms Used by Medieval Writers in Latin to Describe the Inhabitants of Muslim Spain." In *Actas IV Congresso de Estudos Árabes e Islâmicos, Coimbra—Lisboa, 1 a 8 de Setembro de 1968*. Leiden: E. J. Brill, 1971. 253–66.

Barletta, Vincent. *Covert Gestures: Crypto-Islamic Literature as Cultural Practice in Early Modern Spain*. Minneapolis: University of Minnesota Press, 2005.

Barreto, Luís Filipe. "Gomes Eanes de Zurara e o nascimento do discurso historiográfico de transição." In *Descobrimentos e renascimento: formas de ser e pensar nos séculos XV e XVI*. Lisbon: Imprensa Nacional-Casa da Moeda, 1983. 63–125.

Bartels, Emily C. "Making More of the Moor: Aaron, Othello, and Renaissance Refashionings of Race." *Shakespeare Quarterly* 41 (1990): 433–54.

————. "*Othello* and Africa: Postcolonialism Reconsidered." *William and Mary Quarterly* 3d ser. 54 (1997): 45–64.

Bellamy, Elizabeth J. "From Virgil to Tasso: The Epic Topos as an Uncanny Return." In *Desire in the Renaissance: Psychoanalysis and Literature*, ed. Valeria

Finucci and Regina Schwartz. Princeton, N.J.: Princeton University Press, 1994. 207–32.

Benjamin, Walter. *The Origin of German Tragic Drama.* Trans. John Osborne. London: Verso, 1998.

Benoliel, José. *Episódio do gigante Adamastor: Lusíadas, canto V, est. XXXVII–LXX: estudo crítico.* Lisbon: Imprensa Nacional, 1898.

Bethlehem, Louise. "Adamastor, or the Exorbitant Truth of the Fetish." In *Skin Tight: Apartheid Literary Culture and Its Aftermath.* Pretoria: University of South Africa Press; Leiden: Brill, 2006. 38–54.

Bhabha, Homi K. *The Location of Culture.* London: Routledge, 1994.

Blackmore, Josiah. "Africa and the Epic Imagination of Camões." *Portuguese Literary and Cultural Studies* 9 (2002): 107–15.

———. "The Fortunes of Manuel de Faria e Sousa." In *Los quilates de su oriente: La pluralidad de culturas en la Península Ibérica en la Edad Media y los albores de la modernidad. Estudios ofrecidos a Francisco Márquez Villanueva,* ed. M. M. Gaylord, Luis Girón-Negrón, and Ángel Saenz-Badillos. Newark, Del.: Juan de la Cuesta, in press.

———. "Imagining the Moor in Medieval Portugal." *Diacritics* 36.3–4 (2006): 27–43.

———. *Manifest Perdition: Shipwreck Narrative and the Disruption of Empire.* Minneapolis: University of Minnesota Press, 2002.

———. "The Monstrous Lineage of Adamastor and His Critics." *Portuguese Literary and Cultural Studies* 7 (2008): 255–63.

———. "The Moor and the Topography of (Mis)Reading in Zurara." *Hispanófila* 128 (2000): 103–12.

———. "The Poets of Sodom." In *Queer Iberia: Sexualities, Cultures, and Crossings from the Middle Ages to the Renaissance,* ed. Josiah Blackmore and Gregory S. Hutcheson. Durham, N.C.: Duke University Press, 1999. 195–221.

Blake, John William, ed. and trans. *Europeans in West Africa, 1450–1560. Documents to illustrate the nature and scope of Portuguese enterprise in West Africa, the abortive attempt of Castilians to create an empire there, and the early English voyages to Barbary and Guinea.* Vol. 1. London: Hakluyt Society, 1942.

Bovill, E. W. *The Golden Trade of the Moors.* 2d ed. London: Oxford University Press, 1968.

Boxer, Charles R. *João de Barros: humanista português e historiador da Ásia.* Ed. Teotónio R. de Souza. [Lisbon]: Centro Português de Estudos do Sudeste Asiático, 2002.

———. "Three Historians of Portuguese Asia (Barros, Couto and Bocarro)." In *Orientalismo/Orientalism.* Lisbon: Fudação Oriente, 2002. Vol. 2 of *Opera Minora,* ed. Diogo Ramada Curto. 2002. 13–38.

Boxer, C. R. *The Portuguese Seaborne Empire, 1415–1825.* New York: Alfred A. Knopf, 1969.

————. *Race Relations in the Portuguese Colonial Empire, 1415–1825*. Oxford: Clarendon Press, 1963.

————, ed. and trans. *The Tragic History of the Sea*. Foreword and Additional Trans. by Josiah Blackmore. Minneapolis: University of Minnesota Press, 2001.

————. *Two Pioneers of Tropical Medicine: Garcia d'Orta and Nicolás Monardes*. London: Wellcome Historical Medical Library, 1963.

Bowra, C. M. *From Virgil to Milton*. London: Macmillan, 1948.

Braga, Theophilo. *História da Universidade de Coimbra nas suas relações com a instrucção publica portugueza*. Vol. 1 (1289 a 1555). Lisbon: Academia Real das Sciencias, 1892.

Branche, Jerome C. *Colonialism and Race in Luso-Hispanic Literature*. Columbia: University of Missouri Press, 2006.

Brink, André. "A Myth of Origin." In Vladislavić 41–47.

Brooks, George E. *Landlords and Strangers: Ecology, Society, and Trade in Western Africa, 1000–1630*. Boulder, Colo.: Westview Press, 1993.

Bunes Ibarra, Miguel Ángel de. *La imagen de los musulmanes y del norte de África en la España de los siglos XVI y XVII: los caracteres de una hostilidad*. Madrid: Consejo Superior de Investigaciones Científicas, 1989.

Burke, James F. *Vision, the Gaze, and the Function of the Senses in Celestina*. University Park: Pennsylvania State University Press, 2000.

Butler, Judith. *The Psychic Life of Power: Theories in Subjection*. Stanford, Calif.: Stanford University Press, 1997.

Carruthers, Mary J. *The Book of Memory: A Study of Memory in Medieval Culture*. Cambridge: Cambridge University Press, 1990.

Carvalho, Joaquim de. *Estudos sobre a cultura portuguesa do século XV*. Vol. 1. Coimbra: [Universidade de Coimbra], 1949.

————. "A livraria de um letrado do século XVI: Fr. Diogo de Murça." In *Estudos sobre a cultura portuguesa do século XVI*, vol. 2. Coimbra: Universidade de Coimbra, 1948. 111–99.

Casares, Aurelia Martín. "Free and Freed Black Africans in Granada in the Time of the Spanish Renaissance." In *Black Africans in Renaissance Europe*, ed. T. F. Earle and K. J. P. Lowe. Cambridge: Cambridge University Press, 2005. 247–60.

Cass, Jeffrey. "Interrogating Orientalism: Theories and Practices." In *Interrogating Orientalism: Contextual Approaches and Pedagogical Practices*, ed. Diane Long Hoeveler and Jeffrey Cass. Columbus: Ohio State University Press, 2006. 25–45.

Castro, Américo. *España en su historia: cristianos, moros, y judíos*. Barcelona: Crítica, 1983.

Castro, Aníbal Pinto de. *O episódio do Adamastor: seu lugar e significação na estrutura de "Os Lusíadas."* Lisbon: Commissão Executiva do IV Centenário de "Os Lusíadas," 1972.

Cidade, Hernâni. *Luís de Camões II: o épico.* 2d ed. Lisbon: Revista da Faculdade de Letras, 1953.

Clark, Stuart. *Vanities of the Eye: Vision in Early Modern European Culture.* Oxford: Oxford University Press, 2007.

Coates, Timothy J. *Convicts and Orphans: Forced and State-Sponsored Colonizers in the Portuguese Empire, 1550–1755.* Stanford, Calif.: Stanford University Press, 2001.

Cochran, Terry. *Twilight of the Literary: Figures of Thought in the Age of Print.* Cambridge: Harvard University Press, 2001.

Cohen, Jeffrey J. *Medieval Identity Machines.* Minneapolis: University of Minnesota Press, 2003.

Cohen, Jeffrey Jerome. "Monster Culture (Seven Theses)." In *Monster Theory: Reading Culture,* ed. Jeffrey Jerome Cohen. Minneapolis: University of Minnesota Press, 1996. 3–25.

Cohen, Walter. "The Discourse of Empire in the Renaissance." In *Cultural Authority in Golden Age Spain,* ed. Marina S. Brownlee and Hans Ulrich Gumbrecht. Baltimore: Johns Hopkins University Press, 1995. 260–833.

Conley, Tom. *The Self-Made Map: Cartographic Writing in Early Modern France.* Minneapolis: University of Minnesota Press, 1996.

Costa, João Paulo Azevedo de Oliveira e. "La presencia de los portugueses en el Oriente durante el siglo XVI: nuevas perspectivas." In *Extremo oriente ibérico: investigaciones históricas: metodología y estado de la cuestión,* ed. Francisco Solano, Florentino Rodao, and Luis E. Togores. Madrid: Agencia Española de Cooperación Internacional; Centro de Estudios Históricos, 1989. 433–43.

Curto, Diogo Ramada. "Introdução: orientalistas e cronistas." In *Orientalismo/Orientalism.* Lisbon: Fundação Oriente, 2002. Vol. 2 of *Opera Minora.* By Charles Ralph Boxer. Ed. Diogo Ramada Curto. [xiii]–xxii.

———. "Portuguese Imperial and Colonial Culture." In *Portuguese Oceanic Expansion, 1400–1800,* ed. Francisco Bethencourt and Diogo Ramada Curto. Cambridge: Cambridge University Press, 2007. 314–57.

Dangler, Jean. *Making Difference in Medieval and Early Modern Iberia.* Notre Dame: University of Notre Dame Press, 2005.

David-Peyre, Yvonne. "Le Concept de mélancolie à travers quelques dialogues portugais du XVIᵉ siècle." In *L'Humanisme portugais et l'Europe. Actes du XXIᵉ colloque international d'études humanistes, Tours, 3–13 Juillet 1978.* Paris: Fondation Calouste Gulbenkian, 1984. 193–215.

Davis, Elizabeth R. *Myth and Identity in the Epic of Imperial Spain.* Columbia: University of Missouri Press, 2000.

Davis, Natalie Zemon. *Trickster Travels: A Sixteenth-Century Muslim between Worlds.* New York: Hill and Wang, 2006.

Devisse, Jean, and Michel Mollat. *The Image of the Black in Western Art.* Vol. 2, part 2. Trans. William Granger Ryan. Lausanne: Office du Livre, 1979.

Diffie, Bailey W., and George D. Winius. *Foundations of the Portuguese Empire, 1415–1580*. Minneapolis: University of Minnesota Press, 1977.

Dinis, António J. Dias. *Vida e obras de Gomes Eanes de Zurara*. Vol. 1. Lisbon: Agência Geral das Colónias, 1949.

Domingues, José D. Garcia. "A concepção do mundo árabe-islâmico n'*Os Lusíadas*." *Garcia de Orta* (1972): 201–26.

Duffy, James. *Portugal in Africa*. Cambridge: Harvard University Press, 1962.

Earle, T. F. "Autobiografia e retórica numa canção de Camões." *Arquivos do Centro Cultural Português* 23 (1987): 507–21.

Elbl, Ivana. "'Men without Wives': Sexual Arrangements in the Early Portuguese Expansion in West Africa." In *Desire and Discipline: Sex and Sexuality in the Premodern West*, ed. Jacqueline Murray and Konrad Eisenbichler. Toronto: University of Toronto Press, 1996. 61–86.

Elliott, J. H. *Imperial Spain, 1469–1716*. New York: St. Martin's Press, 1964.

Figueira, Dorothy. "Fantasies of Faith." In *Literatura de viagem: narrativa, história, mito*, ed. Ana Margarida Falcão, Maria Teresa Nascimento, and Maria Luísa Leal. Lisbon: Cosmos, 1997. 389–98.

Figueiredo, João R. *A autocomplacência da mimese: uma defesa da poesia, Os Lusíadas e a Vida de Frei Bartolomeu dos Mártires*. Coimbra: Angelus Novus, 2003.

Filgueira Valverde, José. *Camoens*. Barcelona: Labor, 1958.

Fisher, Philip. *The Vehement Passions*. Princeton, N.J.: Princeton University Press, 2002.

Floyd-Wilson, Mary. *English Ethnicity and Race in Early Modern Drama*. Cambridge: Cambridge University Press, 2003.

Folger, Robert. *Images in Mind: Lovesickness, Spanish Sentimental Fiction and Don Quijote*. North Carolina Studies in the Romance Languages and Literatures 274. Chapel Hill: University of North Carolina Department of Romance Languages, 2002.

Fonseca, João Abel de. "A Crónica de Guiné, de Gomes Eanes de Zurara e a etapa henriquina dos descobrimentos." In *Os descobrimentos portugueses no século XV*. Actas do II Simpósio de História Marítima. Lisboa, 20/22 de Abril de 1994. Ed Bernardino Cadete and Jorge Borges de Macedo. Lisbon: Academia de Marinha, 1999. 137–79.

Fonseca, Luís Adão da. "Prologue: The Discovery of Atlantic Space." In Winius, *Portugal, the Pathfinder* 5–17.

Freud, Sigmund. "Mourning and Melancholia." In *On the History of the Psycho-Analytic Movement; Papers on Metapsychology and Other Works*, trans. James Strachey. London: The Hogarth Press and the Institute of Psycho-Analysis, 1957. 243–58.

Friedman, John Block. *The Monstrous Races in Medieval Art and Thought*. Cambridge: Harvard University Press, 1981.

Fuchs, Barbara. "Imperium Studies: Theorizing Early Modern Expansion." In *Postcolonial Moves: Medieval through Modern*, ed. Patricia Clare Ingham and Michelle R. Warren. New York: Palgrave Macmillan, 2003. 71–90.

———. *Mimesis and Empire: The New World, Islam, and European Identities*. Cambridge: Cambridge University Press, 2001.

Garay, René P. "First Encounters: Epic, Gender and the Portuguese Overseas Venture." In *Global Impact of the Portuguese Language*, ed. Asela Rodriguez de Laguna. New Brunswick, N.J.: Transaction, 2001. 77–94.

García-Arenal, Mercedes, and Miguel Ángel de Bunes. *Los españoles y el norte de África: siglos XV–XVIII*. Madrid: Mapfre, 1992.

Gil, Fernando. "O efeito-*Lusíadas*." In *Viagens do olhar: retrospecção, visão e profecia no renascimento português*, ed. Fernando Gil and Helder Macedo. Porto: Campo das Letras, 1998. 13–75.

———. "Viagens do olhar: os mares dos *Lusíadas*." In *Viagens do olhar: retrospecção, visão e profecia no renascimento português*, ed. Fernando Gil and Helder Macedo. Porto: Campo das Letras, 1998. 77–120.

Gil, José. *Monstros*. Lisbon: Quetzal, 1994.

Gillies, John. *Shakespeare and the Geography of Difference*. Cambridge: Cambridge University Press, 1994.

Glaser, Edward, ed. *The "Fortuna" of Manuel de Faria e Sousa: An Autobiography*. Münster Westfalen: Aschendorff, 1975.

———. "Manuel de Faria e Sousa and the Mythology of *Os Lusíadas*." In *Portuguese Studies*. Paris: Fundação Calouste Gulbenkian/Centro Cultural Português, 1976. 135–57.

Godinho, Vitorino Magalhães. "A idea de descobrimento e os descobrimentos e expansão." *Anais do Clube Militar Naval* 120 (1990): 627–42.

Goodman, Jennifer R. *Chivalry and Exploration, 1298–1630*. Woodbridge, UK: Boydell Press, 1998.

Graham, Lucy. "Racializing the Cape of Storms: Adamastor in the White South African Imagination." Cambridge Postcolonial Symposium. Pembroke College. April 2004.

Gray, Stephen. *Southern African Literature: An Introduction*. New York: Barnes and Noble, 1979.

Greenblatt, Stephen. *Marvelous Possessions: The Wonder of the New World*. Chicago: University of Chicago Press, 1991.

Greene, Roland. "Colonial Becomes Postcolonial." In *Postcolonialism and the Past*, ed. Barbara Fuchs and David J. Baker. Special issue of *MLQ* 65.3 (2004): 423–41.

Grubb, Eileen E. McGrath. "Attitudes towards Black Africans in Imperial Spain." *Legon Journal of the Humanities* 1 (1974): 68–90.

Hadfield, Andrew. "General Introduction." In *Amazons, Savages, and Machiavels:*

Travel and Colonial Writing in English, 1550–1630, ed. Andrew Hadfield. Oxford: Oxford University Press, 2001. 1–10.

Hair, P. E. H. "Discovery and Discoveries: The Portuguese in Guinea 1444–1650." In *Africa Encountered: European Contacts and Evidence 1450–1700*. Aldershot, UK: Ashgate, 1997. 11–28.

———. "The Early Sources on Guinea." *History in Africa* 21 (1994): 87–126.

Hall, Kim F. *Things of Darkness: Economies of Race and Gender in Early Modern England*. Ithaca, N.Y.: Cornell University Press, 1995.

Hannaford, Ivan. *Race: The History of an Idea in the West*. Washington, D.C.: Woodrow Wilson Center Press; Baltimore: Johns Hopkins University Press, 1996.

Hanzimanolis, Margaret. "Ultramarooned: Gender, Empire and Narratives of Travel in Southern Africa." Diss., University of Cape Town, 2005.

Hardie, Philip. *Virgil's Aeneid: Cosmos and Imperium*. Oxford: Clarendon Press, 1986.

Hart, Jonathan. *Comparing Empires: European Colonialism from Portuguese Expansion to the Spanish-American War*. New York: Palgrave Macmillan, 2003.

Harvey, E. Ruth. *The Inward Wits: Psychological Theory in the Middle Ages and the Renaissance*. Warburg Institute Surveys 6. London: The Warburg Institute; University of London, 1975.

Harvey, L. P. *Islamic Spain, 1250–1500*. Chicago: University of Chicago Press, 1990.

———. *Muslims in Spain, 1500 to 1614*. Chicago: University of Chicago Press, 2005.

Haydara, Abou. *L'envers de l'épopée portugaise en Afrique (XVe–XXe siècles)*. Paris: L'Harmattan, 2007.

Hegel, Georg Wilhelm Friedrich. *Lectures on the Philosophy of World History. Introduction: Reason in History*. Trans. H. B. Nisbet. Cambridge: Cambridge University Press, 1975.

Helgerson, Richard. *Forms of Nationhood: The Elizabethan Writing of England*. Chicago: University of Chicago Press, 1992.

Helms, Mary W. *Ulysses' Sail: An Ethnographic Odyssey of Power, Knowledge, and Geographical Distance*. Princeton, N.J.: Princeton University Press, 1988.

Hespanha, António Manuel. "O orientalismo em Portugal (séculos XVI–XX)." In *O orientalismo em Portugal*. Comissão Nacional para as Comemorações dos Descobrimentos Portugueses. Porto: Edifício da Alfândega, 1999. 15–37.

Hess, Andrew C. "The Evolution of the Ottoman Seaborne Empire in the Age of the Oceanic Discoveries, 1453–1525." *American Historical Review* 75 (1970): 1892–1919.

———. *The Forgotten Frontier: A History of the Sixteenth-Century Ibero-African Frontier*. Chicago: University of Chicago Press, 1978.

Hilton, J. L. "Adamastor, Gigantomachies, and the Literature of Exile in Camões' *Lusiads*." *Scholia* n.s. 16 (2007).

———. "'Chamei-me Adamastor': Naming the Spirit of the Cape in Luis Vaz de Camões' *Lusiads*." *Nomina Africana* 20.1–2 (2006).

Horta, José da Silva. "O Africano: produção textual e representações (séculos XV–XVII)." In *Condicionantes culturais da literatura de viagens: estudos e bibliografias*, ed. Fernando Cristóvão. Lisbon: Cosmos/Centro de Literaturas de Expressão Portuguesa da Universidade de Lisboa, 1999. 261–301.

———. "Evidence for a Luso-African Identity in 'Portuguese' Accounts on 'Guinea of Cape Verde' (Sixteenth–Seventeenth Centuries)." *History in Africa* 27 (2000): 99–130.

———. "A imagem do Africano pelos portugueses antes dos contactos." In *O confronto do olhar: o encontro dos povos na época das navegações portuguesas, séculos XV e XVI: Portugal, África, Ásia, América*, ed. António Luís Ferronha. Lisbon: Caminho, 1991. 43–70.

———. "Primeiros olhares sobre o Africano do Sara Ocidental à Serra Leoa (meados do século XV–inícios do século XVI)." In *O confronto do olhar* 73–126.

———. "A representação do africano na literatura de viagens, do Senegal à Serra Leoa (1453–1508)." *Mare Liberum* 2 (1991): 209–338.

Huet, Marie-Hélène. *Monstrous Imagination.* Cambridge: Harvard University Press, 1993.

Hulme, Peter. *Colonial Encounters: Europe and the Native Caribbean, 1492–1797.* London: Routledge, 1992.

———. "Tales of Distinction: European Ethnography and the Caribbean." In *Implicit Understandings: Observing, Reporting, and Reflecting on the Encounters between Europeans and Other Peoples in the Early Modern Era*, ed. Stuart B. Schwartz. Cambridge: Cambridge University Press, 1994. 157–97.

Hutcheson, Gregory S. "The Sodomitic Moor: Queerness in the Narrative of *Reconquista*." In *Queering the Middle Ages*, ed. Glenn Burger and Steven F. Kruger. Minneapolis: University of Minnesota Press, 2001. 99–122.

"Inaugurate." *Oxford English Dictionary.* 2d. ed. 1989.

Irwin, Robert. *Dangerous Knowledge: Orientalism and Its Discontents.* Woodstock, N.Y.: Overlook Press, 2006.

Islam, Syed Manzurul. *The Ethics of Travel: From Marco Polo to Kafka.* Manchester: Manchester University Press, 1996.

Jackson, K. David. *Camões and the First Edition of The Lusiads, 1572.* CD-ROM. Dartmouth: Center for Portuguese Studies, University of Massachusetts-Dartmouth, 2003.

———. "Orientalness: Portuguese in the Orient before Orientalism." Portuguese Orientalism. MLA Convention. Loews Hotel, Philadelphia. December 28, 2006.

Jacob, Christian. *The Sovereign Map: Theoretical Approaches in Cartography throughout History.* Trans. Tom Conley. Ed. Edward H. Dahl. Chicago: University of Chicago Press, 2006.

Kaye, Jacqueline. "Islamic Imperialism and the Creation of Some Ideas of 'Europe.'" In *Europe and Its Others*, vol. 1, ed. Francis Barker, Peter Hulme, Margaret Iverson, and Diana Loxley. Colchester: University of Essex, 1985. 59–71.

Kinzel, Ulrich. "Orientation as a Paradigm of Maritime Modernity." In *Fictions of the Sea: Critical Perspectives on the Ocean in British Literature and Culture*, ed. Bernhard Klein. Aldershot, UK: Ashgate, 2002. 28–48.

Klibansky, Raymond, Erwin Panofsky, and Fritz Saxl. *Saturn and Melancholy: Studies in the History of Natural Philosophy, Religion, and Art*. New York: Basic Books, 1964.

Kristeva, Julia. *Strangers to Ourselves*. Trans. Leon S. Roudiez. New York: Columbia University Press, 1991.

La Roncière, Charles de. *La découverte de l'Afrique au moyen âge: cartographes et explorateurs*. Vol. 2. Cairo: La Société Royale de Géographie d'Égypte, 1924–25.

Lahon, Didier. "Black African Slaves and Freedmen in Portugal during the Renaissance: Creating a New Pattern of Reality." In *Black Africans in Renaissance Europe*, ed. T. F. Earle and K. J. P. Lowe. Cambridge: Cambridge University Press, 2005. 261–79.

———. *Os negros no coração do império: uma memória a resgatar, séculos XV–XIX*. Lisbon: Secretario Coordenador dos Programas de Educação Multicultural, Ministério da Educação, 1999.

Lausberg, Heinrich. *Elementos da retórica literária*. Trans. R. M. Rosado Fernandes. 3d ed. Lisbon: Fundação Calouste Gulbenkian, 1982.

Letzring, Monica. "The Adamastor Episode and Eighteenth Century Aesthetic Theory of the Sublime in England." In *Actas da I Reunião Internacional de Camonistas*. Lisbon: Commissão Executiva do IV Centenário da Publicação de "Os Lusíadas," 1973. 407–27.

Lima, J. A. Pires de. *A teratologia n' "Os Lusíadas."* Porto: Maranus, 1949.

Lipking, Lawrence. "The Genius of the Shore: Lycidas, Adamastor, and the Poetics of Nationalism." *PMLA* 111.2 (1996): 205–21.

Little, Arthur L. *Shakespeare Jungle Fever: National-Imperial Re-Visions of Race, Rape, and Sacrifice*. Stanford, Calif.: Stanford University Press, 2000.

Liu, Benjamin. *Medieval Joke Poetry: The* Cantigas d'Escarnho e de Mal Dizer. Harvard Studies in Comparative Literature 50. Cambridge: Harvard University Department of Comparative Literature, 2004.

Livermore, H. V. *A New History of Portugal*. 2d ed. Cambridge: Cambridge University Press, 1976.

———. "On the Conquest of Ceuta." *Luso-Brazilian Review* 2.1 (1965): 3–13.

Loomba, Ania. *Colonialism/Postcolonialism*. 2d ed. London: Routledge, 2005.

Lourenço, Eduardo. *Portugal como destino seguido de Mitologia da Saudade*. Lisbon: Gradiva, 2001.

Lowe, Kate. "Introduction: The Black African Presence in Renaissance Europe." In *Black Africans in Renaissance Europe*, ed. T. F. Earle and K. J. P. Lowe. Cambridge: Cambridge University Press, 2005. 1–14.

Lyons, Bridget Gellert. *Voices of Melancholy: Studies in Literary Treatments of Melancholy in Renaissance England.* London: Routledge and Kegan Paul, 1971.

Macedo, Helder. "O braço e a mente. O poeta como herói n' *Os Lusíadas*." *Arquivos do Centro Cultural Português* 16 (1981): 61–72.

Macedo, José Agostinho de. *Censura dos Lusíadas.* Vol. 1. Lisbon: Impressão Régia, 1820.

———. *Reflexões críticas sobre o episódio de Adamastor nas Lusíadas, canto V. oit. 39. em fórma de carta.* Lisbon: Impressão Régia, 1811.

MacGaffey, Wyatt. "Dialogues of the Deaf: Europeans on the Atlantic Coast of Africa." In *Implicit Understandings: Observing, Reporting, and Reflecting on the Encounters between Europeans and Other Peoples in the Early Modern Era*, ed. Stuart B. Schwartz. Cambridge: Cambridge University Press, 1994. 249–67.

Machado, José Pedro. *Dicionário etimológico da língua portuguesa.* Vol. 5. Lisbon: Livros Horizonte, 1987.

———. *Influência arábica no vocabulário português.* Vol. 2. Lisbon: Revista de Portugal, 1961.

Madureira, Luís. *Imaginary Geographies in Portuguese and Lusophone-African Literature: Narratives of Discovery and Empire.* Lewiston, N.Y.: Edwin Mellen Press, 2006.

Manzalaoui, Mahmoud. Review of *Orientalism* by Edward W. Said. *Modern Language Review* 75 (1980): 837–39.

Margarido, Alfredo. "La Vision de l'autre (africain et indien d'Amérique) dans la renaissance portugaise." In *L'Humanisme portugais et l'Europe. Actes du XXIe colloque international d'études humanistes. Tours, 3–13 Juillet 1978.* Paris: Fondation Calouste Gulbenkian/Centre Culturel Portugais, 1984. 507–55.

Marques, A. H. de Oliveira. *History of Portugal.* Vol. 1. New York: Columbia University Press, 1972.

Matar, Nabil. *Turks, Moors, and Englishmen in the Age of Discovery.* New York: Columbia University Press, 1999.

Mbembe, Achille. *On the Postcolony.* Berkeley: University of California Press, 2001.

McClintock, Anne. *Imperial Leather: Race, Gender and Sexuality in the Colonial Contest.* New York: Routledge, 1995.

Meserve, Jeffrey David. "Narrating the African 'Other': (Re)Reading Camões, *Os Lusíadas*, and Portuguese Encounters with Africa, 1492–1572." M.A. thesis, Yale University, 2005.

Meyerson, Mark D. "Introduction." In *Christians, Muslims, and Jews in Medieval and Early Modern Spain: Interaction and Cultural Change*, ed. Mark D. Meyerson and Edward D. English. Notre Dame: University of Notre Dame Press, 1999. xi–xxi.

Miller, Christopher L. *Blank Darkness: Africanist Discourse in French.* Chicago: University of Chicago Press, 1985.

Mills, Sara. *Discourse.* London: Routledge, 1997.

Miranda, José Carlos Ribeiro. "A lenda de Gaia dos livros de linhagens: uma questão de literatura?" *Línguas e Literaturas (Revista da Faculdade de Letras do Porto),* 2d ser. 5.2 (1988): 483–515.

Monteiro, George. *The Presence of Camões: Influences on the Literature of England, America, and Southern Africa.* Lexington: University Press of Kentucky, 1996.

Morison, Samuel Eliot. *Portuguese Voyages to America in the Fifteenth Century.* Cambridge: Harvard University Press, 1940.

Mudimbe, V. Y. *The Idea of Africa.* Bloomington: Indiana University Press; London: James Currey, 1994.

———. *The Invention of Africa: Gnosis, Philosophy, and the Order of Knowledge.* Bloomington: Indiana University Press; London: James Currey, 1988.

Neves, Leonor Curado. "Uma leitura do episódio do Adamastor: sobre um artigo de António José Saraiva." In *Estudos portugueses: homenagem a António José Saraiva.* Lisbon: Instituto de Cultura e Língua Portuguesa/Ministério da Educação, 1990. 281–92.

Newitt, Malyn, ed. *East Africa.* Aldershot, UK: Ashgate, 2002.

———. "Formal and Informal Empire in the History of Portuguese Expansion." *Portuguese Studies* 17 (2001): 1–21.

———. *A History of Portuguese Overseas Expansion, 1400–1668.* London: Routledge, 2005.

Nicolopulos, James. *The Poetics of Empire in the Indies: Prophecy and Imitation in* La Araucana *and* Os Lusíadas. University Park: Pennsylvania State University Press, 2000.

Nirenberg, David. *Communities of Violence: Persecution of Minorities in the Middle Ages.* Princeton, N.J.: Princeton University Press, 1996.

Padrón, Ricardo. *The Spacious Word: Cartography, Literature, and Empire in Early Modern Spain.* Chicago: University of Chicago Press, 2004.

Pagden, Anthony. *Lords of All the World: Ideologies of Empire in Spain, Britain and France c. 1500–1800.* New Haven: Yale University Press, 1995.

Pap, Leo. "On the Etymology of Portuguese SAUDADE: An Instance of Multiple Causation?" *Word* 43 (1992): 97–102.

Parker, Alexander A. *Polyphemus and Galatea: A Study in the Interpretation of a Baroque Poem.* With verse trans. by Gilbert F. Cunningham. Austin: University of Texas Press, 1977.

Parry, J. H. *The Age of Reconnaissance.* Berkeley: University of California Press, 1981.

Pearson, Michael N. "The Search for the Similar: Early Contacts between Portuguese and Indians." In *Clashes of Cultures: Essays in Honour of Niels Steensgaard,* ed. Jens Christian V. Johansen, Erling Ladewig Petersen, and Henrik Stevnsborg. Odense: Odense University Press, 1992. 144–59.

Penrose, Boies. *Travel and Discovery in the Renaissance, 1420–1620.* Cambridge: Harvard University Press, 1952.

Pérez-Mallaína, Pablo E. *Spain's Men of the Sea: Daily Life on the Indies Fleets in the Sixteenth Century.* Trans. Carla Rahn Phillips. Baltimore: Johns Hopkins University Press, 1998.

Pierce, Frank. "Camões' Adamastor." In *Hispanic Studies in Honour of Joseph Manson,* ed. Dorothy M. Atkinson and Anthony H. Clarke. Oxford: Dolphin, 1972. 207–15.

———. "The Place of Mythology in the *Lusiads.*" *Comparative Literature* 6 (1954): 97–122.

Porter, Dennis. "*Orientalism* and Its Problems." In *The Politics of Theory.* Proceedings of the Essex Conference on the Sociology of Literature, July 1982. Ed. Francis Barker, Peter Hulme, Margaret Iversen, and Diana Loxley. Colchester: University of Essex, 1983. 179–93.

Pratt, Mary Louise. *Imperial Eyes: Travel Writing and Transculturation.* London: Routledge, 1992.

Prestage, Edgar. "The Life and Writings of Azurara." In *The Chronicle of the Discovery and Conquest of Guinea* (1896), trans. Charles Raymond Beazley and Edgar Prestage. Vol. 1. New York: Burt Franklin, n.d. i–lxvii.

Prestholdt, Jeremy. "Portuguese Conceptual Categories and the 'Other' Encounter on the Swahili Coast." *Journal of Asian and African Studies* 36 (2001): 383–406.

Quint, David. *Epic and Empire: Politics and Generic Form from Virgil to Milton.* Princeton, N.J.: Princeton University Press, 1993.

Radden, Jennifer, ed. *The Nature of Melancholy: From Aristotle to Kristeva.* New York: Oxford University Press, 2000.

Ramalho, Américo da Costa. "Aspectos clássicos do Adamastor." In *Estudos camonianos.* Lisbon: Instituto Nacional de Investigação Científica, 1980. 35–44.

———. "Sobre o nome de Adamastor." In *Estudos camonianos.* Lisbon: Instituto Nacional de Investigação Científica, 1980. 27–34.

Raman, Shankar. *Framing "India": The Colonial Imaginary in Early Modern Culture.* Stanford, Calif.: Stanford University Press, 2001.

Randles, W. G. L. "The Atlantic in European Cartography and Culture from the Middle Ages to the Renaissance." In *Geography, Cartography and Nautical Science: The Impact of the Great Discoveries.* Aldershot, UK: Ashgate/Variorum, 2000. 1–28.

———. *L'Image du sud-est africain dans la littérature européenne au XVIᵉ siècle.* Lisbon: Centro de Estudos Históricos Ultramarinos, 1959.

———. "Notes on the Genesis of the Discoveries." *Stvdia* 5 (1960): 20–46.

Read, Jan. *The Moors in Spain and Portugal.* London: Faber and Faber, 1974.

Rebelo, Luís de Sousa. "Providencialismo e profecia nas crónicas portuguesas da expansão." *Bulletin of Hispanic Studies* 71 (1994): 67–86.

Relaño, Francesc. *The Shaping of Africa: Cosmographic Discourse and Cartographic Science in Late Medieval and Early Modern Europe.* Hampshire, UK: Ashgate, 2002.

Richards, Moira. "Adamastor: A Post-Patriarchal Approach." *Scrutiny2: Issues in English Studies in Southern Africa* 4 (1999): 73–74.

Río Parra, Elena del. *Una era de monstruos: representaciones de lo deforme en el Siglo de Oro español.* [Pamplona]: Universidad de Navarra; Frankfurt: Vervuert, 2003.

Rogers, Francis M., trans. *The Obedience of a King of Portugal.* Minneapolis: University of Minnesota Press, 1958.

———. *The Travels of the Infante Dom Pedro of Portugal.* Cambridge: Harvard University Press, 1961.

Rubiés, Joan-Pau. "Futility in the New World: Narratives of Travel in Sixteenth-Century America." In *Voyages and Visions: Towards a Cultural History of Travel,* ed. Jaś Elsner and Joan-Pau Rubiés. London: Reaktion, 1999. 74–100.

———. *Travel and Ethnology in the Renaissance: South India through European Eyes, 1250–1625.* Cambridge: Cambridge University Press, 2000.

Russell, Peter. *Prince Henry "the Navigator": A Life.* New Haven: Yale University Press, 2000.

———. "White Kings on Black Kings: Rui de Pina and the Problem of Black African Sovereignty." In *Facing Each Other: The World's Perception of Europe and Europe's Perception of the World,* part 2, ed. Anthony Pagden. Aldershot, UK: Ashgate, 2000. 503–15.

Russell-Wood, A. J. R. *The Portuguese Empire, 1415–1808: A World on the Move.* Baltimore: Johns Hopkins University Press, 1998.

Said, Edward W. *Orientalism.* New York: Vintage, 1978.

Saive, Denise. "A 'verdadeira notícia': descrição e ficção, prefiguração do discurso colonial na representação do negro em *Tratado breve dos rios de Guiné do Cabo-Verde* de André Álvares d'Almada & *Beschryvinghe ende historische verhael van het Gout Koninckrijck van Gunea* de Pieter de Marees." M.A. thesis, Universiteit Utrecht, 2005.

Santos, Custódio Lopes dos. "A denominação 'Adamastor' em *Os Lusíadas.*" In *IV Reunião Internacional de Camonistas.* Ponta Delgada: 1984. 623–29.

Santos, Maria Emília Madeira. *Viagens de exploração terrestre dos portugueses em África.* 2d ed. Lisbon: Centro de Estudos de História e Cartografia Antiga, 1988.

[S. Luiz, Francisco de.] *Apologia de Camoens contra as Reflexoens Críticas do P. José Agostinho de Macedo sobre o episodio de Adamastor no Canto V. dos Lusiadas.* Santiago: Joam Moldes, 1819.

Saraiva, António José. "Função e significado do maravilhoso n'*Os Lusíadas.*" *Colóquio/Letras* 100 (1987): 42–50.

——. "Lugar do Adamastor na estrutura d'*Os Lusíadas.*" In *Estudos portugueses: homenagem a Luciana Stegagno Picchio.* Lisbon: Difel, 1991. 653–55.

Schiesari, Juliana. *The Gendering of Melancholia: Feminism, Psychoanalysis, and the Symbolics of Loss in Renaissance Literature.* Ithaca, N.Y.: Cornell University Press, 1992.

Schleiner, Winfried. *Melancholy, Genius, and Utopia in the Renaissance.* Wiesbaden: In Kommission bei Otto Harrassowitz, 1991.

Sena, Jorge de. "Introdução." In *Lvsiadas de Lvis de Camões, comentadas por Manuel de Faria e Sousa,* vol. 1. Lisbon: Imprensa Nacional-Casa da Moeda, 1972. 9–56.

Sennett, Richard. *Flesh and Stone: The Body and the City in Western Civilization.* New York: W. W. Norton, 1994.

Silva, Chandra Richard de. "Beyond the Cape: The Portuguese Encounter with the Peoples of South Asia." In *Implicit Understandings: Observing, Reporting, and Reflecting on the Encounters between Europeans and Other Peoples in the Early Modern Era,* ed. Stuart B. Schwartz. Cambridge: Cambridge University Press, 1994. 295–322.

Silva, Innocencio Francisco da. *Diccionario bibliographico portuguez.* Vol. 5. Lisbon: Imprensa Nacional, 1860.

Silva, John de Oliveira e. "Exile under Fire: Reassessing the Poetics and Practice of Manuel de Faria e Sousa." In *Global Impact of the Portuguese Language,* ed. Asela Rodriguez de Laguna. New Brunswick, N.J.: Transaction, 2001. 61–76.

Silva, Tony Simões da. "Raced Encounters, Sexed Transactions: 'Luso-tropicalism' and the Portuguese Colonial Empire." *Pretexts: Literary and Cultural Studies* 11 (2002): 27–39.

Silva, Vítor Manuel de Aguiar e. *Camões: labirintos e fascínios.* Lisbon: Cotovia, 1994.

——. "The Songs of Melancholy: Aspects of Mannerism in Camões." In *A Revisionary History of Portuguese Literature,* ed. Miguel Tamen and Helena C. Buescu. New York: Garland, 1999. 30–57.

Smith, Roger C. *Vanguard of Empire: Ships of Exploration in the Age of Columbus.* New York: Oxford University Press, 1993.

Snead, James A. "Repetition as a Figure of Black Culture." In *Black Literature and Literary Theory,* ed. Henry Louis Gates Jr. New York: Methuen, 1984. 59–79.

Snowden, Frank M., Jr. *Blacks in Antiquity: Ethiopians in the Greco-Roman Experience.* Cambridge: Harvard University Press, 1970.

Sollors, Werner. *Neither Black nor White Yet Both: Thematic Explorations of Interracial Literature.* New York: Oxford University Press, 1997.

Soufas, Teresa Scott. *Melancholy and the Secular Mind in Spanish Golden Age Literature.* Columbia: University of Missouri Press, 1990.

Sousa, Ronald de. "Philosophical Implications of Camões' Use of the Classical Mythological Tradition in the Adamastor Episode of *Os Lusíadas*." *Garcia de Orta* (1972): 535–46.

Stewart, Susan. *On Longing: Narratives of the Miniature, the Gigantic, the Souvenir, the Collection*. Durham, N.C.: Duke University Press, 1993.

Stoler, Ann Laura. *Carnal Knowledge and Imperial Power: Race and the Intimate in Colonial Rule*. Berkeley: University of California Press, 2002.

Strandes, Justus. *The Portuguese Period in East Africa*. Trans. Jean F. Wallwork. Ed. J. S. Kirman. Nairobi: East African Literature Bureau, 1961.

Subrahmanyam, Sanjay. *The Career and Legend of Vasco da Gama*. Cambridge: Cambridge University Press, 1997.

Sweet, James H. "The Iberian Roots of American Racist Thought." *William and Mary Quarterly* 3d ser. 54 (1997): 143–66.

Thomaz, Luís Filipe. "Muçulmanos." In *Dicionário de história dos descobrimentos portugueses*, ed. Luís de Albuquerque. 2 vols. Lisbon: Caminho, 1994.

———. "Le Portugal et l'Afrique au XVᵉ siècle: les débuts de l'expansion." *Arquivos do Centro Cultural Português* 26 (1989): 161–256.

Thornton, John K. "Early Portuguese Expansion in West Africa: Its Nature and Consequences." In Winius, *Portugal, the Pathfinder* 121–32.

———. "The Portuguese in Africa." In *Portuguese Oceanic Expansion, 1400–1800*, ed. Francisco Bethencourt and Diogo Ramada Curto. Cambridge: Cambridge University Press, 2007. 138–60.

Tiffin, Chris, and Alan Lawson. "Introduction: The Textuality of Empire." In *De-scribing Empire: Postcolonialism and Textuality*, ed. Chris Tiffin and Alan Lawson. London: Routledge, 1994. 1–11.

Tinhorão, José Ramos. *Os negros em Portugal: uma presença silenciosa*. Lisbon: Caminho, 1988.

Tofiño-Quesada, Ignacio. "Spanish Orientalism: Uses of the Past in Spain's Colonization of Africa." *Comparative Studies of South Asia, Africa and the Middle East* 23 (2003): 141–48.

Tolan, John V. *Saracens: Islam in the Medieval European Imagination*. New York: Columbia University Press, 2002.

Valladares, Rafael. "No sólo atlántico: Portugal y su imperio." *Revista de Occidente* 281 (2004): 45–58.

van Wyk Smith, M. "Introduction." In *Shades of Adamastor: Africa and the Portuguese Connection: An Anthology of Poetry*, ed. M. van Wyk Smith. Grahamstown: Institute for the Study of English in Africa, Rhodes University; National English Literary Museum, 1988. 1–37.

———. "Ptolemy, Paradise and Purgatory: Portugal and the African Imaginary." In Vladislavić 83–97.

Varisco, Daniel Martin. *Reading Orientalism: Said and the Unsaid*. Seattle: University of Washington Press, 2007.

Vasconcellos, Carolina Michaëlis de. *A saudade portuguesa: divagações filológicas e literar-históricas em volta de* Inês de Castro *e do cantar velho "Saudade Minha—¿Quando Te Veria?"* 2d rev. ed. Porto: Renascença Portuguesa, 1922.

Vaughan, Alden T., and Virginia Mason Vaughan. "Before *Othello*: Elizabethan Representations of Sub-Saharan Africans." *William and Mary Quarterly* 3d ser. 54 (1997): 19–44.

Vieira, Yara Frateschi. "Adamastor: o pesadelo de um ocidental." *Colóquio/Letras* 98 (1987): 25–37.

Vladislavić, Ivan, ed. *T'kama-Adamastor: Inventions of Africa in a South African Painting*. Johannesburg: University of the Witwatersrand, 2000.

Voigt, Lisa. *Writing Captivity in the Early Modern Atlantic: Circulations of Knowledge and Authority in the Iberian and English Imperial Worlds*. Chapel Hill: University of North Carolina Press, forthcoming.

Wack, Mary Frances. *Lovesickness in the Middle Ages: The* Viaticum *and Its Commentaries*. Philadelphia: University of Pennsylvania Press, 1990.

Washburn, Wilcomb E. "The Meaning of 'Discovery' in the Fifteenth and Sixteenth Centuries." *American Historical Review* 68.1 (1962): 1–21.

Wells, Marion A. *The Secret Wound: Love-Melancholy and Early Modern Romance*. Stanford, Calif.: Stanford University Press, 2007.

Williams, David. "Introduction." "An essay on epic poetry." By Voltaire. In *The Complete Works of Voltaire*. 3B. Oxford: Voltaire Foundation, 1996. 121–302.

Willis, Robert Clive. "'Os Lusíadas' and Its Neoclassical Critics." *Ocidente* 83 (1972): 269–86.

Winius, George D. "Bibliographical Essay: Treasury of Printed Source Materials Pertaining to the XV and XVI Centuries." In Winius, *Portugal, the Pathfinder* 373–401.

———, ed. *Portugal, the Pathfinder: Journeys from the Medieval toward the Modern World 1300—ca. 1600*. Madison: Hispanic Seminary of Medieval Studies, 1995.

Yates, Frances. *The Occult Philosophy in the Elizabethan Age*. London: Routledge, 2001.

Index

Adamastor, xxiv, 1, 47, 82, 88, 89, 103, 105–38, 147–54, 165n1, 165n3, 165n4, 166n7, 166n8, 167n15, 169n27, 169n28, 170–71n37, 171n42, 172n50, 172n52, 173–74n61, 174n63, 174n64; and Africa, 119, 120, 122, 129, 130, 144, 146, 164n30, 170n35, 171n40; and embodiedness, 123–24, 126, 128–29, 130, 131, 133, 146, 150, 151, 152, 167n13, 170n33, 173n58; as *figura* (figure), 122, 123, 149, 167n12; and melancholy, 119, 122, 126–44, 148, 149, 150, 168n21, 171n41; as monster, 119, 122–24, 133, 135, 136, 149–53. *See also* Africa; Camões, Luís de; *imaginatio;* melancholy; monsters; monstrosity; Sousa, Manuel de Faria e

Afonso V, King, 44, 55, 94, 98, 156n5, 162n9

Africa, xiii, xv, xvi, xvii, xviii, xix, xx, xxii, xxiii, xxiv, 1, 2, 3, 9, 11, 13, 14, 18, 19, 20, 21, 25, 33, 34, 35, 40, 41, 45, 47, 50, 53, 55, 58, 60, 62, 63, 64, 65, 66, 67, 68, 69, 70, 71, 73, 78, 80, 83, 91, 92, 93, 94, 101, 105, 106, 119, 121, 122, 125, 126, 130, 135, 148, 150, 151, 155n3, 155n5, 156n5, 156n11, 157n1,

157n12, 158n3, 159n19, 160n23, 162n9, 162n12, 164n30, 168n17, 171n38; and blackness, 4, 15, 19, 22–24, 27–29, 89, 97, 100, 130, 159n19, 160n31, 160n34, 161n1, 161n37, 168–69n23, 170n35, 171n37; discovery of, xxi; etymology of, 75, 163n29; as geographic idea, 14, 15–18, 30, 45, 52; as historio-graphic home, 84; as "new world," xxii, 157n11; and papal bulls, 48–49; and "race," 22–24, 29–30, 160n28, 160n29; regions/colors of, 29–32, 51, 52, 61–62, 161n37; and space, 30–32, 52, 54, 61, 74, 75, 161n38; and strangeness, 77. *See also* Adamastor; Alfonso X of Castile; Bojador, Cape; Ceuta; Ethiopia; geohumoralism; Good Hope, Cape of; Guinea; melancholy; Morocco; Nile River; Sahara; Senegal River; Zurara, Gomes Eanes de

Africans. *See* Ethiopia; Guinea; Moors

Alfonso X of Castile, 5, 8, 160n20, 164n37; *Cantigas de Santa Maria,* 4, 5, 6, 158n9; and definition of *moro* (Moor), 5; *General estoria,* 4, 16, 32,

Mármol Carvajal, Luis del, 31, 161n37
marvel, 36, 40, 86, 123, 124, 135
Mauritania, 2, 3, 16, 18, 19, 24, 25, 30,
    45, 65, 158n3, 160n34; and blackness
    of skin, 3; as imprecise term, 3. *See
    also* Africa; Moors
maurophilia, 9
Maurus, 2, 3. *See also* Moors
Mbembe, Achille, 77
McClintock, Anne, 22, 54, 160n27
melancholy, xxiv, 82, 119, 122, 126–43,
    148, 149, 150, 153, 154, 156n11, 165n4,
    168n19, 168n22, 169n26, 170n32,
    170n33, 170n36, 171n41, 171n44,
    172n46; and Africa, 129–30, 134, 138;
    and *amor hereos* (lovesickness),
    132–33, 169n27, 169n29, 170n31; and
    eros, 144; and humoral theory, 128–
    29, 131, 132, 133, 134, 164n38, 168n20,
    168n21, 169n25; in *Leal conselheiro*,
    140–42; and maritime expansion,
    128, 135, 153; and Saturn, 140, 149;
    and *saudade*, 142–43. *See also*
    Adamastor; Africa; *imaginatio*;
    monsters; *saudade*
Melinde (Malindi), xvi, 50, 83, 84, 105
Melville, Herman, 105
Mexía, Pedro (*Silva de varia lección*),
    135
monsters, xxiv, 1, 26, 62, 122, 123,
    124–26, 135, 136, 149, 150, 151, 152, 153,
    165n4, 167n14, 167n15, 167n16, 168n17.
    See also Adamastor
monstrosity, xxiv, 89, 119, 122, 123, 125,
    126, 149, 150, 151
mooring, xvi
Moorishness, xvii, xxiii, 2, 5, 6, 148,
    150, 158n10; and dark skin, 5, 6, 8;
    and sex, 7–8. *See also* Moor
Moors, xvi, xxiii, 1, 2, 4, 5, 6, 9, 10, 11,
    15, 16, 18, 20, 21, 24, 26, 31, 41, 42,

44, 45, 46, 56, 61, 62, 64, 65, 66, 76,
    78, 79, 80, 81, 89, 95, 96, 99, 103,
    104, 150, 152, 156n9, 158n5, 158n6,
    158n13, 160n27, 160n33, 161n34,
    171n30; and birds, xiii–xiv; and
    Christians, 5–6, 7, 8–9; classical/
    medieval definitions of, 2–3, 5; in
    England and Portugal, xvii, 155n4;
    and *imaginatio*, 95, 96, 99–100, 102;
    loss of Spain to, 39; and papal bulls,
    49; and sex, 7, 22, 26, 130; war
    against, xv, 9–11, 39, 40, 41, 44, 61,
    66, 159n14, 162n8. *See also* Africa;
    Alfonso X of Castile; alterity;
    Camões, Luís de; Ethiopia; Guinea;
    Islam; Muslims; Saracens; Zurara,
    Gomes Eanes de
moro, 2, 3, 4. *See also* Moors
Morocco, xiii, xv, xvii, xxi, 3, 9, 10, 41,
    64, 67, 70, 79
mouro, 2, 3, 4, 11, 25, 31, 42, 45, 49, 50,
    62, 89, 98, 99, 158n4, 160n34. *See also*
    Moors
Mudimbe, V. Y., xvi, xxi, 49, 74
Muhammad, 5, 37, 44, 64, 65, 80, 121,
    148, 149, 150, 152, 162n8, 173–74n61,
    174n62. *See also* Islam; Sousa,
    Manuel de Faria e
mulatto, 29
Muslims, xvi, 3, 4, 7, 8, 10, 19, 50, 78,
    156n11, 158n4. *See also* Moors

nautical voyaging, xvi, xxiv, 11, 33,
    47, 50, 52, 53, 54, 57, 73, 122, 150,
    153; erotics of, xxiv, 146; and
    orientation, 59–60
Niger River, 17
Nile River, 15, 16, 17, 18, 65

Orient, xix, xxiv, 13, 17, 18, 20, 63, 68,
    159n15

JOSIAH BLACKMORE is professor in the Department of Spanish and Portuguese at the University of Toronto. He is author of *Manifest Perdition: Shipwreck Narrative and the Disruption of Empire* (Minnesota, 2002) and editor of C. R. Boxer's *Tragic History of the Sea* (Minnesota, 2001).